# U.S. LATINO ISSUES

D0732155

**Recent titles in
Contemporary American Ethnic Issues**

Native American Issues
*Paul C. Rosier*

# U.S. LATINO ISSUES

## RODOLFO F. ACUÑA

Contemporary American Ethnic Issues
*Ronald H. Bayor, Series Editor*

GREENWOOD PRESS
Westport, Connecticut • London

**Library of Congress Cataloging-in-Publication Data**

Acuña, Rodolfo.
    U.S. Latino issues / Rodolfo F. Acuña.
        p.    cm. — (Contemporary American ethnic issues)
    Includes bibliographical references (p. ) and index.
    ISBN 978-0-313-36143-2
    1. Hispanic Americans—Social conditions. 2. Hispanic Americans—Ethnic identity.
    3. Hispanic Americans—Statistics. 4. United States—Ethnic relations. 5. United
    States—Population. 6. United States—Relations—Latin America. 7. Latin
    America—Relations—United States. I. Title. II. Series.
    E184.S75A67    2003
    305.868′073—dc13          2003040844

British Library Cataloguing in Publication Data is available.

Copyright © 2003 by Rodolfo F. Acuña

All rights reserved. No portion of this book may be
reproduced, by any process or technique, without the
express written consent of the publisher.

Library of Congress Catalog Card Number: 2003040844

ISSN: 1543–219X

First published in 2003

Greenwood Press, 88 Post Road West, Westport, CT 06881
An imprint of Greenwood Publishing Group, Inc.
www.greenwood.com

Printed in the United States of America

The paper used in this book complies with the
Permanent Paper Standard issued by the National
Information Standards Organization (Z39.48–1984).

10   9   8   7   6   5   4   3   2

# CONTENTS

# SERIES FOREWORD

Northern Ireland, the Middle East, and South Asia are just some of the places where ethnic/racial issues have divided communities and countries. The United States has a long history of such division that often has erupted into violent conflict as well. In America, a nation of immigrants with many ethnic and racial groups, it is particularly important to understand the issues that separate us from one another. Nothing could be more damaging to our nation of nations than the misconception of others' opinions on controversial topics.

The purpose of this series is to provide the means by which students particularly, but also teachers and general readers, can comprehend the contentious issues of our times. The diverse groups chosen for inclusion are the country's main ethnic/racial minorities. Therefore, the groups covered are African Americans, Native Americans, Asian Americans, Latino Americans, Jewish Americans and Muslim Americans. Each book is written by an expert on that group, a scholar able to explain and discuss clearly in a narrative style the points of friction within the minority and between the minority and majority.

Each volume begins with the historical background of a contemporary issue, including court decisions and legislative action, that provides context. This introduction is followed by the pros and cons of the debate, various viewpoints, the opinion of notables, questions for discussion or paper topics, and recommended reading. Readers of this series will become conversant with such topics as affirmative action and reparations, Indian names and images in sports, undocumented immigrants and border control, intermarriage, separation of church and state, old-world ties and assimilation, and racial profiling. Knowledge of such concerns will help limit conflict, encourage discussion, and clarify the opinions of those who disagree with majority views. It is important, especially for students, to recognize the value of a different point of view.

Also of importance is realizing that some issues transcend ethnic/racial boundaries. For example, stereotypical images are concerns of both Native Americans and Asian Americans, affirmative action and reparations are more than black-white controversies, and separation of church and state affects Muslim as well as Jewish Americans. These subjects are perennial ones in American history and serve to illustrate that they need to be discussed in a way that brings attention to various views.

This type of series would have served a useful purpose during earlier years when Americans searched for answers and clarification for complex issues tied to race and ethnicity. In a nation that has now become more diversified and during a period once again of extensive immigration, it is time to look at our disputes and calmly appraise and discuss.

*Ronald H. Bayor*
*Series Editor*

# ACKNOWLEDGMENTS

I want to acknowledge the support of Ronald Bayor, the series editor, and a longtime scholar in the field of ethnic studies. I have for a long time respected his contributions and thank him for his support. I enjoyed very much working with Wendi Schnaufer, the Senior Acquisitions Editor, who has made this a better book. Without her participation I would have lost interest; she is intellectually challenging. I thank Manley Witten for his reading of the first draft and Debbie Jackson for her clerical support. So much of the learning about Chicanos, Central Americans, and Latin Americans comes from personal contact. I owe a great debt to my Chicano, Mexican, and Central American students. Lastly, I thank my family: my sons, Frank and Walter and their families, and especially my wife, Guadalupe, and my daughter Angela. As any writer knows, writing does not come without a price; the writer steals time from those around him. I have stolen a lot of time from my wife and daughter and I hope this book in some small way compensates for the emotional drain.

# INTRODUCTION

*U.S. Latino Issues* concerns a group of people who the U.S. Census calls Latinos or Hispanics. Although Latinos can be of different nationalities, as with Asian Americans, the census lumps them together for the census count. When and why the Latino identity came about is a more involved story. Essentially, politicians, the media, and marketers find it convenient to deal with the different U.S. Spanish-speaking people under one umbrella.

However, many people with Spanish surnames contest the term *Latino*. They claim it is misleading because no Latino or Hispanic nationality exists since no Latino state exists, so generalizing the term *Latino* slights the various national identities included under the umbrella. Some critics argue that the Latino identity was artificially constructed by the U.S. government. According to the critics, the purpose was to erase the historical memory of the various Spanish-speaking groups. These critics accuse the promoters of the term *Latino* of being cheerleaders for the system that celebrate a false impression that Latinos are making it in society, resulting in flag-waving ceremonies celebrating, "We are number one." Finally, the Latino identity erases the reality that most people under this umbrella are of mixed-race background.

The supporters of the term argue times have changed and national identities as we once knew them are outdated. They believe clinging onto national identities promotes nationalism, factionalism, and thus division. They argue that the term *Latino* is more inclusive. This school of belief is divided into two factions, one preferring the term *Hispanic* and the other preferring *Latino*. The popularity of the terms is greater within professional and business groups who live closest to Anglo Americans and who want to forge a national presence. In turn, government agencies, which for statistical reasons find it more convenient to lump the disparate groups into one, support the trend.

With this controversy in mind, *U.S. Latino Issues* turns to introducing the different nationalities within the contested Latino identity, taking into account their individual realities without debating the political correctness of the term, the definition of which depends on the person's view of the world.

## WHO ARE THEY AND HOW MANY SO-CALLED U.S. LATINOS ARE THERE?

The 2000 census lists 35.3 million Latinos in the United States. Latinos make up 12.5 percent of the nation's population, and by the year 2005 Latinos probably will be the largest minority in the United States, outnumbering African Americans, who total between 34.7 million and 36.4 million. The population of U.S. Latinos grew 60 percent since the 1990 census, when the Census Bureau counted 22.4 million of them. Mexican Americans compose the largest group, making up 58.5 percent of total Latinos, probably more if the census acknowledged that 17.3 percent of the respondents marked Latino or Hispanic without designating a nationality. The Latino population grew the fastest in the Midwest, where the U.S. Latino population rose by 80 percent to 3.1 million during the 1990s and where seven of 10 Latinos are Mexican Americans.[1]

The Lewis Mumford Center for Comparative Urban and Regional Research at University at Albany, State University of New York, has questioned these figures and believes that there has been a serious undercount of new Latino immigrants, that is new immigrants from the Dominican Republic, Central America, and South America. The growth of the new Latino population is creating tension as the numbers of old Latino groups, such as Cuban Americans, who register 1.3 million, are challenged for leadership by the newcomers. The Mumford Center estimates that 1.1 million Dominicans (63 percent foreign-born) and 1.1 million Salvadorans (more than 70 percent foreign-born) lived in the United States in 2000, and that the new Latinos are growing more rapidly than Puerto Ricans, who are by definition U.S.-born, or Cubans, who are 68 percent foreign-born.[2]

U.S. Latinos, especially those of Mexican ancestry, are young compared to the rest of the U.S. population. The median age of Latinos nationally in 2000 was 25.9, almost 10 years below the national median of 35.3. However, the median age of Mexicans nation-wide is even lower at 24.2 years. (Some 36 percent of Mexican Americans were born in Mexico, about half of them immigrating to the United States since 1992.) Almost three-fourths of U.S.

**Table 1**
**2000 U.S. Census Bureau Latino Results**

| Subject | Number | Percent |
|---|---|---|
| Hispanic or Latino origin | | |
| Total population | 281,421,906 | 100.0 |
| Hispanic or Latino (of any race) | 35,305,818 | 12.5 |
| Not Hispanic or Latino | 246,116,088 | 87.5 |
| Hispanic or Latino by type | | |
| Hispanic or Latino (of any race) | 35,305,818 | 100.0 |
| Mexican | 20,640,711 | 58.5 |
| Puerto Rican | 3,406,178 | 9.6 |
| Cuban | 1,241,685 | 3.5 |
| Other Hispanic or Latino | 10,017,244 | 28.4 |
| Dominican (Dominican Republic) | 764,945 | 2.2 |
| Central American (excludes Mexican) | 1,686,937 | 4.8 |
| Costa Rican | 68,588 | 0.2 |
| Guatemalan | 372,487 | 1.1 |
| Honduran | 217,569 | 0.6 |
| Nicaraguan | 177.684 | 0.5 |
| Panamanian | 91,723 | 0.3 |
| Salvadoran | 655,165 | 1.9 |
| Other Central American | 103,721 | 0.3 |
| South American | 1,353,562 | 3.8 |
| Argentinean | 100,864 | 0.3 |
| Bolivian | 42,068 | 0.1 |
| Chilean | 68,849 | 0.2 |
| Colombian | 470,684 | 1.3 |
| Ecuadorian | 260,559 | 0.7 |
| Paraguayan | 8,769 | 0.0 |
| Peruvian | 233,926 | 0.7 |
| Uruguayan | 18,804 | 0.1 |
| Venezuelan | 91,507 | 0.3 |
| Other South American | 57,532 | 0.2 |

*(continued)*

**Table 1**
**Continued**

| Subject | Number | Percent |
| --- | ---: | ---: |
| Spaniard | 100,135 | 0.3 |
| All other Hispanic or Latino | 6,111,665 | 17.3 |
| Checked only other Hispanic | 1,733,274 | 4.9 |
| Write-in Spanish | 686,004 | 1.9 |
| Write-in Hispanic | 2,454,529 | 7.0 |
| Write-in Latino | 450,769 | 1.3 |
| Not elsewhere classified | 787,089 | 2.2 |

*Source:* Bureau of the Census, *Census 2000 Summary File 1,* in *The Hispanic Population: Census 2000 Brief.*

Mexicans are younger than age 35—the youngest of the U.S. Latinos. The second largest Latino group was the Puerto Ricans, who numbered 3.4 million, or 9.6 percent of the Latino total. Puerto Ricans had a median age of 27.3 years. Central Americans number 1.68 million, or 4.8 percent of the total, and had a median age of 29.2. (Caution: the Mumford Center has revised these figures upward.) Dominicans total 765,000, or 2.2 percent of Latinos, with a median age of 29.5. (Note that the Mumford Center estimates the total U.S. Dominican population at 1.1 million.) About 1.2 million Cubans, whose median age is 40.7, live in the United States.

Because U.S. Latinos are young, they have a higher birthrate than white Americans. These figures are even more dramatic considering that by the year 2030, Latinos will compose half of all Texans,[3] and that in 1998, 47.5 percent of infants born in California were Latinos. Meanwhile, Euro-American mothers accounted for 33.9 percent of infants born, followed by Asians and Pacific Islanders with 10.7 percent, African Americans with 6.8 percent and Native Americans at 0.5 percent (see Table 1).[4]

Apart from differences in nationality among U.S. Latinos, class and gender differences also exist. U.S. Latinos are represented in all classes. Recent studies show that Latino middle-class households earning more than $40,000 have increased by 80 percent in the past 20 years.[5] Nearly 42 percent of native-born or U.S.-born Latino households were middle class in 1998 (up from 39 percent in 1979). The percentage of native-born Latinos with a college education rose from 10.7 percent in 1979 to 15.4 percent in 1998, a gain of 43.9 percent (see Table 3). Yet this gain was smaller with Mexican

**Table 2**
**Mumford Estimates of U.S. Latino Population for 2000**

| | |
|---|---|
| Mexican | 23,060,224 |
| Puerto Rican | 3,640,460 |
| Cuban | 1,315,346 |
| Dominican | 1,121,257 |
| Central American | 2,863,063 |
| Costa Rican | 111,672 |
| Guatemalan | 657,329 |
| Honduran | 362,171 |
| Nicaraguan | 294,334 |
| Panamanian | 164,371 |
| Salvadoran | 1,117,959 |
| Other Central American | 181,228 |
| Argentinean | 168,991 |
| Bolivian | 70,545 |
| Chilean | 117,698 |
| Colombian | 742,406 |
| Ecuadorian | 396,400 |
| Paraguayan | 14,492 |
| Peruvian | 381,850 |
| Uruguayan | 30,010 |
| Venezuelan | 149,309 |
| Other South American | 97,969 |
| Other Hispanic | 1,135,799 |

*Source:* John R. Logan, *The New Latinos: Who They Are, Where They Are.* Lewis Mumford Center, 10 September 2001.

Americans and U.S. Central Americans because these populations had more immigrants and were younger. From 1979 to 1998, about 60 percent of Anglo families had become middle class while only 35 percent of all Latino households, which included native born, were middle class. Significantly, poverty increased during this period as families making less than $20,000 a year rose from 1.2 million to 2.6 million. In sum, the middle-class Latino popu-

**Table 3**
**2000 U.S. Census Comparison of Education and Poverty**

| | Central American and Mexican | Puerto Rican | Cuban | South American | Other Hispanic | Non-Hispanic |
|---|---|---|---|---|---|---|
| Educational attainment Latino origin | | | | | | |
| Bachelor's degree | 5.1 | 8.6 | 13.9 | 11.8 | 8.9 | 18.1 |
| Advanced degree | 1.8 | 4.4 | 9.2 | 5.6 | 5.6 | 9.1 |
| Less than high school diploma | 49.0 | 35.7 | 27.0 | 35.7 | 28.4 | 13.0 |
| Family type and poverty status | | | | | | |
| Below poverty level | 21.2 | 23.0 | 15.0 | 16.3 | 18.1 | 8.0 |
| Married-couple families below poverty level | 16.7 | 8.1 | 10.3 | 9.9 | 8.9 | 3.9 |
| Male householder, no spouse present below poverty level | 15.8 | 19.0 | 19.8 | 19.0 | 17.5 | 10.7 |
| Female householder, no spouse present below poverty level | 38.4 | 47.4 | 33.8 | 32.0 | 40.0 | 26.1 |
| Earnings | | | | | | |
| $50,000 to $74,999 | 7.4 | 13.1 | 10.1 | 8.6 | 12.0 | 19.8 |
| $75,000 and over | 2.1 | 4.3 | 11.7 | 4.1 | 7.0 | 14.3 |

*Source:* Bureau of the Census, *Current Population Survey, March 2000,* Ethnic and Hispanic Statistics Branch, Population Division. Internet Release Date: 6 March 2001.

lation was growing, making assimilation into U.S. society easier for many U.S. Latinos. Nevertheless, the poverty rate for Latino children was also three times that of non-Latino white children. In other words, while the U.S. Latino middle class was expanding, the poor were becoming poorer. Poverty among Latinos became more acute as the government reduced benefits such as food stamps.[6] The cause of this poverty among Latinos was not that Latinos were not working. In 2000, 80.4 percent of Latino males were working compared with 74.3 percent of non-Latino white males, suggesting that Latinos were poor not because they did not work, but because employers did not pay Latinos sufficiently.[7]

As with class status, gender played a varying role within each nationality. In 2000, Latino males—18,161,795 of them—outnumbered the 17,144,023 Latinas. (With whites, Asians, and blacks, the female population outnumbered the male population.)[8] However, this statistic adjusted itself as the population entered their 20s, and by age 40 Latinas outnumbered Latino males. Latinas also differed from their male counterparts in education, faring better in comparison to Latino males than to white women. For example, Latinas were less likely to take the SAT exam than their white or Asian female counterparts, and when they did, Latinas scored lower. Simultaneously, Latinas outnumbered Latinos in taking the SAT exam.[9] Contributing to this education gap is the fact that Latinos and Latinas are more likely to attend schools with lower percentages of certified teachers than are white or Asian students. In addition, Latino students overall are underrepresented in Head Start, early childhood developmental programs, after-school programs, and academic courses such as advanced placement courses.[10]

Apart from this inequality, Latino families are four times more likely to be living in poverty than white families (14.2 percent compared with 3.3 percent) while Latino families headed by females were twice as likely as their white counterparts to be living in poverty (38.8 percent compared with 18.6 percent). In addition, 31.7 percent of Puerto Rican children lived in poverty.[11] According to Census 2000, the median full-time earnings for Latinas were $20,527, compared to white men who had earnings of $37,339.[12] Taken as a whole, Latina women in 1999 had a median income of $11,314 compared to $14,771 for black women and $30,594 for white women.[13] Among women, 56.5 percent of Latinas work outside the house compared to 60.8 percent of white women.[14]

## WHERE DO LATINOS LIVE?

Where Latinos live greatly depends on when they came to the United States and on their economic class. Of the Latino nations, Mexico is the closest in proximity to the United States. Thus, at first Mexicans resided primarily in the border states and on the West Coast, but during the 1990s this changed and Mexicans spread throughout the nation. Most of the new Latinos (close to 1.4 million) live in New York State and on the U.S. mainland. At least 1.1 million Puerto Ricans of the 3.4 million on the mainland live in New York State (Puerto Ricans are U.S. citizens and the island of Puerto Rico belongs to the United States, so Puerto Ricans are not considered to be typical immigrants). Dominican immigration represents the second largest number of Caribbean-Latino immigration, and they are concentrated in the Northeast. More than half of all Cuban Americans live in Miami; in fact, more than 85 percent live in four states: Florida, New Jersey, New York, and California. In recent years, the arrival of other Latino groups has challenged Cuban Americans. About 850,000 new Latinos arrived in Florida in the 1990s, and more than 500,000 Puerto Ricans live in Florida, along with about 400,000 Mexicans.[15] There are also 350,000 Puerto Ricans and 500,000 new Latinos in New Jersey. Of the new immigrants, Central Americans are the most mobile, emigrating primarily from El Salvador, Nicaragua, and Guatemala, and residing in California, Florida, New York, Texas, and Illinois. In contrast to other Latinos, most South Americans came to the United States for professional and, to a lesser extent, political reasons, and most hold white-collar, scientific, or executive positions; in recent years, however, a core of lower middle- and working-class South Americans have emigrated to the United States. About 500,000 South Americans live in New York State, many of whom are new arrivals.[16] Ecuador and Peru also have large concentrations of immigrants on the East Coast.

According to Census 2000, half the nation's Latinos live in two states: California and Texas. More than one in five Latinos live in the Los Angeles region. California had almost as many new Latinos arriving during the 1990s as did New York, close to 1.4 million, though the Mexican population eclipses them. Southern California houses four of the top 10 communities of at least 100,000 Latinos nationwide. Unincorporated East Los Angeles ranks first and is 96.8 percent Latino, mostly of Mexican origin. The city of Santa Ana ranks seventh, El Monte, eighth and Oxnard ninth. California houses one-third of U.S. Latinos; about one-quarter of its overall population is of Mexican ancestry. People of Mexican background also represent about one-quarter of all Texans.[17]

Mexican Americans compose a large portion of the Latino population of Harris County, Texas, which includes Houston (1.1 million); and Cook County, Illinois, which includes Chicago (1.1 million). New Mexico has the largest percentage of U.S. Latinos of any state with 42 percent. But New Mexico is sparsely populated, so each of the above counties actually has more

U.S. Latinos than New Mexico. Cubans dominate Miami-Dade (1.3 million) in Florida. According to the census, 43.5 percent of the U.S. Latino population lives in the West, 32.8 percent in the South, 14.9 percent in the Northeast, and 8.9 percent in the Midwest. Texas is much more diverse than in the 1980s, with 400,000 new Latinos arriving in the 1990s.

Thus, the growth and dispersal of the U.S. Latino population will have a dramatic impact on the nation. Social scientists can no longer generalize that all Mexicans live in the Southwest or that all Latinos are Mexican or Puerto Rican. In the future, Latinos will challenge American society, both culturally and politically.

## THE HISTORY

Some Americans of Mexican descent were in the Southwest long before the Anglo Americans arrived in what is now the United States. The Southwest became part of the United States because of two wars, the Texas War of 1836 and the Mexican American War that ended in 1848 in which the United States took half of Mexico's land, and the Gadsden Purchase of 1853. The large-scale Mexican immigration throughout the twentieth century augmented their numbers. Various factors drove Mexican immigration to the United States, including the uprooting of Mexicans in the last quarter of the nineteenth century as the railroads, financed by foreign capital, advanced the commercialization of agriculture, displacing many small farmers. In addition, industrialization created a demand for Mexican workers in the United States. Labor contractors recruited them to work on the railroads, mines, farms, stockyards, and in other industries. As the need for labor pulled Mexicans into the United States, each wave of Mexican immigration met with intense discrimination as Mexicans established colonies *(colonias)* and enclaves *(barrios)* and their own community, religious, and labor organizations. During the first quarter of the twentieth century, the bulk of the Mexican migration to the United States was to Texas and Arizona. However, by the second quarter of that century, California became a favorite destination for Mexicans.

During the 1980s, Mexican immigrants continued overwhelmingly to settle in California. Changes took place, and during the 1990s the trends shifted. Work opportunities in poultry plants, slaughterhouses, and restaurants pulled Mexican immigrants to the South and Midwest. Mexicans also harvested tobacco and other crops there. Besides a large population in California, Mexicans, along with other Latinos, now make up almost one-quarter of the population in some counties of North Carolina, Georgia, Iowa, Arkansas, Minnesota, and Nebraska. This movement has transformed the Mexican American population from a regional minority to a national presence. This migration also paved the way for other Latinos, who in previous decades had primarily moved to large cities.

Puerto Rico became a possession of the United States in 1898 after the Spanish-American War and the signing of the Treaty of Paris. In reality, Puerto Ricans did not have a choice in this annexation. Ever since the annexation, Puerto Ricans have struggled to define themselves, with some wishing to become a state within the American republic and others fighting for the independence of Puerto Rico. Technically, Puerto Ricans became American citizens in 1917 under the Jones Act, but conditions on the island resembled those of some third-world countries. Puerto Ricans began trickling into the United States soon after annexation, and the 1920 census registered 41,094 Latinos in New York City alone. Of these, 21.2 percent were Cuban and West Indian, 17.9 percent Puerto Rican, and 18.9 percent were Central and South American. The rest of the Latino population, almost 36 percent, was from Spain. This number grew to 110,223 ten years later, and the Puerto Rican population grew to 40.7 percent (44,930).[18] The Puerto Rican migration quickened and spread to other parts around World War II. In the state of New York, the Puerto Rican population rose from 61,463 in 1940 to 811,843 in 1970.[19]

After 1959, with the success of the Cuban Revolution, Cuban political refugees came in larger numbers to the United States. From 1959 to 1963, 215,000 Cubans arrived in the United States. The 1966 Cuban Adjustment Act gave Cubans political asylum and made Cubans eligible for government-sponsored and subsidized programs.[20] Cubans dominated Miami, the closest city to Cuba, and formed a sizeable number in New York and New Jersey. The Miami Cuban community grew from 50,000 to 580,000 between 1960 and 1980. The white upper- and middle-class composition of Cubans gave them more power and visibility than other Latinos. Despite economic and social advantages, however, Cubans suffered discrimination. Cubans also have remained culturally cohesive, acculturating rather than assimilating into American society. Cuban Americans are far from homogeneous, however. Although the first wave was mostly whites of Spanish origin (*criollo*), other waves in the 1980s included working-class Africans as well as white and mixed blood Cubans.[21] Cuban leader Fidel Castro allowed 125,000 Cubans to leave the island in four months during the Mariel boat lift (named after the Port of Mariel) in 1980. Meanwhile, economic conditions on the island worsened as subsidies from the Soviet Union ended and a U.S. embargo isolated the Cuban government economically.

The Dominican Republic shares the large island of Hispaniola with Haiti, once a French possession. By 1960, 13,293 Dominicans lived in New York City; 10 years later, 66,914 resided there. The Dominican migration accelerated in 1960 with the assassination of dictator Rafael Trujillo, a favorite of the United States. This first wave of migration consisted of many wealthy Dominicans who had benefited from the Trujillo regime. The United States invaded the Dominican Republic in the mid-1960s, and between 1966 and 1978 the dictatorship drove many progressives out of the country. According to one observer, the Dominicans "[I]n steadily rising numbers but almost unnoticed . . . have been arriving for almost four decades now. Outside New York City and a few other places in the northeast, not many Americans seemed to have noticed their growing presence."[22] Perhaps the Dominican Republic is best known for is its baseball superstars such as Sammy Sosa, Alex Rodríguez, and Manny Ramírez. Between 1961 and 1986 some 400,000 Dominicans migrated to the United States, primarily to New York City, with another 44,000 migrating to Puerto Rico. (Today there are more than 300,000 Dominicans in Puerto Rico.) While Census 2000 counted 764,945 Dominicans, other sources estimated that there were 1.5 million Dominicans by 2000. (The Dominicans have a sizeable undocumented population.) While many Dominicans are poor, the population has a sizeable middle class that fled the island after the overthrow of Trujillo, and who now operate businesses in the United States.[23]

Central Americans are the newest arrivals, representing 4.8 percent of the U.S. Latino presence. (This probably is a dramatic undercount.) In 20 years, Central Americans have developed many eateries and community organizations. In addition, 1979 was a watershed year for Central America, and larger numbers began arriving in the United States because of the instability back home. The overthrow of dictator Anastacio Somoza in Nicaragua destabilized the region, and rebels launched wars of liberation in Guatemala and El Salvador, where the military killed 200,000 and 50,000, respectively. To a lesser extent, Panamanians, Hondurans, and Costa Ricans also migrated north. Generally, Central Americans as a group are less educated, work at menial employment, and are darker than South Americans and Cubans. Most live in Latino neighborhoods, keeping their first culture intact.

In Nicaragua after the overthrow of Somoza, the Sandinista Party assumed control of the government. The Sandinistas sought economic aid, which the Soviet Union volunteered. The United States funded the counterrevolutionaries, whom Americans called *Contras,* and because of the U.S. economic embargo, the Sandinista government was unable to stabilize. In the 1980s, one-tenth of Nicaraguans left their country, a third of them college-educated, white-collar workers, or businesspeople. Many Nicaraguans entered the United States as political refugees and many settled in the Miami area. In 1980, an estimated 25,000 Nicaraguans lived in the United States; in 2000 the census reported the number rose to 177,684.[24]

The largest group of Central Americans is Salvadoran, who have large populations in Southern California, Houston, Washington, D.C., and New York. Most came to the United States because a bloody civil war ripped through the country from 1980 to 1992. After Puerto Rico, El Salvador is the most densely populated country in Latin America. The Civil War there had many causes, not the least of which was the monopoly of the country's land by slightly more than a dozen elite families. During the 1980s, the military imposed a dictatorship as the guerrilla forces under the Farabundo Marti National Liberation Front (FMLN) fought to break this control. The 1980 census counted about 30,000 Salvadorans in the United States; the 2000 Census counted 655,165 Salvadorans. The number is likely to be closer to one million. Salvadorans have been very active in the United States, building an impressive organizational infrastructure, integrating into trade unions, and bringing lawsuits over their immigration status.

Guatemala has been in political turmoil for much of its existence. The latest civil war came about when the CIA sponsored the overthrow of President Jacob Arbenz in 1954 when he threatened the plantations of the United Fruit Co. The civil war escalated in the 1980s as the United States supported the military government, and the military killed more than 200,000 Guatemalans. The 1980 census showed about 71,000 Guatemalans living in the United States This number grew from 230,000 in 1990 to 372,487 in 2000. According to some sources, most of the Guatemalans in the United States are of Mayan origin for whom Spanish is a second language. Many Guatemalans are former villagers whom the military drove off their land. Guatemalans are more dispersed within areas than Salvadorans and live primarily in Los Angeles, San Francisco, Chicago, Houston, and Washington, D.C., where they share space with other Latinos. Many also are farm workers.

Although Honduras did not experience the civil turmoil of El Salvador, Nicaragua, and Guatemala, Honduras was used as a base of operations by both the CIA and the Nicaraguan *Contras.* The 2000 census recorded 217,569 Hondurans in the United States; Hondurans have settled in California, southern Florida, and New York. The Honduran population is diverse, with a large community of Honduran *Garifuna,* black English-speaking Hondurans from the Caribbean coast, settling in the Bronx and parts of Brooklyn in New York. Although wealthier Hondurans also have migrated to the United States, a sizeable number work as migrant farm workers.

The other Central American nations have sent fewer immigrants to the United States. Costa Rica has enjoyed relative peace and prosperity, and therefore has not sent large numbers of immigrants. The largest concentration of Costa Ricans is in the Miami area, because Miami is a major financial and business center for Latin America. However, Costa Ricans are also found in Los Angeles and New York City.

A construct of the United States, Panama came about in the early 1900s when the United States wanted to build a canal. The United States fomented a revolution there, which caused Panama to get its independence from Colombia in 1903. Like most people of the region, many Panamanians are of mixed blood—Indian and Spanish; however, the African admixture (West Indians brought to the canal to work and never taken back) has been significant, along with some of Chinese and Hindu ancestry.[25]

Before the 1980s, most South Americans were either political exiles or they were wealthier than the other U.S. Latino groups and lived apart from them. Today, South Americans account for 3.8 percent of the Latino total. The South American bloc is smaller than the rest largely because of distance and the cost of transportation, which until recently was prohibitive for most people. A good number of South American immigrants are political refugees, and as a group, most are better off than the rest of U.S. Latinos. For example, many Argentines came to the United States between 1976 and 1983 during the Dirty War. In addition, many Argentine Jews fled the country because of anti-Semitism. One in five Argentines who fled settled in the New York City area and another part settled in Miami. The current economic crisis is also driving them out of Argentina. Their numbers, however, remain relatively low. Fewer immigrants have entered from Bolivia because the cost and difficulty of travel keep them from migrating in larger numbers.

The Colombian migration took place during the 1950s and early 1960s during the civil war called *La Violencia* (The Violence), in which hundreds of thousands of Colombians were killed. Many middle-class Colombians and merchants migrated to the United States during this period. The growth of the drug cartels created instability during the late 1970s, which encouraged more Colombians to migrate out of the country. The Colombian American population stood at 77,000 in the 1970s and escalated to around 470,000 by the year 2000. Colombians live primarily in New York City, New Jersey, and Miami.[26]

Bad governments have afflicted Ecuador and have caused hundreds of thousands of Ecuadorians of all classes to migrate to the United States. Cheaper transportation has made emigration easier for Ecuadorians. Miami became a sort of Ellis Island for Ecuadorians and other immigrants from South America. Some 60 percent live in New York City, and another 10 percent live in Los Angeles.

The pattern of Peruvians entering the United States was similar to other South Americans, with the wave in the 1950s and 1960s being primarily middle class, followed by a larger wave of 100,000 Peruvians in the second half of the 1980s as political and economic instability gripped the country. An estimated 200,000 Peruvians live in the New York tri-state area, and another 230,000 are spread out nationally. Educator Félipe Reinoso became the first Peruvian American elected as a Connecticut state senator in 2000.[27]

Venezuelans arrived during the 1980s because of an economic crash. Before this, Venezuela had enjoyed relatively good times and did not have much emigration because of the boom in oil. Today fewer than 100,000 live mostly in Florida, New York City, and other major East Coast cities.

Many Chileans arrived after the CIA's overthrow of Chilean president Salvador Allende in 1973. More than a million Chileans left the country between 1973 and 1990; however, few migrated to the United States. Many Chileans returned to Chile after military dictator Augusto Pinochet left office, leaving about 69,000 Chileans currently living in the United States. The other Latin American countries—Bolivia, Paraguay and Uruguay—have a relatively small presence.

Some U.S. Latino organizations consider immigrants from non-Spanish-speaking Latin American countries such as Brazil and West Indies as U.S. Latinos. This argument also makes sense for French-speaking Haitians who share the island with the Dominican Republic. The boat people from Haiti should be considered Latinos as much as those of other nations. Haitians are from Latin America, and many U.S. Latinos can trace back their ancestry to Africa. About 514,000 Haitians and West Indians, natives of the Bahamas, Barbados, Jamaica, Trinidad, and Tobago, live in Florida. That makes Florida the West Indians' second most popular destination, slightly behind the state of New York, which has received Jamaicans and Haitians for decades. Haitians and West Indians also have migrated to Boston.[28] Many of these immigrants speak English or French as do smaller number of Belizeans. Brazilians are considered Latinos; however, Brazilians speak Portuguese and do not have a strong national presence in the United States.

## THE CONTESTED IDENTITY

Identity among Latinos is contested because they are composed of disparate races and nationalities. Roughly 60 percent of Latinos were U.S.-born, with great variations from group to group. (Puerto Ricans, for instance, are U.S. citizens.) The rate of immigration plays a decisive role in Latino population growth: many native-born Latinos are in fact the children of new immigrants, who themselves tend to be young and have comparatively high fertility rates. Racially, Latinos are diverse. For example, Mexicans are mostly *mestizos*, a mixture of Indian and Spanish (and to a lesser extent African and Asian); Puerto Ricans are a mixture of African and Spanish and some Indian; whereas Nicaraguans are a mixture of Indian, Spanish, and African. Latinos are similar to one another in that Latinos were all colonized; Spain conquered and controlled most of them for more than 300 years. Consequently, most U.S. Latinos speak Spanish, although with different intonations, something that is often not reflected in contemporary Hollywood movies. Latinos all have a strong sense of connection with their mother countries, bringing with them historical memories and cultural variations. At home, many continue eating foods favored in their mother countries, and these cuisines often differ from Mexican cuisine, which the Mexican Indian has heavily influenced. Enchiladas, tacos, and mole are all Mexican foods, and other U.S. Latinos do not necessarily eat spicy foods.

So why, if Latinos are different, do people use *Hispanic* or *Latino* as terms to describe their origin? The best and most logical reason is that various federal programs require data on the ethnic makeup of the community for federal affirmative action plans, community reinvestment reports, and public health service requirements.[29] Not everyone has the same needs, however. As mentioned, there is no one *Hispanic* or *Latino* nationality. The terms themselves are misleading, since *Hispanic* technically means Spanish, and Latin American countries fought wars of independence against Spain and formed separate nation-states. In addition, the designation *Latino* refers to an Italian language. Both words have political baggage, especially for Mexican Americans who, to avoid discrimination and to differentiate themselves from darker Mexicans, often call themselves Spanish Americans or Latin Americans. Moreover, many Mexican Americans prefer the term *Chicano*, which was adopted during the 1960s as a political term embracing collective responsibility to bring about social change for their community and within the country.

In short, considerable controversy exists within the disparate Spanish-speaking populations about whether *Latino* and/or *Hispanic* are valid terms. Because the same words are used to refer to different notions of their identities, confusion is apt to result when speakers do not realize they are using these words with different senses. When people use notions of race and gender, they understand and use them in different ways. When they use terms such as *Hispanic* and *Latino,* are they referring to ethnicity, caste, or nationality? Being precise is important, because these terms carry with them different meanings and interests. Realistically, are U.S. Latinos ready to surrender their individual histories? This has not been the case with Jewish Americans, Irish Americans, and others.

Using the term Latino also raises a concern of African Americans. In the view of some African Americans, the broadness of the term, *Latino* has cut ever-shrinking civil rights entitlements too many ways. Critics charge that all too often Latinos stretch the notion of the entitlements of the civil rights acts. African Americans argue that entitlements should be limited to identifiable racial and ethnic minorities who have suffered historical discrimination that has resulted in economic, social, and political disadvantages. African Americans point out that Spaniards and Italians do not meet this criterion.[30]

## ABOUT THIS BOOK

The book is divided into 10 chapters, each addressing an important and controversial issue pertinent to Latinos. A background section introduces each chapter about U.S. Latino communities and their history, then frames each issue, after which arguments for and against the issue are presented, followed by a section with questions for the students to discuss and debate. At the end of the chapter there are selected readings for the student who wants further information as well as relevant Web sites. Additional Internet sites can be found through Google, America Online, or other search engines.

The first chapter is on race classifications. In the 2000 census, close to half the Latino population classified itself as white. This has led to a debate about the reasons for this. Opinions range. Some say that classifying Latinos as white dilutes the identity of white Americans. Others respond that it does not matter. The question here is presented so it introduces students to the notion of race, which has been one of the most overriding and divisive issues in U.S. history. It is an issue that potentially divides U.S. Latinos, hence the term *contested identity.*

Chapter 2 is about assimilation. Historically assimilation meant almost complete absorption into American society, leaving only symbolic veneers to the immigrant identity. For example, cynics may ask what remains of Italian culture among Italian Americans other than pizza and the *Godfather* movies. In reality, the question of assimilation has wider implications. American conservatives are waging a culture war in America concerning whether minorities should forget the past and melt in. Arguments are presented from both sides.

Chapter 3 deals with bilingual education. The debate over bilingual education has raged in most parts of the country, with opponents trumpeting that the official language of America is English and that bilingual education dilutes that mission and divides people. Most U.S. Latinos have interpreted this attitude as an attack on them and have responded negatively to ballot initiatives such as California's Proposition 227. The issue has divided many Americans and promises to continue raising questions in the future as U.S. Latino, as well as Asian, populations grow and seek to retain their original languages.

Chapter 4 is about borders. The United States shares about 2,000 miles of borders with Canada and Mexico. Because of the higher standard of living in the United States—Americans consume about 50 percent of the world's resources—it is a desirable place for those wanting to emigrate. Consequently, large waves of both authorized and unauthorized immigrants have entered the United States since the 1970s, touching off nativist reactions from some white Americans worried that people who differ racially and culturally may not assimilate (or will assimilate) into American society.

Chapter 5 addresses the issue of affirmative action, which is again part of an ongoing national debate on how best to achieve equality in our society. Affirmative action is a wedge issue that divides society between liberals and conservatives and between whites and people of color. The debate is part of the culture war in the United States, which raged during the second half of the 1990s and still demands attention.

Chapter 6 involves interracial dating and marriage. With Latinos, the acceptance of interracial dating and marriage depends on housing patterns and regional differences, as well as the country of origin and the darkness of the individual U.S. Latino's skin. The acceptance of interracial dating also depends on whether the minority partner conforms to the majority culture. For example, interracial dating and marriage is much more problematic in Georgia and Mississippi than it is in Florida. The issue is also a question of different generational responses.

Chapter 7 explores public funding for education and health services to undocumented immigrants and their families. The issue of immigration is complex. Some estimates say there are as many as 7 million to 8 million undocumented immigrants in the United States. American-first groups say the U.S. taxpayer should not pay for the education and medical care of people who have broken the law and are in the United States illegally. Others respond that 80 percent plus of the U.S. Latino population work and pay taxes (in comparison to slightly less than 75 percent of white males) and contribute to society and that everyone has a constitutional right to an education. They argue that the reason that undocumented and other poor Latinos have to seek subsidized medical care is because employers are not paying for the cost of social production. These arguments often are heated, with one side accusing the other of being un-American or racist.

Chapter 8 addresses immigration and amnesty for unauthorized immigrants. Again, the pro and con arguments verge on the personal, with many Americans asking why those without papers should be rewarded and given preference over applicants who followed the law and are waiting their turn in line. This mind-set generates an equally vehement response from supporters of amnesty, who say that the debate is not about something as trivial as buying tickets to a movie theater, but about gaining entrance to a country. Either directly or indirectly, pro-immigrant forces say the United States has created the conditions that have led to the unauthorized migration and that amnesty just periodically adjusts for a phenomenon that gets out of hand.

The last two chapters concern the question of sovereignty and other issues specifically regarding Cuba and Puerto Rico. Chapter 9 discusses the military and political presence of the United States in Cuba. While the various nationalities under the U.S. Latino label are alike, often looking and sounding alike to the majority culture, showing that there are differences is important. Whether the United States is violating the sovereignty of Cuba is discussed with regards to the U.S. base at Guantánamo Bay and how the Cuban government wants the United States out. Also discussed is the U.S. economic embargo of Cuba, which does not allow American farmers or many other countries to trade with Cuba and does not allow Americans to travel there. Having troops on Cuban soil and the embargo are hot issues on which not all of the U.S. Latino groups agree.

Finally, chapter 10 centers on Puerto Rico, which is part of the United States and has commonwealth status. The chapter presents the question: what rights do the Puerto Rican people have to limit military exercises on the adjoining island of Vieques? The answers are complex, controversial, and involve different points of view, even among Puerto Ricans.

In sum, the format of the book is designed to encourage discussion, and the topics are more often controversial than not, which will hopefully open the door to further debate. Scholars keep talking about the search for truth, but we package much of our knowledge in sound bytes, and what we know as we reduce truth to acceptable paradigms is that we are free to deduce the answer without going outside the official model to explore other possibilities.

## NOTES

1. George Benge, "NAHJ Focuses on Impact of Hispanic Culture, Growth in Communities," *Gannett Co. Inc.,* http://www.gannett.com/go/newswatch/2001/July/ nw0706–1.htm, accessed 23 July 2003. Also see Rev. Lawrence Dowling, "US Bishops Reflect on Pastoral Impact of Fewer Priests," National Federation of Priests' Councils (excerpt from Fall 2000–Touchstone), http://www.nfpc.org/RESEARCH-RPTS/ pastoral-impact.html, accessed 1 August 2003.

2. John R. Logan, "The New Latinos: Who They Are, Where They Are," Lewis Mumford Center, 10 September 2001, http://mumford1.dyndns.org/cen2000/ HispanicPop/HspReport/HspReportPage1.html, accessed 23 July 2003.

3. Mark Babineck, "Demographer: Texas Likely to Become Majority Hispanic in 2030s," *Associated Press Newswires,* 19 December 2001, http://www.amarillonet.com/ stories/12201/tex_facesof.html, accessed 23 July 2003. The Texas State Data Center released three sets of projections.

4. Reuters News Service, "Majority of Babies Born in California Are Hispanic," *Deseret News,* 20 December 2001.

5. Valeria Godines, "Hispanic Incomes Gaining: ICI Professor Measures a Commonly Overlooked Group, the Latino Middle Class," *The Orange County Register,* 11 April 2001; "National Study Finds 80 Percent Growth in Latino Middle Class Over Past 20 Years," *NoticiasWire.com,* www.noticiaswire.com/experts_research/midlat/print.html, accessed 23 July 2003.

6. Jim Jaffe and Michelle Bazie, "Poverty Rates Fell in 2000 as Unemployment Reached 31-Year Low: Upturn in Unemployment Combines with Weakness in Safety Net Raise Red Flags for 2001," *Center on Budget and Policy Priorities,* 26 September 2001, www.centeronbudget.org/9-25-01pov.htm, accessed 23 July 2003.

7. Raul Yzaguirre, "Census Shows Disparity in Education of Latino Children," *Hispanic Online Hispanic Magazine.com,* April 2001, www.hispanicmagazine.com/2001/apr/Forum, accessed 23 July 2003.

8. Bureau of the Census, *Census 2000 Briefs,* http://www.census.gov/populations/www/cen2000/briefs.html, accessed 23 July 2003. Also see Denise I. Smith and Renee E. Spraggins, *Gender 2000: Census Brief,* September 2001, http://www.census.gov/prod/2001pubs/c2kbr01-9.pdf, accessed 23 July 2003.

9. "Are American's Schools Leaving Latinas Behind? New Report Identifies Steps to Advance Educational Outcomes," *Noticiaswire Press Release,* http://www.noticiaswire.com/experts_research/lat_behind, accessed 23 July 2003.

10. Raul Yzaguirre, "Census Shows Disparity in Education of Latino Children," *Hispanic Online Hispanic Magazine.com,* April 2001, www.hispanicmagazine.com/2001/apr/Forum, accessed 23 July 2003.

11. Ibid.

12. "Race and Pay Equity," *POLICY BRIEF: National Committee for Pay Equity,* http://www.feminist.com/fairpay/brief.htm, accessed 23 July 2003.

13. Census Information Center, "Hispanic Income Fact Sheet," *National Council of La Raza,* November 2000, http://www.nclr.org/policy/census.html, accessed 23 July 2003. This Web site provides links to various studies.

14. Georgia Pabst, "Census Data Show Impact for Latinos but Future Work Force Continues to Struggle, Group's Report Says," *Milwaukee Journal Sentinel,* 16 July 2001, http://www.jsonline.com/news/census2000/jul01/census16071501.asp, accessed 23 July 2003. "More than one-third of Latinos are under the age of 18, and half are under the age of 26."

15. John R. Logan, "The New Latinos: Who They Are, Where They Are," Lewis Mumford Center, 10 September 2001, http://mumford1.dyndns.org/cen2000/HispanicPop/HspReport/HspReportPage1.html, accessed 23 July 2003.

16. Ibid.

17. According to Jeffrey Passel, a demographer at the Urban Institute, a Washington, D.C., think-tank, "The Mexican-origin population is what's driving the growth in the Hispanic population," quoted in Patrick J. McDonnell, "Mexicans Change Face of U.S. Demographics Census: Study shows Latinos on rise, settling in many parts of country," *Los Angeles Times,* 10 May 2001. See also Bureau of the Census, *The Hispanic Population: Census 2000 Brief,* May 2001, http://www.census.gov/Press-Release/www/2001/cb01-81.html, accessed 23 July 2003.

18. Agustin Laó-Montes, introduction to *Mambo Montage: The Latinization of New York City,* ed. Agustín Laó-Montes and Arlene Dávila (New York: Columbia University Press, 2001), 19–20.

19. See http://www.boricua.com, accessed 31 July 2003. It is a valuable tool in accessing contemporary Puerto Rican Web sites.

20. "Latinos in the United States," *The National Association of Hispanic Journalists,* http://www.nahj.org/resourceguide/chapter_3c.html, accessed 23 July 2003. A good overview of disparate groups.

21. Susan A. Vega García, "Recommended U.S. Latino Web Sites Diversity and Ethnic Studies," http://www.public.iastate.edu/~savega/us_latin.htm, accessed 24 July 2003. Gives a good overview and links of available Latino Web sites.

22. See the Dominican Studies Institute at the City University of New York, http://www.ccny.cuny.edu/dsi/about.htm, accessed 24 July 2003.

23. Max J. Castro, "Making Pan Latino: Latino Pan-Ethnicity and the Controversial Case of the Cubans," http://personal.law.miami.edu/~fvaldes/latcrit/archives/harvard/castro.htm, accessed 24 July 2003; see also "Latinos in the United States," *The National Association of Hispanic Journalists,* http://www.nahj.org/resourceguide/chapter_3c.html, accessed 23 July 2003.

24. "Latinos in the United States," *The National Association of Hispanic Journalists,* http://www.nahj.org/resourceguide/chapter_3c.html, accessed 23 July 2003.

25. Ibid.

26. "Latinos in the United States," *The National Association of Hispanic Journalists,* http://www.nahj.org/resourceguide/chapter_3c.html, accessed 23 July 2003; Juan González, *Harvest of Empire: A History of Latinos in America* (New York: Penguin, 2000); Earl Shorris, *Latinos Biography of a People* (New York: Norton, 1992); Roberto Suro, *Strangers among Us: Latinos' Lives in a Changing of America* (New York: Vintage Books, 1999).

27. "Latinos in the United States," *The National Association of Hispanic Journalists,* http://www.nahj.org/resourceguide/chapter_3c.html, accessed 23 July 2003.

28. Miranda Leitsinger, "West Indian Numbers Boom; Florida 'Capitol of the Caribbean'," *Associated Press Newswires,* 15 December 2001; Sosyete Koukouy (Haitian group), http://www.librerimapou.com/cultural.html, accessed 24 July 2003; Jamaica Awareness, Inc., http://www.jamaicaawareness.com, accessed 24 July 2003; Leslie Casimir, "Census: 36 Percent of City Foreign-Born," *New York Daily News,* 21 November 2001, http://www.npg.org/states/statenews/ny_listserv.html, accessed 24 July 2003. More than a third of New Yorkers were born in another country. New York's West Indian population is estimated at 589,000 and consists largely of Jamaicans (220,085) and Haitians (147,911).

29. Bureau of the Census, "Why a Question on Hispanic or Latino Origin? Various Federal Programs Require Data on the Ethnic Make-Up of the Community," http://www.census.gov/mso/www/rsf/racedata/tsld010.htm, accessed 24 July 2003.

30. *Jose Cisneros et al. v. Corpus Christi Independent School District et al.* Civ. A. No. 68-c-95. United States District Court for the Southern District of Texas, Houston Division 324 F. Supp. 599; 1970 U.S. Dist. LEXIS 11469. 4 June 1970. This decision held that Mexican Americans were "an identifiable ethnic class who have suffered de jure and de facto segregation, who are protected as a class under the Fourteenth Amendment and the laws of the United States, who are now being subjected to a dual school system in violation of the Fourteenth Amendment and the laws of the United States, and who the court has found should be, and are, protected, and who should be in a unitary school system."

## SELECTED WORKS

Acuña, Rodolfo. *Occupied America: A History of Chicanos.* 5th ed. New York: Longman, 2003.

Cruz, Jose E. *Identity and Power: Puerto Rican Politics and the Challenge of Ethnicity.* Philadelphia, Pa.: Temple University Press, 1998.

Dávila, Arlene. *Latinos Inc.: The Marketing and Making of a People.* Berkeley, Calif.: University of California Press, 2001.

Garza, Hedda, and James Cockcroft. *Latinas: Hispanic Women in the United States.* Albuquerque, New Mexico: University of New Mexico Press, 2001.

González, Juan. *Harvest of Empire: A History of Latinos in America.* New York: Penguin Books, 2000.

Grenier, Guillermo J., Lisandro Pérez, and Nancy Foner. *Legacy of Exile: The Cubans in the United States.* Allyn & Bacon New Immigrants Series. New York: Allyn & Bacon, 2003.

Grieco, Elizabeth M., and Rachel C. Cassidy. *Overview of Race and Hispanic Origin.* U.S. Census Brief, March 2001. http://www.census.gov/prod/2001pubs/c2kbr01-1.pdf. Accessed 24 July 2003.

Guzmán, Betsy. *The Hispanic Population. Census 2000 Brief.* U.S. Census Bureau. May 2001. http://www.census.gov/prod/2001pubs/c2kbr3sp.pdf. Accessed 24 July 2003.

Hamilton, Nora, and Norma Stoltz Chinchilla. *Seeking Community in a Global City: Guatemalans and Salvadorans in Los Angeles.* Philadelphia, Pa.: Temple University Press, 2001.

Laó-Montes, Agustín and Arlene Dávila, eds. *Mambo Montage: The Latinization of New York City.* New York: Columbia University Press, 2001.

"Latinos in the United States." *The National Association of Hispanic Journalists,* http://www.nahj.org/resourceguide/chapter_3c.html. Accessed 23 July 2003.

Logan, John R. *The New Latinos: Who They Are, Where They Are.* Lewis Mumford Center, 10 September 2001. http://mumford1.dyndns.org/cen2000/Hispanic Pop/HspReport/HspReportPage1.html. Accessed 24 July 2003.

Mahler, Sarah J. and Nancy Foner, eds. *Salvadorans in Suburbia: Symbiosis and Conflict.* New York: Allyn & Bacon, 1996.

Márquez, Benjamin and James Jennings, "Representation by Other Means: Mexican American and Puerto Rican Social Movement Organizations," *PS: Political Science and Politics* 33 (3): 541ff (September 2000).

Menjivar, Cecilia. *Fragmented Ties: Salvadoran Immigrant Networks in America.* Berkeley, Calif.: University of California Press, 2000.

Oboler, Suzanne. *Ethnic Labels, Latino Lives: Identity and the Politics of (Re)presentation in the United States.* Minneapolis, Minn.: University of Minneapolis Press, 1995.

Paley, Grace. *A Dream Compels Us: Voices of Salvadoran Women.* Cambridge, Mass.: South End Press, 1990.

Pardo, Mary. *Mexican American Women Activists: Identity and Resistance in Two Los Angeles Communities.* Philadelphia, Pa.: Temple University Press, 1998.

Rodríguez, Clara E. *Changing Race: Latinos, the Census, and the History of Ethnicity in the United States.* New York: New York University Press, 2000.

———. *Puerto Ricans: Born in the U.S.A..* Boulder, Colo.: Westview Press, 1991.

Santa Ana, Otto. *Brown Tide Rising: Metaphors of Latinos in Contemporary American Public Discourse*. Austin, Tex.: University of Texas Press, 2002.

Shorris, Earl. *Latinos Biography of a People*. New York: Norton, 1992.

Smith, Denise, and Renee E. Spraggins. *Gender: 2000*. U.S. Census. September 2001. http://www.census.gov/prod/2001pubs/c2kbr01-9.pdf. Accessed 23 July 2003.

Suro, Roberto. *Strangers among Us: Latinos' Lives in a Changing of America*. New York: Vintage Books, 1999.

# 1

# RACE CLASSIFICATION

## BACKGROUND

Race is one of the most pressing, controversial, and potentially divisive issues in American society. Historically, a person's race has determined success and failure, acceptance and rejection. Despite its importance, the definition of race in America has been arbitrary, depending greatly on the dominant society's definition. The United States once applied the simplistic standard of determining a person's race by deeming that if a person had one drop of African blood, he or she was Negro. In the case of Latinos, this standard has varied, largely depending on their class.

Many government entities before World War II classified working-class Mexicans as belonging to the Red race, or just simply the Mexican race. For instance, in the 1930 census, the U.S. Bureau of the Census listed them as Mexican. In that census the bureau instructed census takers that "[p]ractically all Mexican laborers are of a racial mixture difficult to classify, though usually well-recognized in the localities where they are found. In order to obtain separate figures for this racial group, it has been decided that all persons born in Mexico, or having parents born in Mexico, who are not definitely white, Negro, Indian, Chinese, or Japanese, should be listed as Mexican ('Mex')."[1] In the 1940 census, the instructions were, "Mexicans are to be regarded as white unless definitely of Indian or other nonwhite race." The 1950 Census Report required "'white' (W) for Mexicans unless they are definitely of Indian or other nonwhite race." The importance of race was not lost on Mexican American organizations. Aware that being white carried privileges in the

United States, they pressured the federal government to label Mexicans as Caucasian, which the Census Bureau finally did in 1948.[2] Mexican Americans were not the exception. The United States is a country of immigrants, and there have been changing perceptions of the race of other groups. For example, in 1909 the census listed Armenians as Asiatics. Because of pressure from Armenians, a court held that year that Armenians were white. In 1922, the U.S. Supreme Court ruled that people from India, although technically Caucasian, were not white. Before the 2000 census, Congress held hearings attempting to decide a classification for Middle Eastern Arabs.[3] To this day the U.S. Census Bureau has not decided what U.S. Latinos are and avoids defining them as a race. The most recent census (2000) classified Latinos as an ethnic group. The changes made by the Bureau have not satisfied everyone, however. Even Latinos disagree as to what race they belong.

The racial diversity among U.S. Latinos also has formed particular notions of race, making it even more difficult to categorize Latinos racially. The 300 to 400 years of Spanish colonialism in Latin America constructed racial categories to benefit those of Spanish blood. The more Spanish blood the Spanish subjects had, the more privileges they acquired. In fact, the Spaniards attempted to impose an elaborate categorization of race mixtures (see Tables 1.1 and 1.2). These racial classifications were listed on the individual's baptismal records for most of the colonial period. However, because much of the colonial population was mobile and people did not carry their baptismal certificates with them, the colonial subjects identified themselves without records. The standard classification was based on how Spanish or white a person looked. By the end of the eighteenth century, the race categories had dwin-

Table 1.1
Racial Categories in Mexico during the Spanish Colonial Period

| Year | Total Percent | Europeans | Africans | Indians | Creoles | Afro-Mestizos | Indio-Mestizos |
|------|------|------|------|------|------|------|------|
| 1570 | 100.0 | 0.2 | 0.6 | 98.7 | 0.3 | 0.1 | 0.1 |
| 1646 | 100.0 | 0.8 | 2.0 | 74.6 | 9.8 | 6.8 | 6.0 |
| 1742 | 100.0 | 0.4 | 0.8 | 62.2 | 15.8 | 10.8 | 10.0 |
| 1793 | 100.0 | 0.2 | 0.1 | 61.0 | 17.8 | 9.7 | 11.2 |
| 1810 | 100.0 | 0.2 | 0.2 | 60.0 | 17.9 | 10.2 | 11.5 |

*Source:* Gonzalo Aguirre Beltran, *Poblacion Negra De Mexico* (Mexico: Fondo de Cultura Economica, 1972), 233.

dled to Spaniard, mestizo, Spanish-mestizo, Indio-mestizo, African-mestizo, and Negro. People understood the social and political importance of being white or nearly white. The term *mestizo*, for example, was almost synonymous with not being Indio.

Vigorous race mixing characterized the Latin American colonies of Spain (see Table 1.2). The Spaniards and other Europeans brought Africans to the plantations of the New World to replace the millions of native Indians in the

**Table 1.2**
**Rough Spanish Categorization of Race Mixtures**

**Basic categories:**

Peninsulare, Spaniard born in Spain

Criollo, Spaniard born in the colonies

Indio

Negro, African

**Various mixtures or** *castas:*

Spaniard and Indian produce Mestizo

Spaniard and Mestiza produce Castiza

Spaniard and Castiza produce Spaniard

Mestizo and Indian produce Coyote

Black and Spaniard produce Mulatto

Mulatto and Spaniard produce Morisco

Spaniard and Morisca produce Albino

Spaniard and Albino produce Black-Return Backwards

Black and Indian produce Wolf (lobo)

Wolf and Indian produce Zambaiga

Zambaigo and Indian produce Albarazado

Albarazada and Indian produce Chamizo

Chamizo and Indian produce Cambuja

Albarrado and Indian produce Chachimboreta

Indian and Cambuja produce Wolf-Return-Backwards

Wolf-Return-Backwards and Indian produce Hold-Yourself-in-Mid-Air

*Source:* "Castas," http://www.emory.edu/COLLEGE/CULPEPPER/BAKEWELL/
thinksheets/castas.html.

West Indies who had died.[4] The Spaniards repeated this scenario throughout Latin America. For example, Mexico had a population of 25 million indigenous people, and 75 years later, hardly more than 1 million were left. In central Mexico, 95 out of every 100 people perished. In western and central Honduras, 95 percent of the native people were exterminated within the span of half a century. In western Nicaragua, 99 percent died, with the population falling from more than 1 million people to fewer than 10,000 in 60 years. The causes were the rapid spread of European diseases, overwork, warfare, and often the enslavement of the native American. Spanish colonialism created a racist regime, which drew its justifications from an appeal to biblical authority. Racial stereotypes were constructed, such as the idea that the Indians lacked reason, and that Indians were like infants who had to be educated by *gente de razón* (rational people), that is, Christian people who were adults. The Spaniards also rationalized the enslavement of Africans by saying that they did not have a soul or that they were biologically inferior to whites. Racial stereotypes went a long way in justifying a cruel and exploitive system in both Latin America and the United States, where labor systems allowed others to be treated as less than Spanish or as less than American.

The race admixture of the different Latin American countries varied; however, an individual's status and consequent treatment within society depended on race. In Cuba and Puerto Rico, the three major ethnic groups are African, Spanish, and mulatto, whereas Nicaragua has a blend of all three. In Argentina, people are mostly European in the Buenos Aires area, but are mainly mestizos in the Pampa area. The mixture in Mexico is characterized as Spanish, Indian, and Mestizo; however, there is growing evidence that there are also African and Asian admixtures there.

Supporting the idea of various admixtures in Mexico is anthropologist Eric Wolf, who wrote in his book *Sons of the Shaking Earth,* "The total number of Spaniards who migrated to Middle America has been estimated at 300,000. With the Spaniard came another element of population, the African slave. Roughly 250,000 were imported into Mexico during the three centuries of the slave trade. . . . No part of Middle America is without Negro admixture, although the physical evidence of this admixture has probably been submerged."[5] After denunciating the African influence, Wolf states, "Negroes were not the only slaves imported into Middle America. Small numbers of Indians, Burmese, Siamese, Indonesians, and Filipinos were also brought in to serve in similar capacity."[6] Theodore G. Vincent, in a recent book on Mexican President Vicente Guerrero, who had both Indian and African blood, posits that an "estimated 100,000 Asians [were] brought to Mexico in slavery on the Manila-to-Acapulco galleons. The Spaniards labeled the Asians 'African' because the Spanish wanted more slaves, and by law only

Africans could be slaves."[7] Little is known about the importation of Asians into colonial Mexico, but it is important to think about it in the context of race.[8] What is known is that racial mixing took place in every corner of the Spanish empire and affected the social construction of race.[9] If Latinos, similar to other colonized people, wanted to move up in racial categories, then white was right.

It is no wonder, then, that almost half of U.S. Latinos (48 percent) would classify themselves as "white only" on the 2000 census. Some 42 percent chose another race, and only 4 percent said they were black or African American alone; approximately 6 percent reported two or more races.[10] The contradiction is noticeable even in identifying nationality; 17 percent did not list a nationality and called themselves Latino or Hispanic.[11] Thus, it is not surprising that 3.06 million, or 80.5 percent, of island Puerto Ricans also list themselves as white. The census lists only 302,933, or 8.0 percent, of island Puerto Ricans as African; 158,415, or 4.2 percent, as two or more races; and 3.76 million, or 98.8 percent, as Latino.[12] (By 1867, Puerto Rico had 656,328 inhabitants; its population recorded as 346,437 whites and 309,891 of color; the *castas* racial category included blacks, mulattos, and mestizos.) To this day, in Mexico or in the Southwest United States, indigenous-looking Mexicans will vehemently protest that they are white. This is surprising, since most sources say that 60 percent of Mexicans are mestizos, 30 percent are predominately Amerindian, 9 percent white, and 1 percent other.[13] Throughout Mexico, apart from their indigenous features, there are those with African blood who still insist they are mestizos or white.

This is not a new phenomenon, and the responses are consistent with history. In 1980, 53.2 percent of Mexican Americans claimed to be white, 1.8 percent black, and 45 percent of another race. In that year, 47.7 percent of Mexican Americans in California claimed to be white, and 51.9 percent of other race. Around 62 percent of Mexican American *Tejanos* (Texans) claimed to be white and 37.5 percent of other race. Why are the percentages different in Texas? Could the fact that Texas once was a confederate state have any bearing?[14] In the 1990 census, 50.6 percent of Mexican Americans identified themselves as white. Some 1.2 percent said they were black, and 46.7 percent claimed to neither be white nor black. Of Mexican Americans in California in 1990, 45.2 percent claimed to be white, and 53.6 percent of another race; in Texas, the numbers were 58.3 percent and 40.9 percent respectively.

In the 2000 census, only about 2 percent of U.S. residents, or 5.5 million people, selected two or more racial categories. Approximately 211.5 million people, or 75 percent of the total population, reported only white. Meanwhile, close to 7 million Americans identified themselves as belonging to more than one race. (Of these, 20 percent said they were white, American

Indian, and Alaska native; 16 percent white and Asian; and 14 percent white and black.)[15] The results from the disparate Latino groups were not broken down. For example, would Cuban Americans be more apt to designate themselves as white than would Puerto Ricans and Dominicans? Would mainland Puerto Ricans be more apt to designate themselves as black than would island-raised Puerto Ricans? What is the difference between those who are Mexican-born, Central American-born, and U.S.-born? What role does history play in conditioning the respondent to mark white, considering the privileges that being white has historically held? In truth, most Mexicans and Salvadorans are mestizos, which means they are at least two races.

This confusion has led Jamaican-born Harvard sociologist Orlando Patterson to argue in 2001 that white people are not becoming a minority in the United States because Latinos are white. Patterson argues that claiming America is becoming less white fuels the fears of the white majority. Patterson writes, "The *New York Times* reported that 71 of the top 100 cities had lost white residents and made clear only in the third paragraph of the article that it is really 'non-Hispanic whites' who are now a minority in these cities." According to Patterson, what this and other articles fail to take into account is "the fact that nearly half the Hispanic population is white in every social sense of this term; 48 percent of so-called Hispanics classified themselves as solely white, giving only one race to the census taker." Thus, if the Hispanic population is added to "a robust 69.1 percent of the total population of the nation," whites are 75.14 percent of the total population, down by only 5 percent from the 1990 census. According to Patterson, "[r]ecent studies indicate that second-generation Hispanic whites are intermarrying and assimilating mainstream language and cultural patterns at a faster rate than second generation European migrants of the late nineteenth and early twentieth centuries." While one may not agree with Patterson, his arguments have some merit in questioning the Census Bureau's policies of race categorization.

On one hand, the census has allowed citizens to classify themselves in as many racial ways as they wish, shaking the notion that races are immutable categories. This raises the question, however, whether dismantling of racial constructs in America is a good thing. What other system of identification would take its place? Patterson is correct that Latinos, similar to blacks, have used race to identify inequality and needs and to justify entitlements such as affirmative action and voting rights. Many minorities fear that without race as a factor, it will be impossible to assess the needs of Latinos and implement programs to correct inequalities.[16] It also raises the following questions: even if Latinos are classified as white, does that make them white? Do most Americans look at them as white? Will their inequality go away by itself?[17]

Thus, critics maintain that the U.S. census takers and other social scientists have confused matters by avoiding the question of race-constructing identities that many Latinos contest. Indeed, the term *ethnicity* is a new term, largely a creation of the 1930s. The word *ethnic* came from the Greek *ethnos,* which was from the word *ethnikos,* originally meaning heathen or pagan. Over time *ethnic* referred to other tribes, and the word gradually took on racial characteristics. Because of the different nationalities that came to the United States, the word *ethnics* became known sometime around World War II as a polite way of referring to non-WASP Americans. In the 1960s, it became synonymous with minority groups and cultural constructs. However, the discussion of ethnicity has always been present and Anglo Americans have blurred the lines between race, ethnicity, and nationality.[18]

Given this discussion, it is not totally surprising that many Americans are confused about what race they are. Using the three racial categories—Caucasian, Asian, and Negroid—what test should be used to decide what race a person is? During the eighteenth century in colonial New Spain (Mexico), the priest would look at the person and say, "*Tiene parecido de español*" ("He looks like a Spaniard"). This was the standard, and everyone strived to look like Spaniards because looking like one brought substantial privileges. Indians and Africans wanted to look like mestizos because it made them look more like Spaniards, which again moved them up in status. Similarly, in the United States, being an American was being white, so light-skinned African Americans had more privileges than darker-skinned African Americans. Many lighter-skinned African American slaves worked in the big house instead of in the fields. The rape of some slaves by their white owners produced lighter-skinned offspring. Over the years, African Americans who had light skin sometimes chose to pass as white to take advantage of the privileges that accrued to white people. It is not surprising that members of ethnic minorities also have striven to be white and even have changed their last names to English equivalents in the hope of acceptance.

Determining race or ethnicity is not an easy chore. Which test will you apply—the United States one drop test that makes a person an other, or the Spanish colonial test where if a person looks like a European, she is white? Why is race important? The consequences of racism still harm a wide body of people. Racial stereotyping is not a relic of the past. In some countries such as the United States, Great Britain, and Australia, racism is revealed when governments opt to eliminate the potential for conflict by simply denying or severely limiting entry of non-Europeans. In 1986, Japanese Prime Minister Yasuhiro Nakasone remarked that the average American intellectual standard is lower than the average Japanese standard because of the blacks and Latinos in the United States. The Japanese Prime Minister said the source of Japan's strength lies in its "racial homogeneity."[19] In 1997, University of Texas Law School Professor Lino Graglia remarked that "Blacks and Mexican-Americans are not academically competitive with whites in selective institutions. . . . It is the result primarily of cultural effects. They have a culture that seems not to encourage achievement. Failure is not looked upon with disgrace."[20]

## SHOULD U.S. LATINOS BE CLASSIFIED AS WHITE?

### For

Some U.S. Latinos argue that the U.S. census historically has listed them as Caucasian. There are only three races to choose from—Caucasian, Asian, and Negroid. U.S. Latinos are clearly neither Asian nor African, so this leaves them with the choice of Caucasian. They argue that being white is important because of the racist history of this country and because society must counteract this historical racism. So in order to become American, Latinos must follow the example of Jews and Italians and become white. According to this reasoning, this position is not anti-African American, but it does recognize that lumping Latinos in with blacks conveys the status of second-class Americanism and gives racists reason to discriminate against U.S. Latinos.

When Orlando Patterson raised the question of whether U.S. Latinos were white, anti-immigrant proponent Steve Sailer came out with a series of articles titled "Pondering Patterson: OK, How White Are Hispanics?"[21] Sailer argued that only 9 percent of the residents of Mexico are white, that 30 percent of Mexicans are predominantly Indian, and 60 percent are mestizos. While these statistics are probably correct, they become a pretext and a negative justification for discriminating against U.S. Latinos in the context of U.S. history. Listing Latinos as non-white also gives Sailer and others the opportunity to divide Latinos into races, thus weakening the group by setting up a scenario where lighter-skinned Mexicans are accepted as Latinos or Hispanics and darker-skinned Latinos are relegated to an underclass.

Requiring a person to list her race on the 2000 census is a racist act. Race has been used to distinguish people. For example, race has been included in the census since 1790, when Negroes were listed as "all other persons."[22] The 1940 census helped the government round up people of Japanese ancestry for the purpose of internment; race justified this confinement. Even during World War II, race was used to exclude non-white people, which is why Mexican American organizations fought to be white; to be other than white was to be inferior. The courts also recognized this. In *Hernandez v.*

*State* (1952), the Texas Court of Appeal ruled that Mexicans were "not a separate race but are white people of Spanish descent," and the lawyers for the Mexican American community did not dispute this rationale. The court held that Mexicans were members of and within the classification of the white race, as distinguished from members of the Negro race.[23]

The strategy of Mexican American civil rights organizations was to claim the racial identity of the majority of Americans. They argued that the Treaty of Guadalupe Hidalgo (1848) made Mexican Americans citizens and recognized them as white. Mexican American organizations eventually won the legal battle, and most courts declared that Mexicans were white. This was a tremendous victory because in 1930 a Texas state court held that Mexican American public school students could not be segregated from children of other white races because of their ethnicity. Mexican Americans guarded this white status because they knew that in this country being white brought many privileges. So when the 1930 census identified Mexican Americans as "other race," Latino civil rights organizations protested, and they reclassified Mexicans, in 1950, as white. Being called white was a right because Mexican Americans fought for the United States during World War II. Today the Census Bureau includes the designations "white, of Hispanic origin" and "white, of non-Hispanic origin." The Census Bureau should abolish these classifications, and it should classify all Latinos as white. As mentioned previously, the Treaty of Guadalupe Hidalgo guarantees Mexicans the right of citizenship, and because non-whites could not be citizens, it was logical that the Treaty recognized Mexicans as white. To accept the label non-white or even "other white" is demeaning and a surrender of Treaty rights.

Since 1970, the job of determining race has been given to the individual. In 1980, the census classified Latinos as an ethnic group. Latinos could choose from 15 race categories.[24] The Latino identity, however, goes beyond race; it is a cultural identity. Culture unites all Latinos. The notion of race is also absurd. Race is a human construct, and it has little to do with science.

Why should Latinos want to identify as non-white? African Americans do not consider Latinos non-white. Would blacks consider Latinos black if they chose to list themselves as black? What is the difference between white and black racism? Because of the distorted construction of race in this country, many blacks such as Professor Patterson are resentful and consider Latinos white; thus Latinos will never be part of their world. African Americans believe whites have decided to let Latinos in the club. Many African Americans also believe that they created the civil rights movement, and it was through their sacrifices that civil rights gains were made. Why should Latinos beg to be accepted by blacks? Economically it makes more sense to try to fit in.[25]

### Against

Race is a social construct, and eugenics is an inexact science at best.[26] The Census Bureau has added to the confusion by classifying Latinos as an ethnic and not a racial group. The reality is that historically, race has been more divisive for Latinos than other groups because Latinos come in different colors. The Census Bureau has thus given Latinos the option of being white or other, in other words, of being white or black. Given the choice, Latinos will choose white because it has more privileges. According to newspaper columnists Patrisia Gonzales and Roberto Rodríguez, this has the effect of "whitening" the country via "demographic genocide." They posit that "[a] check of any encyclopedia will show that between 85 percent and 90 percent of all Mexicans and Central Americans are either indigenous or indigenous-based mestizos."[27] The columnists correctly point out that the European population in Latin America was never large enough to be dominant outside countries such as Argentina and Uruguay.

For 300 years of Spanish rule and 180 years of U.S. rule, Mexicans and other Latinos have been conditioned to accept that being white is superior to Indian. The Census Bureau itself has refused to accept admixtures, and it was only in the 2000 census that the reason for this choice became clear. By lumping all Spanish-speaking peoples under the rubric of Hispanic/Latino, the Census Bureau confuses identification and encourages a crossover, which some Latinos have come to accept. The exercise of identifying oneself as white is a joke among Latinos. In Mexico, for example, a person may call him or herself white, but others will wink and comment "*y no mas le faltan las plumas!*" (he or she is "only missing his, or her, feathers!"). People should be proud of their heritage and not strive to be white; pride is what adds value to a person.

Worse still is that the Census Bureau's policies of respecting self-identity in the 1997 census have skewed the results. The Census Bureau estimates 95 percent of Hispanics are white and 3 percent black. The Census Bureau has complicated matters further in the 2000 census by not giving the respondent the option of marking mestizo/mulatto. The result was that many U.S. Latinos were encouraged to deny their Indian or African heritage.

The census is supposed to clarify the racial landscape but instead had confused and scrambled it. The policies of the Census Bureau are as much an ideological battle as they are an attempt to count people. The censuses allow social scientists the room to invent and exaggerate differences. They confuse the strategies that the disparate Latino groups should use to bring about equality. For example, some scholars believe that Mexican Americans should follow the route of the European ethnics and assimilate, and that they should separate themselves from African Americans.[28] If Latinos would follow the latter strategy, it would be divisive. Latinos and African Americans live side by side, struggling for the same space, and they share common problems. Labeling Latinos white would abandon the mission of many U.S. Latinos to bring about equality, a goal that European immigrants largely abandoned as they were accepted as white. They assimilated as individuals, became white, and in the process left the poor behind.[29]

Rather than changing the way a person thinks about race, the designation of U.S. Latinos as white further complicates the process. The Census Bureau argues that self-identification gives Latinos more options. However, history shows otherwise. Under the Spanish system, the look-alike test was no better than the drop of black blood test. Spanish subjects would tell the priest that they were Spanish and he would sarcastically note, "*dice que es español!*" ("He says he is Spanish!"). Just thinking that he or she is white gives that person the illusion of inclusion.[30]

## QUESTIONS

1. To what race do you believe U.S. Latinos belong? What test did you apply to reach this conclusion? Conduct a poll among your friends, including a cross section of different racial and ethnic groups. Ask them for their opinion and two reasons for their conclusion.

2. Do you believe that the U.S. Census Bureau was justified in treating U.S. Latinos as an ethnic rather than a racial group? Why do you think it took the bureau so long to decide this question?

3. Bring in photographs of U.S. Latino friends or entertainers, apply the one-drop or the sight test to each figure, and determine their race.

4. What is the difference between racism, ethnocentrism, and nationalism? Based on the background narrative, how has this contributed to the confusion as to the race of U.S. Latinos?

5. Do movies or commercials ever have stereotypes of Latinos? Do they condition the public's attitude of Latinos? How do these stereotypes suggest that the advertisers consider Latinos white?

6. Why did the Spaniards during the colonial era use such complicated racial categories to identify the different racial mixtures? Were their categories racist? Why or why not?

7. Most U.S. Latinos are of mixed blood. Why do you believe that close to 50 percent of them designate themselves as white? Do you believe the Spanish system of identifying the different categories of races conditioned U.S. Latinos to want to be white? Given the facts, why would they want to be white? Remember that more U.S. Latinos designated themselves non white. Why is this significant?

8. Many Mexican and American historians say Americans individually invaded

Texas, and later, U.S. troops invaded Mexico. How would these attitudes condition American views of Mexicans and other Latinos? In what way does racism become a pretext or justification for aggression?

9. Explain what you agree and disagree with in the *For* and *Against* positions of this chapter.

10. How do you think African Americans would feel knowing that nearly half of U.S. Latinos identify themselves as white? How would you explain why Latinos are identifying themselves as white? Would it be fair to say that all Latinos prefer white to black, based on the census results? Why might the census be structured this way?

11. The *Jose Cisneros et al. v. Corpus Christi Independent School District et al.* (1970)[31] decision indicated the opinion that "Mexican-Americans are an identifiable ethnic class who have suffered de jure and de facto segregation, who are protected as a class under the Fourteenth Amendment and the laws of the United States, who are now being subjected to a dual school system in violation of the Fourteenth Amendment and the laws of the United States, and who the court has found should be, and are, protected, and who should be in a unitary school system. " Based on this opinion, do you believe U.S. Latinos would be disadvantaged if they were white, which implies European?

12. Do you agree with the proposition that Americans generally considered a person was White Anglo-Saxon Protestant (WASP) in assessing whether he was really white or American? How has this standard changed over time? Are African Americans considered Americans? Are U.S. Latinos considered Americans? How would U.S. Latinos pass or fail the test?

13. How was the WASP test similar to the Spanish *"tiene parecido de español"* ("he or she looks like a Spaniard") test? What was the end result?

14. Is the discussion of race divisive? Why or why not? Will it go away by not talking about it?

15. Are U.S. Latinos a race, an ethnic group, or a nationality? Who constructed the Latino identity—history, Latinos, or the U.S. government?

16. How would you interpret the U.S. Latino remark that a plurality of Latinos identify themselves as white, but more identify themselves as other or black?

17. Would a Latino from Latin America look at race differently from a U.S. Latino? Why or why not?

## NOTES

1. Angela Walton-Raji, "African–Native American Genealogy Forum," http://www.afrigeneas.com/forume/index.cgi?read = 817, accessed 24 July 2003.

2. Rodolfo F. Acuña, *Anything but Mexican: Chicanos in Contemporary Los Angeles* (London: Verso, 1996); Theodore W. Allen, "'Race' and 'Ethnicity': History and the 2000 Census," http://eserver.org/clogic/3–1&2/allen.html, accessed 24 July 2003. Historically, being white was important and Mexicans were classified as white by the Treaty of Guadalupe Hidalgo (1848), which ended the Mexican American War where the United States took half of Mexico's land from it. At the time, U.S. citizenship was

limited to white people, and the treaty guaranteed them citizenship and thus whiteness although the majority of Americans did not consider them white. Thus, Mexican American organizations in the 1930s were appealing for acceptance as white. A change occurred in the 1960s as the Fourteenth and Fifteenth Amendments and the Civil Rights laws became more than dead letters and were enforced, and both Mexicans and Puerto Ricans were classified as white. How could they be protected on the basis of race or color?

3. Clara E. Rodríguez, *Changing Race: Latinos, the Census and the History of Ethnicity in the United States* (New York: New York University Press, 2000); Paul Butler, "A Mix of Colors: Country's Swirling Demographics Put New Twist on Meaning of 'Minority,'" *Dallas Daily News* 3 June 2001; Kenneth Prewitt, "Demography, Diversity, and Democracy. The 2000 Census Story," *Brookings Review* 20, no. 1 (winter 2002): 6–9, http://www.brookingsinstitution.org/dybdocroot/press/review/oldtoc. htm, accessed 24 July 2003; Nathan Glazer, "American Diversity and the 2000 Census," *The Public Interest* (Summer 2001), http://thepublicinterest.com/archives/2001 summer/article1/html, accessed 24 July 2003; Anthony S. Wohl, "Racism and Anti-Irish Prejudice in Victorian England," *The Victorian Web*, http://www.victorianweb. org/victorian/history/race/Racism.html, accessed 24 July 2003.

4. Jalil Sued-Badillo, "Christopher Columbus and the Enslavement of the Amerindians in the Caribbean; Columbus and the New World Order 1492–1992," *Monthly Review* 44, no. 3 (July 1992): 77ff; David E. Stannard, "Genocide in the Americas: Columbus's Legacy," *The Nation* 255, no. 12 (1992): 430ff.

5. Eric Wolf, *Sons of the Shaking Earth: The People of Mexico and Guatemala—Their Land, History, and Culture* (Chicago: Phoenix Books, 1959), 29.

6. Ibid., 30.

7. Theodore G. Vincent, *The Legacy of Vicente Guerrero, Mexico's First Black Indian President* (Gainesville: University Press of Florida, 2001), 1; For more information, see links to "Black Indian Mexico and Related Fields," http://hometown.aol.com/fsln/, accessed 24 July 2003; Gonzalo Aguirre Beltrán, *La Población Negra de México: Estudio Ethnohistórico.* (Xalapa: Universidad Veracruzana, 1992); Vincent Villanueva Mayer, Jr., "The Black Slave on New Spain's Northern Frontier: San Jose De Parral 1632–1676," (Ph.D. diss., University of Utah, 1975), 78. Blacks were among the army assembled at Vera Cruz by Hernando Cortés in his assault on Mexico City. Mayer argues that the importation of African slaves was tied to the problem of labor and the epidemics that ravaged New Spain in 1531, 1545, 1564, and 1576–77. From a calculated 25 million, the number of Indians fell to fewer than 2 million in 1595. Later successive epidemics decimated the population. Between 1519 and 1650 the Viceroyalty imported an estimated 120,000 black slaves, which is two-thirds of all slaves imported into the Spanish possessions in the New World.

8. The Manila Galleon sailed between 1570 and 1815 annually, and 50 to 80 percent of the crew was Filipino. "By one account, some 60,000 Filipinos sailed on the galleons from Manila to Acapulco." These were not slaves, although slaves were probably part of the cargo. "There were also many who belonged to the mestizo class, products of intermarriages between Spanish and native Filipinos who traveled as merchants, technicians or functionaries." Jonathan Best, "Endless War in Mindanao," *Philippine Daily Inquirer,* 2 July 2000. Given what we know about the Spaniards in Mexico and their justification for using war as a pretext for making prisoners slaves, many Filipinos were probably enslaved during these bloody wars. The division of the

Philippines into Moslem and Christian as a consequence of Imperialism is harvesting bitter fruits today. See also Howard M. Federspiel, "Islam and Muslims in the Southern Territories of the Philippine Islands during the American Colonial Period," *Journal of Southeast Asian Studies,* (1 September 1998) 1ff..

9. Traders from Asia and Europe, such as the Portuguese and then the Dutch, traded with the islands. Kerry Nguyen-Long, "Vietnamese Ceramic Trade to the Philippines in the Seventeenth Century," *Journal of Southeast Asian Studies* 30, no. 1 (1 March 1999): 1ff. Slavery was a terrible institution that made huge profits for Europeans and those engaged in it and dispersed people around the globe. Jose S. Arcilla, S. J., "Roots: The Philippines in the 1600s," *BusinessWorld* (Philippines), 21 February 2000. Arcilla writes, "Philippine slavery, for example, was condemned by the first Manila Synod of 1583–86, but it was a dead law. Spaniards and Filipinos continued to have slaves." A 12-year-old boy in 1687 sold for 50 pesos in the Philippines.

10. Elizabeth M. Grieco and Rachel C. Cassidy, *Overview of Race and Hispanic Origin,* U.S. Census Brief, March 2001, 10, http://www.census.gov/prod/2001pubs/ c2kbr01-1.pdf, accessed 24 July 2003; Martin Kasindorf and Haya El Nasser, "Impact of Census' Race Data Debated," *USA Today,* 13 March 2001, http://www. usatoday.com/news/nation/census/2001-03-13-census-impact.htm, accessed 24 July 2003.

11. Tim Funk, "'Latino' Preferred in Great Label Debate," *seattletimes.com,* 18 August 2001, available in online archives of *Seattle Times,* accessed 24 July 2003; Elizabeth M. Grieco and Rachel C. Cassidy, *Overview of Race and Hispanic Origin,* U.S. Census Brief, March 2001, 10, http://www.census.gov/prod/2001pubs/c2kbr01-1.pdf, accessed 24 July 2003; Amitai Etzioni, "Inventing Hispanics: A Diverse Minority Resists Being Labeled," *Brookings Review* 20, no. 1 (winter 2002): 10 (4), http://www.brookingsinstitution.org/press/review/oldtoc.htm, accessed 24 July 2003; Kenneth Prewitt, "Demography, Diversity, and Democracy: The 2000 Census Story," *Brookings Review* 20, no. 1 (winter 2002): 6–9; Theodore W. Allen, "'Race' and 'Ethnicity': History and the 2000 Census," http://eserver.org/clogic/3-<1&2/allen.html, accessed 24 July 2003. It is a thorough but caustic treatment; Martin Kasindorf and Haya El Nasser, "Impact of Census' Race Data Debated," *USA Today,* 13 March 2001.

12. QT-P3. Raza e Hispano o Latino: 2000 Conjunto de Datos: Datos del Componente de 100 Por Ciento del Compendio de Datos 1 (SF1) del Censo 2000 Área geográfica: Puerto Rico, http://factfinder.census.gov/servlet/BasicFactsTable?_lang =es&_vt_name=DEC_2000_SF1_U_QTP3&_geo_id=04000US7, accessed 24 July 2003.

13. CIA—The World Factbook—Mexico, http:/www.cia.gov/cia/publications/factbook/geos/mx.html, accessed 24 July 2003. See also Gregory Velazco y Trianosky, "Beyond Mestizaje: The Future of Race in America," in *New Faces in a Changing America: Multiracial Identity in the Twenty-First Century,* ed. Herman L. deBose and Loretta I. Winters (Thousand Oaks, Calif.: Sage Publishing, 2002).

14. Peter Skerry, *Mexican Americans: The Ambivalent Minority* (New York: Free Press, 1991), 16–17.

15. Elizabeth M. Grieco and Rachel C. Cassidy, *Overview of Race and Hispanic Origin,* U.S. Census Brief, March 2001, http://www.census.gov/prod/2001pubs/ c2kbr01-1.pdf, accessed 24 July 2003; John R. Logan, "How Race Counts for His-

panic Americans," Lewis Mumford Center for Comparative Urban and Regional Research, University at Albany, 14 July 2003, http://mumford1.dyndns.org/cen2000/BlackLatinoReport/BlackLatino01.htm, accessed 24 July 2003.

16. Orlando Patterson, "Race by the Numbers," *New York Times,* 8 May 2001. Patterson has been criticized even by conservatives for his article protesting that Latinos are not white; Steve Sailer, "Pondering Paterson [I-VI]: OK, How White Are Hispanics?," *VDARE,* http://www.vdare.com/sailer/pondering_patterson_1.htm, accessed 24 July 2003. Sailer states that many African Americans look white; Nathan Glazer, "American Diversity and the 2000 Census," *The Public Interest* (summer 2001), www.thepublicinterest.com/archives/2001summer/article1.html, accessed 24 July 2003. Glazer goes through the history of race classification in census; Laurent Belsie, "As Census Report on White Population Comes Out, Some Academics Say This Ethnic Definition Is Changing," *csmonitor.com,* 14 August 2001, http://www.csmonitor.com/2001/0814/p2s1-ussc.htm, accessed 24 July 2003; Carlos D. Conde, "One People, Many Faces: Perception of Hispanics' Numbers, Diversity Doesn't Match Reality," *HoustonChronicle.com,* http://www.mexico-info.com/leadstories/chron/manyfaces.htm, accessed 24 July 2003.

17. See also Orlando Patterson, "Race Over," *New Republic Online,* 30 December 1999; Orlando Patterson, *Rituals of Blood: Consequences of Slavery in Two American Centuries* (New York: Basic Books, 1998).

18. Theodore W. Allen, "'Race' and 'Ethnicity': History and the 2000 Census," http://eserver.org/clogic/3-1&2/allen.htm, accessed 24 July 2003. This is a 22 page paper. The category reads "'White.' Persons 'of Spanish culture or origin.'—Mexicans, Puerto Ricans, Cubans or Central Americans, and unspecified others, are collectively classed as an 'ethnic group,' regardless of race."

19. Claude Lewis, "Minorities Feel Japanese Sting," *Journal of Commerce,* 26 August 1991.

20. "UT Professor Blasts Efforts for Diversity on Campus," *The Houston Chronicle,* 11 September 1997.

21. Steve Sailer, "Pondering Paterson [II]: OK, How White Are Hispanics?" *VDARE,* http.vdare.com/sailer/pondering_patterson_2.htm, accessed 24 July 2003.

22. Bob Curtis, "The 'Race' Question on the U.S. Census Is Racist. Why This Is So and What to Answer Instead," April/May 2000, http://sodabob.com/Constitution/Census.asp, accessed 24 July 2003.

23. Ian F. Haney López, "Race, Ethnicity, Erasure: The Salience of Race to LatCrit Theory," LatCrit: Latinas/os and the Law: A Joint Symposium by California Law Review and La Raza Law Journal, *California Law Review* 85, no. 5 (1997): 1143–211.

24. Bob Curtis, "The 'Race' Question on the U.S. Census Is Racist. Why This Is So and What to Answer Instead," http://sodabob.com/Constitution/Census.asp, accessed 24 July 2003.

25. Jerald E. Podair, "Blacks and Latinos: The Next Racial Divide," *Insight on the News,* 5 February 2001, 44, http://members.tripod.com/~Campello/hispanic.html, accessed 24 July 2003.

26. Eugenics is the study of human genetics and of methods to improve the inherited characteristics, physical and mental, of the human race. Efforts to improve the human race through bettering housing facilities and other environmental conditions are known as euthenics.

27. Patrisia Gonzales and Roberto Rodríguez. "Census Demographic Suicide" Column of The Americas, Universal Press Syndicate, week of 17 March 2000, http://www.voznuestra.com/Americas/_2000/_March/17, accessed 24 July 2003; Peter Skerry, *Mexican Americans: The Ambivalent Minority,* (reprint; Cambridge: Harvard University Press, 1995). Originally written in the 1980s.

28. Peter Skerry, *Mexican Americans: The Ambivalent Minority,* (reprint; Cambridge: Harvard University Press, 1995). Originally written in the 1980s.

29. Peter Skerry, "The Black Alienation: African Americans vs. Immigrants," *The New Republic,* 30 January 1995, also available in online archives of the Brookings Institute; Amitai Etzioni, "Inventing Hispanics: A Diverse Minority Resists Being Labeled," *Brookings Institution* 10, no. 1 (winter 2002): 10ff, http://www.brookingsinstitution.org/press/review/winter2002/etzioni.htm, accessed 24 July 2003.

30. Cindy Rodríguez, "Latinos Give U.S. New View of Race," *Boston Globe,* 2 January 2000, available in online archives of the *Boston Globe.*

31. *Jose Cisneros et al. v. Corpus Christi Independent School District et al.* Civ. A. No. 68-c-95. United States District Court for the Southern District of Texas, Houston Division 324 F. Supp. 599; 1970 U.S. Dist. LEXIS 11469, 4 June 1970.

## SELECTED WORKS

Acuña, Rodolfo F. *Anything but Mexican: Chicanos in Contemporary Los Angeles.* London: Verso, 1996.

García, Jorge J. E. and Pablo De Greiff, eds. *Hispanics/Latinos in the United States: Ethnicity, Race, and Rights.* New York: Routledge, 2000.

Gonzales, Patrisia and Roberto Rodríguez. "Census Facilitates 'Demographic Genocide.'" Column of The Americas, Universal Press Syndicate, week of 17 March 2000.

Gossett, Thomas F. *Race: The History of an Idea in America (Race and American Culture).* 2d ed. New York: Oxford University Press, 1997.

Grieco, Elizabeth M. and Rachel C. Cassidy. *Overview of Race and Hispanic Origin.* U.S. Census Brief, March 2001. Http://www.census.gov/prod/2001pubs/c2kbr01-1.pdf. Accessed 24 July 2003.

Guzmán, Betsy. *The Hispanic Population. Census 2000 Brief.* U.S. Census Bureau, May 2001. Http://www.census.gov/prod/2001pubs/c2kbr3sp.pdf. Accessed 24 July 2003.

Haney López, Ian F. "Race, Ethnicity, Erasure: The Salience of Race to LatCrit Theory." LatCrit: Latinas/os and the Law: A Joint Symposium by *California Law Review* and *La Raza Law Journal. California Law Review* 85, no. 5 (1997): 1143–211.

———. *Racism on Trial: The Chicano Fight for Justice.* Cambridge, Mass.: Belknap Press, 2003.

Logan, John R. "How Race Counts for Hispanic Americans." Lewis Mumford Center for Comparative Urban and Regional Research. University at Albany, 14 July 2003. Http://mumford1.dyndns.org/cen2000/BlackLatinoReport/BlackLatino 01.htm. Accessed 24 July 2003.

Menchaca, Martha. *Recovering History Constructing Race: The Indian, Black, and White Roots of Mexican Americans.* Austin: University of Texas Press, 2001.

"Metropolitan Racial and Ethnic Change Initiative Census 2000." Lewis Mumford

Center for Comparative Urban and Regional Research. Http://mumford. cas.albany.edu/MumfordContact/censusbrochure.pdf. Accessed 24 July 2003.

Nelson, William Javier. "Latinos and Their Escape Hatches." *Interracial Voice.* Http:// www.webcom.com/intvoice/nelson2.html. Accessed 24 July 2003.

Nobles, Melissa. *Shades of Citizenship Race and the Census in Modern Politics.* Stanford, Calif.: Stanford University Press, 2000.

Patterson, Orlando. "Race by the Numbers." *New York Times,* May 8, 2001. Http:// www.racematters.org/racebythenumbers.htm. Accessed 26 July 2003.

Race & Ethnicity, http://eserver.org/race/. Accessed 24 July 2003.

Rodríguez, Clara E. *Changing Race: Latinos, the Census and the History of Ethnicity in the United States.* New York: New York University Press, 2000.

Sailer, Steve. "Importing Mexico's Worsening Racial Inequality." Steve Sailer Archive. Http://www.vdare.com/sailer/sailer_mexico_part2.htm. Accessed 24 July 2003.

Santa Anna, Otto. *Brown Tide Rising: Metaphors of Latinos in Contemporary American Discourse.* Austin: University of Texas Press, 2002.

Skerry, Peter. *Counting on the Census? Race, Group Identity, and the Evasion of Politics.* Washington, D.C.: Brookings Institute Press, 2000. http://www.brookings institution.org/SCHOLARS/PSKERRY.htm. Accessed 24 July 2003.

———. *Mexican Americans: The Ambivalent Minority.* New York: Free Press, 1991.

Universal Black Pages. "Knowledge Based Consulting Services." 19 April 2000. http://www.ubp.com/. Accessed 24 July 2003.

# 2

## ASSIMILATION

### BACKGROUND

Although Americans have not always welcomed immigrants historically, Americans have insisted that immigrants to this country assimilate. This has not always been easy because assimilation has often meant different things to different people. For some, assimilation has been synonymous with Americanization, which *Webster's Dictionary* defines as "becoming American in character, manners, methods, [and] ideals." Many Americans have interpreted this to mean the total absorption of immigrant cultures into the main cultural body.[1] In other words, immigrants were expected to reject their past and act American.

During the first decade of the twentieth century, President Theodore Roosevelt wanted to Americanize immigrants so that they would not threaten American culture. Roosevelt believed that Americans had a unique culture and that the language and customs of foreigners corrupted it. Roosevelt had an "America: Love It or Leave It" attitude toward immigrants, and in his view, immigrants had to surrender their old-world culture and their historical memories, or they should go back to Europe. For Roosevelt the ethnic ghettos of his times were a threat to an American way of life, and he wanted to get rid of them.[2]

The antipathy toward immigrants went beyond culture, and during the first two decades of the twentieth century, most Americans, like Roosevelt, considered people of color and other cultures as threats to the American race, which at the time was considered to be composed of people who spoke

English, had British features, and were Protestant. Roosevelt said in 1906 that "race purity must be maintained" and warned of the falling birth rate among native-born white women, saying that it amounted to "race-suicide" and threatened the survival of the white race.[3] Roosevelt did not consider Latin Americans white, and, therefore, they would not have met his definition of American.

Because large numbers of non-English-speaking and non-English-looking immigrants entered the country during the first two decades of the twentieth century, Americans hotly debated the question of assimilation and what an American should be. For some, continued immigration of people who did not fit the White Anglo-Saxon Protestant (WASP) prototype was a danger to what their definition of American should be. The Daughters of the American Revolution, the Daughters of the Confederacy, and the League of the South were active in seeing that schools taught the official version of U.S. history.[4] Groups such as the American Legion became active in advocating Americanization after World War I. The Legion promoted American history, English language classes, and American cultural classes to immigrants. The end desire was to make them good Americans, to instill the Protestant ethic of hard work, and to have them accept the superiority of American values.

The 1921 and 1924 Immigration Acts were a response to this debate, and represented an effort to preserve the American culture and race. To this end, the National Origins Act–1921 Act limited the number of immigrants entering the country to 350,000, and set a quota for each nationality in any fiscal year to 3 percent of the number of persons of such nationality who were residents in the United States according to the census of 1910. The 1924 Act lowered the ceiling to 165,000 immigrants and limited each nationality to 2 percent of the 1890 census, and, as with the previous act, excluded Asians. Congress called these acts national origins because they placed countries on a quota system and gave preference to northern Europeans, limiting the number of Central and Southern Europeans immigrating to the United States. Latin Americans, because of the opposition of the Western growers who were dependent on them to pick crops, were not put on the quota. The consequences of these acts were far-reaching, and over the next 40 or so years the United States, by limiting the immigration of Southern and Central Europeans, became culturally and racially homogenous. Meanwhile, the Southern and Central Europeans became similar to the majority culture and were assimilated because the second- and third- generations rapidly outnumbered the small immigrant population. Without immigrants constantly reinforcing language and customs, most of the grandchildren of immigrants spoke only English by the third generation. In other words, most European ethnics had assimilated American customs and speech, and they thought of themselves as Americans.

However, the apparent assimilation of European immigrant groups did not end the debate over assimilation or Americanization. In the 1950s, there were still enclaves of Irish, Polish, Italian, Jewish, and other groups throughout the United States, and religion was still an issue in presidential elections. Latinos, Asian Americans, Native Americans, and African Americans also remained apart from the majority culture. Within each of these groups the rate of assimilation differed, according to the size of the ethnic or racial enclave. Economic class also played a role in the assimilation of the different groups. For example, assimilated Europeans with money were able to move out of the ghetto.

The 1960s renewed the question of identity as the children and the grandchildren of immigrants resurrected the notion of identity. During the sixties, many Americans grew conscious of the harsh treatment of immigrants, African Americans, and others in American history. Many Americans felt uncomfortable with the fact that the country had once excluded Asians, whom Congress was permitting to enter the country in limited numbers. In the context of the socially conscious sixties, Congress passed the 1965 Immigration Act, which opened the door for Asians to enter the country on a quota. For the first time, because of the insistence of nativists and American trade unions, Latin Americans were placed on a quota. Despite objections, the 1965 Act was considered a progressive step forward because it changed government immigration policy from national origins to family preferences. That is, to reunite families with the new immigrants, close relatives were given visas in preference to other applicants. Throughout the 1970s and 1980s, large numbers of Asians and Latin Americans migrated to the United States to reunite with their families. The entry of large numbers of Asians, Middle Easterners, and Latin Americans renewed the arguments of nativists that separate national identities were creating division and making assimilation more difficult.

Meanwhile, African Americans, U.S. Latinos, women, and others challenged the prevailing paradigm and wanted programs to maintain their individual identities. This debate over identity shook not only nativists but moderate scholars who called for Americanization. One of the most prominent voices criticizing the demands of African Americans and other minorities to hold on to their identities was that of the American historian Arthur M. Schlesinger, Jr., who wrote the following in his book *The Disuniting of America:*

George Washington was a sternly practical man. Yet he believed no less ardently in the doctrine of the "new race." "The bosom of America," Washington said, "is open . . . to the oppressed and persecuted of all Nations and Religions." But he counseled newcomers against retaining the "Language, habits and principles (good or bad) which they bring with them." Let them come not in clannish groups but as individuals, prepared for "intermixture with our people." Then they would be "assimilated to our customs, measures and laws; in a word, soon become *one people*."[5]

Schlesinger argues that the United States has been relatively successful at avoiding the fragmentation that plagued Europe, and he cautions that there is an alarming tendency among Americans to balkanize their country. Schlesinger appealed to his brand of Americanism, and posited that Americans should renounce old loyalties and melt away ethnic differences, saying that in this way Americans can forge a new culture and a new national identity.[6]

According to Schlesinger, having a set of common values is essential, which the nation can only accomplish through a common interpretation of a past and through a shared national identity and shared historical experiences.[7] Schlesinger condemned the multiculturalists and minorities who harped at what was wrong with America, and he accused the multiculturalists and Afrocentric black scholars of exaggerating past injustices. He argued that minorities should not teach history to promote group self-esteem, but instead they should teach history to promote an understanding of the world and the past. The role of the public school system was to Americanize students and teach them the American creed. It was the schools' job to unify Americans. An obsession with differences led to separatism, and "[s]eparatism nourishes prejudices, magnifies differences and stirs antagonism."[8]

Again, the question of assimilation and who should determine it is a debate that has been raging since the founding of the United States. This debate has fluctuated according to the times. When Schlesinger published his book in the 1990s, the country was in the midst of a culture war in which conservative scholars challenged the pluralistic model of many liberal scholars. Schlesinger and others favored the idea of American society as a melting pot whereas so-called multiculturalists looked at society as a salad bowl where people mixed but were not melted down. Immigrants and, by extension, their descendants were free to keep their individual identities while being part of the salad. The multiculturalists attacked the assimilationists, accusing them of wanting to impose conformity, while ultraconservatives accused the other side of being un-American and joining forces with Marxists to attack Western Civilization.[9]

Calling Schlesinger a nativist would be incorrect since his attack was not on immigrants but instead on the identity politics of un-assimilated minorities and others. Schlesinger's ideas merely coincided with those of nativists who felt that immigration was threatening American culture and race. Historically, they have called those against immigration nativists because they claim to be Native Americans and champions of American culture. Nativism had re-emerged as a force in politics in the 1980s when nativists revitalized their

American-First movement, in form of English-only groups. Nativists revived the question of assimilation and called for an immediate end of immigration. They argued that when immigrants moved to U.S. territory, they agreed to abide by an implied social contract, which American law, traditions, and heritage shaped. The immigrant agreed to assume a common identity—an American identity, agreeing to abandon the past in favor of a new reality. Nativists accused immigrants of straining the social contract by their refusal to assimilate. (Ironically, it was not the immigrant who was refusing to assimilate but instead the second and third generations.)

On the other side, critics did not deny that a social contract existed, but they challenged the right of individuals or groups to define what the duties and obligations of the individual were under this social contract. According to them, the U.S. Constitution and laws formed the social contract and defined the parameters of behavior. Pro-immigrants and activists also challenged the broadness of the social contract's interpretation. Did the newcomers renounce their cultural past? Did immigrants agree not to criticize anything American? Did the descendants of immigrants have the right to retain their ethnic and, for that matter, racial identity?

Americanization as a prerequisite to assimilation is as thorny a subject as it is problematic.[10] Many proponents of Americanization claim that unassimilated immigrants are ethnically balkanizing America. Like in the past, many of these nativists are concerned about having too many foreign-looking and foreign-sounding strangers in their midst and worry about the impact immigrants are having on what they consider unique American values. Nativists see this as a much greater threat than what took place during the first three decades of the twentieth century, when foreigners were clustered in Eastern cities. Today the newcomers are more geographically dispersed, non-European, and darker than the early twentieth century immigrants.

Will U.S. Latinos eventually go the path of the Irish, German, Polish, and Italian nationalities? For many U.S. Latinos, identity is important, and consequently assimilation has been slower for them than for Europeans. Moreover, conditions are not the same for Latinos. While European immigrants had to cross an ocean at a time when travel was slow, Mexico shares a 2,000-mile border with the United States. Latin Americans can reach the United States in a matter of hours. Thus, U.S. Latinos have more contact with their homelands. Telephones also keep them in constant touch with relatives. Further, the masses of Latinos are darker than Europeans, and while Southern and Central Europeans could change their surnames and be assimilated, many U.S. Latinos remain un-assimilated to the fourth and fifth generation from their original immigrant ancestors.

The experiences of the Irish, Poles, and Italians must be put into a historical context. Europeans came to the United States in response to the industrial revolutions of the nineteenth century and the uprooting caused by the transformations of their economies. Europeans arrived in the United States at a time when there was opportunity. Non-English-speaking Europeans suffered discrimination; however, the main obstacles to their assimilation were language, culture, religion, and economic class. European ethnics easily overcame the first two variables. Over time Americans became more tolerant of Catholicism, and the expansion of heavy industry allowed some upward mobility for European ethnics. Some of these immigrants changed their last names, and even their religions were accepted as American.

U.S. Latinos migrating to the United States had different experiences. Some Mexicans were in the United States before the Treaty of Guadalupe Hidalgo of 1848, which ended the Mexican War. Other Mexicans came to the United States throughout the nineteenth century, working on ranches and farms along the Río Bravo. The railroad helped industrialize the Southwest and Mexico and both pushed and pulled Mexicans into the United States. Mexican migration was constant throughout the twentieth century as labor contractors actively recruited Mexican workers for menial labor. Mexicans did not work in heavy industry in any significant numbers until World War II. Additionally, Mexicans assimilated into American society at varying stages. For example, lighter-skinned and middle-class Mexicans were accepted more readily than dark-skinned and working-class Mexicans.

Overall, U.S. Latinos have assimilated, just at different rates. The majority culture influences anyone who listens to TV or the radio or who goes to school. The question is, what constitutes assimilation? Some of the factors that should be considered are as follows:

1. How well does the person speak English? What language is spoken at home?

2. Does the person have an accent?

3. What color skin does the person have?

4. What is the person's level of education and income level?

5. What generation is the person?

6. What type of food is eaten at home?

7. What type of music does the person prefer?

8. Where does the person live? Is it a segregated or integrated neighborhood?

9. What is the race or ethnicity of the person's friends?

Lastly, how much discrimination has the person suffered? Racism plays a determining role in assimilation. Within this quagmire, it is important to discuss the question of assimilation or acculturation.[11]

Remember, not all immigrants are resisting assimilation. What is often the case is that second-, third-, and fourth-generation Latinos are the ones resisting total assimilation, or surrender, as some put it. Some immigrants wish to forget the past entirely, and others want to maintain their national identity. The reality is that once immigrants come into the United States they are part of the nation-state called the United States of America. Their nationality, however, does not change. For example, the Maya Indians in Mexico are part of the Mexican nation-state, but they have a separate national identity. Ultimately the question is, do the immigrants who want to maintain their mother cultures have the right to preserve elements of the past, such as language and history, in the United States?

## SHOULD U.S. LATINOS ASSIMILATE?

### For

The United States has always been similar to a melting pot, welcoming the unwanted of the world. The Statue of Liberty symbolizes that beacon of

Dancers in costume during the 33rd annual Hispanic Day Parade in 1997 in New York. (AP/Wide World Photos)

democracy. When people come here, they leave the prejudices and divisions of the old world behind them. George Washington believed that to hold on to the old ways is divisive, and Arthur Schlesinger believes this as well. Why should blacks want to know about Africa, or why should Latinos want to know about Latin America? If things had been so good in their own countries, immigrants would not have come here. Moreover, everybody accepts the fact that English is the most used language in the world. It is the language of science, so to accept it is to accept progress. If more proof is needed, just look at the border towns of Mexico or go to the Island of Puerto Rico and see whether they would not be better off assimilating American values, culture, and language.

Linda Chávez, a well-known Hispanic columnist, discusses her view of assimilation:

I've always used Chávez professionally. It's, in part, because of my, I think, attachment to my father. It's a name I like. I'm very proud of my heritage and have always been. And it's one of the things I think people misunderstand. I'm an assimilationist. I believe in assimilation. I think that assimilation is the only model that works in a society as diverse as ours, that if each and every group keeps its primary attachment to the ethnic group or the racial group . . . that it's divisive. Having said that, though, one of the unique characteristics about American assimilation is that we do feel that we have some connection to the past. I mean, we eat different foods; we have different kinds of traditions in our homes and celebrations. And I think that so long as the ethnic part is private, so long as public funds are not being used to promote it that there's nothing wrong with it and it, in fact, can make a richer nation and make a richer life. It's when the public gets involved and when we begin expending public money to promote attachment to ethnicity or race that I have a problem.[12]

Those opposing assimilation should read American history and realize how republican values have made this country more democratic. Latinos have to make the choice as to whether they wish to be a part of American history or a part of a history of revolution and chaos. Following the lead of the African American will lead to a backlash, and it will make it more difficult to be accepted. Latinos have to ask themselves why the Irish, Italians, and Jews have made it and why so many Latinos are stuck in the underclass. They also have to ask why the public should support special cultural programs for Latinos. In addition, why should public support go to ethnic studies programs for people who don't want to assimilate? In Afrocentric classes they teach a worldview where Africa is at the center of study. Do we want to teach history, language, and culture using Latin America as the center?

With rights come duties, with privileges come responsibilities, and the first responsibility of U.S. Latinos is to be loyal to this country and show appreciation by studying its history and its culture, which means the study of Western civilization. To quote Arthur Schlesinger, "Separatism nourishes prejudices, magnifies differences, and stirs antagonism."[13] We live in a color-blind society, and our differences cause prejudices. By perpetuating the differences we are perpetuating racism.

A Committee of Scholars in Defense of History, led by Drs. Schlesinger and Diane Ravitch and other leading U.S. historians, issued a manifesto on June 29, 1990, in the *New York Times* titled, "NY Should Teach History, Not Ethnic Cheerleading," in which they criticized changes in the New York curriculum, which officially included Afrocentric materials:

> The Western tradition is the source of ideas of individual freedom and political democracy to which most of the world now aspires. The West has committed its share of crimes against humanity, but the Western democratic philosophy also contains in its essence the means of exposing crimes and producing reforms. This philosophy has included and empowered people of all nations and races. Little can be more damaging to the psyches of young blacks, Hispanics, Asians and Indians than for the State of New York to tell them that the Western democratic tradition is not for them.
>
> And little can have more damaging effect on the republic than the use of the school system to promote the division of our people into antagonistic racial groups. We are after all a nation—as the poet Walt Whitman said, "a teeming Nation of nations"—and history enables us to understand the bonds of cohesion that make for nationhood and a sense of the common good: unum e pluribus. In conclusion, Latinos came to the U.S. to become Americans, if not they would have stayed in their respective countries.

## Against

Arthur M. Schlesinger's argument is simplistic. U.S. Latinos have never had the choice whether to assimilate, or, for that matter, who in the group would or would not be allowed to join the American club. Assimilation is a one-way street, and it has been the white way or no way. Society has reached a point where assimilation involves the majority society acculturating and adopting the positive values and cultural assets of U.S. Latinos, who have more to offer than just good food and music. It should not be a question of cultural abandonment, which is what assimilation is, but one of cultural preservation.

The reality is that unlike immigrants who came to the United States at the turn of the century, U.S. Latinos have kept their original culture intact. Latino immigrants did not have to swim an ocean, and the nearness of their mother land makes it easy to keep contact. Latinos are in constant contact with relatives in the old country. Today both communication by telephone and air travel are quick and cheap. The electronic media—including movies, television, video recordings, and the Internet—allow for the continuation of the cultural experience initiated in their countries of origin. So it is more a question of whether Latinos want to acculturate than assimilate. It is their business if they choose to learn a second culture and not abandon their first culture in favor of American culture, as Schlesinger insinuates.

The fact is that most Latinos *are* acculturated and speak better English than Americans speak Spanish. Latinos are just not assimilated in the way some want them to be assimilated. For instance, why should history be distorted to please some people? The United States is not perfect, and it would be intellectually dishonest to say, for instance, that Mexico provoked the United States into invading it or that Puerto Rico was not incorporated into the United States by force. Slavery, racism, and inequality existed, and if some Americans think that minorities are creating division by mentioning it, they are being divisive.

The reality is that diversity makes Latinos a richer people. However, Latinos find acceptance and opportunities in the mainstream, depending on the color of their skin. The evidence shows that educated Latinos who have no accent have the option of being white and crossing over.[14]

Besides, Latinos are the majority in many parts of the United States. The marketplace is dictating that white merchants learn Spanish and Latino culture to get Latino business. Anglos have a choice. As one Chicano activist once warned Anglo Americans, "Smell the refried beans!"[15] Latinos are not going away, so let them acculturate rather than expect them to abandon their culture. Again, Puerto Rico and Mexico did not choose to become part of the United States. Puerto Ricans became part of the country because the United States took Puerto Rico in 1898.[16] The United States in 1836 and 1849 took more than half of Mexico's land. Afterward the United States exploited Mexico's natural resources and recruited its workers to build the Southwest. Other Latinos have come to the United States because of U.S. intervention and control of the world economy. Yet Puerto Ricans and Mexicans have fought in American wars for more than 100 years, often in disproportionate numbers. In the recent Iraq war, some 37,000 immigrants who were not citizens filled the ranks of the American military.

Latinos do not deserve to be told, "America, love it or leave it." Latinos respect this country but reject the idea that they have to abandon their past. The essence of good citizenship is the ability to choose in which culture a person wants to operate at a given time. The foremost barrier to assimilation is neither speaking Spanish, enjoying Latino music and culture, nor is it learning about self-identity, but it is simply racism.

## QUESTIONS

1. Is there a difference between assimilation and acculturation? If so, what is it?

2. Considering the histories of Puerto Rico and Mexico and the annexation of

their territories to the United States, would the social contract apply to them? Why or why not? Many Mexican Americans and Central Americans say they are indigenous to the Americas. How does the social contract of assimilation apply to indigenous peoples? Under what conditions should the social contract be modified?

3. To what extent, if any, should we revoke the basic principles of a constitutional democracy in order to grant a right not to be assimilated?

4. On page 12 of Schlesinger's *Disuniting of America* (1993), he writes, "What is the American? He is an American, who leaving behind him all his ancient prejudices and manners, receives new ones from the new mode of life he has embraced, the new government he obeys, and the new rank he holds. The American is a new man [sic], who acts upon new principles. . . . Here individuals of all nations are melted into a new race of men." Do you agree or disagree with this statement? Why or why not?

5. In the same book on page 17, Schlesinger claims, "Separatism, however, nourishes prejudices, magnifies differences and stirs antagonisms." By assimilating, does one have to lose ethnicity? Who causes separatism?

6. Many Latinos want to obtain an education so as to return to Latino barrios and *colonias* to teach Latino students to be proud of their history and culture. Would Schlesinger agree with those who want to educate America about Latino culture to help fellow Latinos assimilate into society? Would you agree? Why or why not?

7. Many scholars disagree with the meaning of assimilation. Some scholars interpret assimilation as meaning a total surrender of the immigrant's national identity and the adoption of American culture and identity. Others say that assimilation is more like acculturation—the learning of and functioning within two cultures. Why is there confusion as to the meaning of assimilation? What do you think "Assimilation, American Style" means? List the preconditions for assimilation. Discuss your criteria.

8. Do you believe that immigrants often suffer isolation from assimilated Latinos? Is this a form of discrimination? Some sociologists suggest that this is a form of discrimination that is internalizing the biases of the society. Would you agree or disagree? Why or why not?

9. How do Latinos differ from the Irish, the Italians, and the Jews? Why is it that today it is easier for Latinos to retain their culture? Considering the variables of language, culture, class, and race, will it be easy or difficult for Latinos to assimilate or acculturate?

10. David E. Hayes-Bautista and Gregory Rodríguez in "California; Cultural Assimilation Is Bad for Your Health," *Los Angeles Times*, 17 December 1995, argue that Latino food is healthier than American food, so perhaps this aspect of their culture should not be assimilated. Read the article and comment. This article is also available at the Center for the Study of Latino Health and Culture, the University of California at Los Angeles, http://www.cesla.med.ucla.edu/html/opeds.htm, accessed 26 July 2003.

11. What role does the majority society play in the assimilation of Latinos?

12. Summarize the arguments in favor of assimilation by writing a brief speech or essay.

13. Summarize the arguments against assimilation and strengthen the argument by looking at the selected works listed below.

14. Two films—*Crossover Dreams* (1985, directed by Leon Ichaso) and *Selena* (1997, directed by Gregory Nava)—talk about crossing over into Anglo societies with different messages. Discuss the films.

## NOTES

1. Amy Long, "Fighting a Losing Battle: Theodore Roosevelt's Americanization Machine," History 153, Paper number 2, 17 October 2001, http://www.ups.edu/faculty/dsackman/153%20papers/paper2153a.html, accessed 24 July 2003.

2. Ibid.

3. "1990. Eugenic and Racist Premise of Reproductive Rights and Population Control," http://www.hsph.harvard.edu/Organizations/healthnet/SAsia/depop/Chap7.html, accessed 24 July 2003.

4. The Daughters of the American Revolution were formed with the purpose of promoting understanding of the American Revolution. They have restricted their membership to people who can document that they are descended from someone in the American Revolution. This works to exclude non-Anglo-Saxon immigrants in the nineteenth and twentieth century. Critics accused the organization of bringing the idea of hereditary caste into America, being a blatant separatist group, and spawning Confederate organizations such as the United Daughters of the Confederacy and the Sons of Confederate Veterans. According to one source, "[Arthur]Schlesinger's real complaint is that the minorities in history are getting uppity and rejecting wholesale the history and paternalism of himself and his colleagues." "POS334-L: The Race and Ethnicity Book Review Discussion List," Arthur M. Schlesinger Jr. "Disuniting of America," (Norton, 1991, 1992), http://lilt.ilstu.edu/gmklass/pos334/archive/schlesin.htm, accessed 24 July 2003; "The Pious Humbug of Arthur Schlesinger on Separatism," http://www.templeofdemocracy.com /ArthurSchlesinger.htm, accessed 24 July 2003.

5. Arthur M. Schlesinger, Jr. *The Disuniting of America: Reflections on a Multicultural Society* (New York: W. W. Norton, 1992), 30.

6. Arthur M. Schlesinger, Jr. *The Disuniting of America: Reflections on a Multicultural Society* (1993 Edition), 13.

7. Ibid., 137.

8. Ibid., 17.

9. Schlesinger also headed a Committee of Scholars in Defense of History. The group criticized Afrocentricism and the growth of ethnic studies and women's studies programs and their attempted revision of U.S. history. According to the Committee of Scholars, minorities were in league with radical feminists and others determined to destroy Western civilization. Other scholars joined Schlesinger and accused multiculturalists and Afrocentric scholars of substituting "ethnic cheerleading" for scholarship. Many of the country's leading historians seconded the Committee of Scholars in Defense of History, which objected to the adoption by the state of New York of U.S. history books giving the so-called multiculturalist interpretation.

10. Mark Krikorian, "Will Americanization Work in America?" *Freedom Review.* Center for Immigration Studies (fall 1997), http://www.cis.org/articles/1997/freedom_review.html, accessed 24 July 2003.

11. Sung Chang Chun, "Theory of Ethnicity and Christianity: Assimilational and Plural Models for Explaining the Role of Religion in the Adaptation of Immigrants," Department of Sociology, Notre Dame University, http://www.nd.edu/~schun/research.htm, accessed 24 July 2003; Milton Gordon, *Assimilation in American Life: The Role of Race, Religion and National Origins* (New York: Oxford University Press, 1964), 71.

12. "Linda Chávez, (1947– )," LasCulturas.Com, http://www.lasculturas.com/aa/bio/bioLindaChavez.php, accessed 24 July 2003.

13. *The Disuniting of America* (1993 Edition), 17.

14. Alberto Sándoval-Sánchez, "Working Text: Latinos and Cultural Exchange De-Facing Mainstream Magazine Covers: The New Faces of Latino/a Transnational and Transcultural Celebrities," *Latino Intersections* Volume 1 Issue 1 (2003), http://journals.dartmouth.edu/webobjbin/WebObjects/Journals.woa/xmlpage/2/article/85m accessed September 3, 2003.

15. Bill Boyarsky, "Battle Over Hermosillo: It Is Just the Start," *Los Angeles Times,* 25 August 1993.

16. Marisabel Brás, "The Changing of the Guard: Puerto Rico in 1898," in *The World of 1898: The Spanish-American War,* Hispanic Division, Library of Congress, http://www.loc.gov/rr/hispanic/1898/bras.html, accessed 24 July 2003.

## SELECTED WORKS

Acuña, Rodolfo F. *Sometimes There Is No Other Side: Chicanos and the Myth of Equality.* Notre Dame, Ind.: Notre Dame University Press, 1998.

Balcazar, Hector; Jennifer L. Krull; Gary Peterson. "Acculturation and Family Functioning Are Related to Health Risks among Pregnant Mexican American Women." *Behavioral Medicine* 27, no. 2 (summer 2001).

Chávez, Linda. "The New Politics of Hispanic Assimilation." In *Beyond the Color Line: New Perspectives on Race and Ethnicity in America.* Edited by Abigail Thernstrom and Stephan Thermstrom. Stanford, CA: Hoover Institution 2002. Pp. 383–390.

Cruz, Jose E. *Identity and Power: Puerto Rican Politics and the Challenge of Ethnicity.* Philadelphia, Pa.: Temple University Press, 1998.

Farley, Reynolds and Richard Alba. "The New Second Generation in the United States." *International Migration Review* 36, no. 3 (fall 2002): 669ff.

Gordon, Milton. *Assimilation in American Life: The Role of Race, Religion and National Origins.* New York: Oxford University Press, 1964.

Gurza, Agustin. "Positives about Latinos Bring out Negatives in Some." *Los Angeles Times,* 15 February 2000.

Logan, John R. "How Race Counts for Hispanic Americans." Lewis Mumford Center for Comparative Urban and Regional Research. University at Albany, 14 July 2003. http://mumford1.dyndns.org/cen2000/BlackLatinoReport/BlackLatino01.htm. Accessed 24 July 2003.

Ochoa, Alberto M. "Succeeding in America; Latino Immigrants are Finding a New

World and More Challenges in Assimilating than Immigrants of a Century Ago." *San Diego Union-Tribune*, 20 July 2003.

Ono, Hiromi. "Assimilation, Ethnic Competition, and Ethnic Identities of U.S.-Born Persons of Mexican Origin." *International Migration Review* 36, no. 3 (fall 2002): 726ff.

Orfield, Gary. "The Resegregation of Our Nation's Schools: A Troubling Trend." *Civil Rights Journal* 4, no. 1 (fall 1999): 8ff.

Orfield, Gary and Susan E. Eaton. "Back to Segregation." *The Nation* 276, no. 8 (3 March 2003): 5ff.

Rodríguez, Gregory. "150 Years Later, Latinos Finally Hit the Mainstream," *New York Times,* 15 April 2001.

Rosales, Rodolfo. *The Illusion of Inclusion: The Untold Political Story of San Antonio.* Austin: University of Texas Press, 2000.

Schlesinger, Jr., Arthur M. *The Disuniting of America: Reflections on a Multicultural Society.* New York: W. W. Norton, 1992.

# 3

# BILINGUAL EDUCATION

## BACKGROUND

In recent years, bilingual education has become a political issue. In 1998 a businessman from Silicon Valley, California, named Ron Unz sponsored an initiative in California called "English for the Children" that would eliminate bilingual education. The initiative known as Proposition 227 passed; it purported to give preference to English-language programs for immigrant children. The proposition further reduced the length of time children would remain in special programs. Further, it mandated that the state spend 50 million dollars a year to teach English to adults. The consequence was that the initiative immediately divided Californians along ethnic and ideological lines.

Even bilingual education critics conceded that bilingual education was "a special effort to help immigrant children learn English so that they can do regular schoolwork with their English-speaking classmates and receive an equal educational opportunity."[1] However, they accused supporters of bilingual education of building a billion-dollar industry out of an untested program that resulted in segregating non-English-speaking students, promoting cultural separatism, and encouraging Latino students to drop out. Still others objected to the added stipend that bilingual teachers received because of their knowledge of Spanish.

The defenders of bilingual education claimed that Proposition 227 had nothing to do with education and everything to do with politics. They alleged that it was an attack on immigrants overall and Latinos and Asians in partic-

Ron Unz addresses the media and proponents of the proposal to end bilingual education in Los Angeles Tuesday, June 2, 1998. Proposition 227 divided Californians. It passed even though Latinos voted overwhelmingly against it. (AP/Wide World Photos)

ular. The "English for the Children" initiative came on the heels of Proposition 187 (1994), which took services away from residents without documents, and Proposition 209 (1996), the anti-affirmative action initiative that banned the use of race as a criterion for employment, state contracts, or admission into institutions of higher education. Bilingual education supporters pointed out that the sponsors of Proposition 227 were the U.S. English activists who placed and passed Proposition 63 in California in November 1986. According to University of Colorado law professor Richard Delgado, a string of ultra-right-wing foundations financed the English Only movement, of which Proposition 227 was part.[2]

Opponents argued that Proposition 227 was confusing voters and that bilingual education was pedagogically sound. Bilingual education had two goals: the development of academic English and school success and the development and maintenance of the student's first language. Educator Stephen Krashen argues it makes no sense to let students sit in a class and have a limited grasp of the subject matter while they learn English. According to Krashen, a "child who understands history [in the native language] . . . will have a better chance understanding history taught in English than a child without this background knowledge."[3] Krashen posited that "there is strong evidence that literacy transfers across languages, that building literacy in the primary language is a short-cut to English literacy."[4] Most bilingual educators conceded that some bilingual programs were not meeting the goals but quickly added that public education overall was falling short of educating not only Latino students, but all students. In both cases the quality of the implementation and the funding governed the outcome of the program.

White voters overwhelmingly approved Proposition 227.[5] Latinos voted two to one against the initiative with many describing it as discriminatory; 37 percent voted yes, and 63 percent voted no.[6] The tally was reversed with white voters (see Table 3.1.).

Since the victory in California, Unz has made the abolishment of bilingual education a national crusade. Speaking after the terrorist destruction of the Twin Towers buildings on September 11, 2001, Unz said, "A few weeks ago, Americans witnessed the enormous devastation that a small handful of fanatically committed individuals can wreak upon society. Perhaps it is now time for ordinary Americans to be willing to take a stand against those similarly tiny groups of educational terrorists in our midst [i.e., advocates of bilingual education], whose disastrous policies are enforced upon us not by bombs or even by knives, but simply by their high-pitched voices."[7] Unz relentlessly took his campaign through Arizona, Colorado, Massachusetts, and on to New York City.[8] Unz claimed that after California replaced bilingual education with English immersion, reading test scores soared, and he planned to liberate non-English-speaking children from bilingual classrooms.[9] A minority of conservative Latino newspaper columnists supported Unz.[10]

What then makes bilingual education so controversial? Is bilingual education the invention of the 1960s or of U.S. Latinos? In reality, bilingual education has been part of the European immigrant tradition. Newcomers often enrolled their children in bilingual or non-English-language public and private schools. They wanted to keep their native languages alive. In 1839, Ohio adopted a bilingual education law, authorizing German-English instruction at parents' request. In 1847 Louisiana authorized the teaching of French and English, and the New Mexico Territory did so for Spanish and English in 1850. By the end of the nineteenth century, around a dozen states passed bilingual education laws. These states were not unique, and many smaller localities offered bilingual instruction in languages as diverse as Norwegian, Italian, Polish, Czech, and Cherokee.

Before World War I, at least 600,000 public and parochial school students received some or all of their schooling in German—some 4 percent of all American children in the elementary grades—which was larger than the percentage of students enrolled in Spanish-English programs today. World War I

Table 3.1
Proposition 227: How the Vote Breaks Down (June 1998)*

| Percentage of voters | Voters | Percentage who voted Yes | Percentage who voted No |
|---|---|---|---|
| 69 | White | 67 | 33 |
| 14 | Black | 48 | 52 |
| 12 | Latino | 37 | 63 |
| 3 | Asian | 57 | 43 |
| Party registration | | | |
| 48 | Democrats | 47 | 53 |
| 6 | Independents | 59 | 41 |
| 40 | Republicans | 77 | 23 |
| 25 | Democratic men | 48 | 52 |
| 26 | Democratic women | 48 | 52 |
| 25 | Republican men | 81 | 19 |
| 19 | Republican women | 72 | 28 |
| Political ideology | | | |
| 20 | Liberal | 36 | 64 |
| 43 | Moderate | 59 | 41 |
| 37 | Conservative | 77 | 23 |
| Annual family income | | | |
| 10 | Less than $20,000 | 49 | 51 |
| 20 | $20,000 to $39,999 | 56 | 44 |
| 22 | $40,000 to $59,999 | 61 | 39 |
| 16 | $60,000 to $74,999 | 65 | 35 |
| 32 | $75,000 or more | 64 | 36 |

*61 percent yes, 39 percent no. Won in every county except San Francisco and Ala-
meda (Oakland and East Bay). Rejected 2–1 by Latino voters.
*Source:* Los Angeles Times/CNN exit poll conducted on Tuesday, June 2, 1998.

changed this, and an anti-German sentiment led most states to enact English-only laws designed to Americanize foreigners. People of German extraction even changed their last names to Americanized versions, and local school boards banned the study of foreign languages in the early grades, which the courts declared unconstitutional in 1923. By the mid-1920s, school districts had largely dismantled bilingual schooling. School authorities expected immigrant children to learn in English only, and they prohibited them from speaking Spanish or any other foreign language in school. Teachers often punished Latino students when they broke the no-Spanish-spoken rule. Schools called this method of teaching English sink-or-swim, or the immersion method.

This instruction in English became moot with the European ethnics as they moved into the third and fourth generations away from the original immigrants. Mexicans and Puerto Ricans, as well as other Latino immigrants, remained isolated in rural and urban enclaves where many received limited schooling. School boards segregated many Latino students from English-speaking children, which also retarded the Latinos' learning of English. Older Latinos to this day tell horror stories about their experiences in these schools.

Congress passed the Bilingual Education Act of 1968 during an era of growing immigration and a militant civil rights movement. It allocated federal funding to encourage local school districts to try approaches incorporating native-language instruction. Most states followed the lead of the federal government, enacting bilingual education laws of their own or at least decriminalizing the use of other languages in the classroom.[11] The notion came from President Lyndon Johnson, who, according to former U.S. Rep. Edward R. Roybal, raised the idea of bilingual education on an Air Force One flight. Johnson based his concern on his teaching experience in a Mexican school where he observed that the Mexican children were smart, but that they did not know how to speak English. This would keep them in the same grade year after year, falling behind in crucial subjects like math and science, which Mexican students could understand in Spanish. Mexican American educators also pointed out that teachers often punished Mexican students for speaking Spanish at school. Studies showed that school districts would often label non-English-speaking Mexican American students as mentally retarded.

From the beginning, the process was fraught with politics, with some educators and politicians opposing bilingual education unless it emphasized teaching Mexican Americans how to speak English. Eventually, the bill passed, ironically with little support from the White House. This lack of support was because of President Johnson's problems with the Vietnam War and the politics of the war on poverty. Much of the funding for the first bilingual program came from the media giant, the Hearst Corporation.[12]

Soon after Congress passed the Bilingual Education Act of 1968, the U.S. Supreme Court held in *Lau v. Nichols* that leaving limited-English students in English-only classrooms to sink or swim made "a mockery of public education." The court held that education should be equally available to all students. *Lau v. Nichols* required schools to take "affirmative steps" to overcome language barriers hampering children's access to the curriculum. Congress immediately reinforced this in the Equal Educational Opportunity Act of 1974.[13] Neither the Bilingual Education Act nor the Lau decision requires any specified methodology for teaching limited-English students. However, bilingual education was clearly considered a civil right that required educational programs to offer equal opportunities for limited-English children.[14]

Influencing the discourse of bilingual education is that most Americans have never been fond of foreign languages. Although business becomes more global, for example, most institutions of higher learning dropped or lowered foreign language requirements. Between 1966 and 1979, U.S. colleges and universities scaled back requirements for foreign language as a qualification for admission, and the number of institutions of higher education requiring a foreign language for admission dropped from 34 percent to 8 percent. Meanwhile, many children of European ethnics who were becoming teachers resented that many school districts were requiring some knowledge of Spanish, and said if people lived in the United States, they should speak English. They believed it was up to the students to adjust to the system. To make their point, they explained how their grandparents had come to the United States and how they had to learn English.

Many U.S. Latino leaders countered that Americans had a low opinion of the Spanish language and culture, and that the best way to counteract this ethnocentricism was to give Spanish language and culture greater importance in the educational scheme. By this time, Mexican Americans and Asians were not the only U.S. proponents of bilingual education. Cuban immigrants, many of them highly educated, called for quality schooling for their children, an education that would preserve the Cubans' Spanish culture. Puerto Ricans were equally outspoken in their demands. In New York City, ASPIRA (ASPIRE), a Puerto Rican cultural organization, sued the school board for effective bilingual programs.

Meanwhile, the dreams of many Latinos that everyone would speak two languages were scaled back, and by 1983 the National Association for Bilingual Education advocated transitional bilingual programs and abandoned its demand for language maintenance. It accepted the primacy of English and said the native tongue should be considered a second language. The American Federation of Teachers (AFT) opposed bilingual education because its leader believed it was keeping Latinos from assimilating. Although U.S. Latinos had increased in population, they lacked the voting and economic power to fight back the pressure of English Only groups.

The fluctuation in the economy in the eighties and nineties increased strains and heightened nativist sentiments throughout the United States. Deindustrialization, that is, the sending of factories overseas, had severely curtailed the stepping stone many working-class Americans had into the middle class by eliminating higher paying union scale jobs. Rising property values also made it more difficult to qualify for purchasing a house. With this downturn, nativism increased, and bilingual education came under heavy fire as funding for education decreased, from kindergarten through to institutions of higher learning. Conservative think tanks played an important role in cultivating this discontent and associating the disaffectedness and the decline in education with many reforms of the 1960s. The rising conservatism expressed itself through a growing resistance to taxes, blaming unemployment on immigrants, and a growing resentment toward immigrants and bilingual education. A sense that the United States was losing ground to Japan and Western European nations seemed to justify the curtailing of special programs such as bilingual education and ethnic studies.

Within this context, a polarization occurred within American society. A conservative surge countered the civil rights reforms of the 1960s, and in the late 1970s, ultraconservatives became much more active in forming think tanks and organizations. According to University of Colorado law professor Richard Delgado, "The Reagan era was a time of consolidation and experiment. Supply-side economics came and went. Religion, family values, and patriotism came to stay."[15] These struggles thrust this movement into the mainstream in the early 1990s, fanned by a severe depression during which many politicians blamed immigrants for the economic recession. Former California Governor Pete Wilson resurrected his political career by blaming immigrants for California's problems. Wilson contributed greatly to Proposition 187, the anti-immigrant initiative, in 1994; Proposition 209, the anti-affirmative action initiative, in 1996; and Proposition 227, the anti-bilingual education initiative in 1998. Meanwhile, most U.S. Latinos became more defensive, interpreting the anti-bilingual education mood as directed against them.

The fight for bilingual education is far from over. Many U.S. Latinos believe that a knowledge of the Spanish language is a strong part of their identity and essential in this era of globalization. The issue of bilingual education binds most U.S. Latino organizations with a common cause. ASPIRA (New York), the Puerto Rican Legal Defense Fund, and the Mexican American Legal Defense and Education Fund all filed amicus briefs in *Lau v. Nichols*.[16]

Puerto Ricans had a strong sense of identity even before being incorporated into the United States in 1898.[17] In New York City in 1980, 91 percent of Puerto Ricans spoke Spanish at home compared with 90 percent of Cubans and 64 percent of Mexicans. Why? In the past, Puerto Rico's isolation from the mainland allowed for the formation of close family and cultural ties.[18] But probably more important was the role of U.S. colonialism and American racism both on the island and on the mainland.

Mexicans have a different experience with racism than other Latinos, engendering a strong sense of identity among Mexicans. The Mexican Revolution of 1910 contributed to the forging of this identity. The constant waves of Mexicans coming from Mexico have revitalized their sense of Mexicanness; intermarriage between immigrants and citizens has been common throughout the generations. Identity is also important to Cubans and has been reinforced by their exile status.

In addition, most South Americans and Central Americans are recent arrivals and also have a strong sense of identity, having gone through almost 200 years of nation-state building. Salvadorans, for example, come from a densely populated area, and a war and their collective migrations to the United States have reinforced Salvadoran identity.

Because of this, the victory of the English Only forces in California did not end the debate over bilingual education. Thus, as Latinos got more political clout and more of them were elected to office, Latino politicians and organizations began to challenge the act. The way they saw it was that an estimated 1.5 million public school students in California spoke little, if any, English, and that this problem had to be addressed. The powerful state Sen. Richard Polanco, D-Los Angeles, chair of the Latino Legislative Caucus in 2001, pushed legislation that would require "appropriate instruction, curriculum, and materials" for limited-English students.[19] Unz and company reacted and warred with the state over how school authorities should implement the law in classrooms. Meanwhile, just 12 percent of the state's 1.5 million language minority students remained in bilingual programs. One reason for this was the negative publicity given to bilingual education. Another was the inability of the state to hire adequately trained Spanish-speaking teachers. Yet another reason was that many school districts failed to inform parents of the option to keep their children in bilingual programs.[20]

Out of the discourse on bilingual education a third camp has emerged, which recognizes that both immersion and bilingual programs have been deficient. This camp states that test scores can go either way and that many teachers are not teaching the subject matter by training students to take particularized exams. They point to the inequality of schools and cite the lack of certified teachers in Latino and African American schools. Because of this, the American Civil Liberties Union (ACLU) has sued in California, alleging that "the state is providing its poorest students with an inferior education." The ACLU expected to expand its suit to cover all the state's 1,100 districts and their 5.8 million students.[21]

The Center for the Future of Teaching and Learning in Santa Cruz found that one in seven teachers in California was uncredentialed and that "low-income children are more likely than ever to be stuck in a classroom with the state's least experienced, least prepared teachers."[22]

## SHOULD PUBLIC SCHOOLS OFFER BILINGUAL EDUCATION?

### For

Most Americans do not know what bilingual education is. They are instinctively against bilingual education because it sounds foreign. Accordingly, Americans feel threatened by other languages. From the reaction of a sizeable group of Americans it could be said that if you know three languages, you are trilingual; if you know two languages, you are bilingual; and if you know one language, you are American. Ironically, many oppose bilingual education just when business and government want more people proficient in foreign languages.

Saying that the reason for opposing bilingual education is based on the needs of the child is disingenuous. The common argument that people have succeeded without it is open to question. For example, many German Americans received bilingual education, and they were among the most successful of the European immigrants. Jewish Americans have had Hebrew schools that supplemented their public education, as did the Japanese Americans, and that education did not detract from their learning or assimilation into society. Many other ethnic groups, such as the Italians and Poles, did not have as extensive bilingual education networks, but that is no reason that Latinos or any other newcomers should suffer through their language barriers.

What it comes down to is that Latino children have certain needs. Many studies show that students coming from places such as Mexico do better in school than U.S.-born Mexicans, and that those coming to the United States having completed the first six grades do better than those having completed only one grade. The ability to read transfers across languages, even when the writing systems are different. Instead of blaming bilingual education for the system's failure, educators should study what it is in American education that takes away the child's motivation to learn.

Limited-English-speaking children would benefit from bilingual education just as most Americans would benefit from knowing two languages. This is especially true in an age when the United States is reaching international free-trade agreements, such as NAFTA (North American Free-Trade Agreement),

with Latin American countries. Even corporations conducting business recognize this and have called for more foreign languages taught in the schools.
Yet the fact is that schools have enrolled only a small percentage of Latino
students in bilingual education: In California, for example, only 15 percent
were in full bilingual programs.

What is ironic is that many of the same forces that are calling for prayer in
the schools are the same ones who are opposing the teaching of bilingual
subjects, which leads one to believe they base the argument against bilingual
education more on emotion than reason. Opponents of bilingual education
tell us that the public is against bilingual education. Most studies, however,
do not show this to be the case. For example, why did U.S. Latinos in California vote two to one against Proposition 227? Especially since English Firs-
ters say a person can get a better job by learning English. However, African
Americans speak English and most graduate from high school, but they have
not made significant gains. Indeed, many are worse off than Latinos. Moreover, with the globalization of the U.S. economy, it seems that knowing more
than one language is an asset, not a liability.

The fact is that it is the quality of the schools and the skills they impart
that determine success. People can know all the English they want, but if
they do not have skills in math they are limited, and they do not have to
know English to understand math. A well-rounded knowledge of one's first
language can be helpful in providing background knowledge. This is not to
say that all bilingual programs are doing a good job. Just as with English-
based programs, some are good and some are bad. Yet it is a bit too much
to blame bilingual education for the high dropout rate of Latinos as if poverty
and bad schools did not play a role. For example, in South Central Los Angeles barely one-third of their teachers are certified. In white areas in the San
Fernando Valley, most teachers are certified. Is it really fair or rational to say
this discrepancy plays no role in the students' outcome?

Latinos know Latino children have problems and that their schools are in
bad shape. This is why Latinos want to improve bilingual education. Frankly,
if the schools were doing an excellent job of educating non-Latino students,
it would be easy to say, "give it a try." If those people who oppose bilingual
education really had Latino children's interests in mind, it would be easy to
say, "give it a try." However, people who are anti-bilingual usually oppose
immigration, affirmative action, and civil rights.

The immersion method, which is the sink-or-swim method, makes no
sense. Society is beyond the times when people would throw their kids into
a river and tell them to swim or drown. If society wants to help Latinos then
it needs to get the parents better jobs, improve housing, bring schools up to
the level of the best schools in the state, and provide certified teachers. Be-

tween 1952 and 1972, government spending for education in schools and colleges increased more than 700 percent, from $8.4 billion to $67.5 billion. During that period, the school median of white students increased substantially. It was not until the 1970s, when Latinos and other minorities started to approach a majority in many local school districts dominated by white school board officials, that support for education was abandoned.

## Against

If a person lives in America, he or she should speak English. Bilingual education is expensive, ineffective, retards the learning of English, and retards Americanization. The most effective and quickest way to teach children a language is to immerse them. Immersion programs make the immigrant child speak and learn only in English. Bilingual education discriminates against other students since most of the bilingual programs are for Latino students.

Bilingual education is an experiment that went wrong. The founders had the best of intentions, but it was wrongheaded. Bilingual education is part of a civil rights movement that catered to African Americans and was hastily put together for Latinos who believed the schools had victimized them. Supporters held out bilingual education as a cure-all for the drop-out problem and a program to motivate students to stay in school. Instead, bilingual education isolated Latino students and created pockets of different languages. From that point, it went astray.

Bilingual education by any standards has been ineffective. The schools have impaired the learning of English and the assimilation of immigrant students by segregating them in Spanish-language classes, which has in fact worsened the high drop-out rates for Latino students, and consequently fewer Latino students graduate from high school. The inability to speak English has kept Spanish speakers at the bottom of the economic and educational ladder in the United States. Everyone knows that more people speak English than any other language. English is the language of science, technology, diplomacy, international trade, and commerce. In Europe they conduct business in English. In universities around the world, most scientists speak English. The United States leads the world in the field of computers, and English is absolutely necessary to be a computer scientist and to be a player in the information age. Without English, immigrants will be prisoners in languages that will soon be obsolete.

The mission of the public schools is to make students good citizens, and bilingual education frustrates that mission. The advocates of bilingual education are separatists who want to keep students captives. Their goal is not simply to make students proficient in two languages but to make them cultural separatists. This is the reason that they call it bilingual-bicultural education. The real aim of bilingual education is to promote the criticism and erosion of traditional American values. Because of their extremism, bilingual proponents can alienate Americans voters.

Bicultural programs have diverted Hispanic students from fields such as engineering and computer science, which have been seriously neglected by Chicanos and Puerto Ricans. Finally, funds to support bilingual programs are going to foreigners rather than native-born Americans. Most Mexican Americans and other U.S. Latinos don't need bilingual education, they understand almost no Spanish; English is widely spoken in Mexican American and U.S. Latino homes. English is the official language of America, and the schools should make its teaching mandatory.[23]

## QUESTIONS

1. Why did bilingual education come about? What caused the original public rejection of bilingual education? Is there any parallel between then and now? How does bilingual education conflict with Americanization? If so, how?

2. Many bilingual proponents say that foreign languages have never been popular in the United States to the point that, "if you know three languages, you are trilingual; if you know two, you are bilingual; and if you know only one, you are American." Is this a fair criticism? Why or why not?

3. Describe the tensions between the advocates and critics of bilingual education. Do you believe they could have avoided this clash? Why are there no winners and the students losers in cases such as this?

4. Drawing from two or more sources, summarize the arguments against bilingual education and those for it.

5. Was the bilingual education conflict over good education or was it political? Study the table showing the percentage of those voting for or against Proposition 227. What do the results tell you about who was for or against?

6. Read Peter Duignan, "Commentary; Ethnic Politics Fails Our Schoolchildren; Prop. 227: Is a Power Play Masked as Education, Denying Students the Key Tool for Success, English Literacy," *Los Angeles Times*, 26 May 1998. Do you think that Duignan's arguments are pedagogical or political in nature? Discuss the article. (Additional works by Peter Duignan, "Bye-Bye, Bilingual," Hoover Institution, *Hoover Digest* no. 3 (1999), http://www-hoover.stanford.edu/pub lications/digest/993/duignan.html, accessed 26 July 2003.)

7. Julie Cart, in "Campaign 2000; Tribal Languages Unintended Target in English-Only Drive; Measure: Largely Aimed at Spanish Programs, the Arizona Proposition Could Curb the Teaching of Native American Languages. Latino and Indian Groups Oppose It," *Los Angeles Times*, 4 November 2000, reported an unintended consequence of Proposition 203 was that the English-only edict aimed at the state's growing number of Spanish-speaking students also could

restrict the teaching of the imperiled languages spoken among Arizona's 21 Native American tribes. What do you think?

8. Read Agustin Gurza, "Bilingual Ed: The Truth behind Test Gains," *Los Angeles Times,* 22 July 2000. The author is of the opinion that Ron Unz is often first in line to take credit for the hard work of teachers and students. Here, Unz was taking credit for the success of San Juan Elementary in Orange County, California, where poor Latino students posted double-digit advances in some grades and subjects on the Stanford 9 test. "Here's what Unz would have us believe: San Juan switches decisively to English and does great; Santa Ana schools stick stubbornly to bilingual instruction and don't do so well." The editorialist says that San Juan students in the immersion program overall did no better at most grade levels than students at Walker Elementary in Santa Ana, a school where half the kids still are enrolled in bilingual education, and that students at Walker Elementary actually did better in the math scores at selected grade levels. "'The Santa Ana district officials looked at test results for 11 schools with high numbers of students in bilingual classes, compared with 13 schools with low bilingual enrollment. There was no difference between the two groups in terms of their performance progress,' said Linda Kaminski, chief academic officer for Santa Ana Unified." What is the significance of this story?

9. Read Nick Anderson and Louis Sahagun, "Bilingual Classes Still Thriving in Wake of Prop. 227; Education: in L.A. Unified, about 10 Percent Return to Native-Language Instruction; Figure Is as High as 90 Percent Elsewhere. Measure Allows Parents That Choice," *Los Angeles Times,* 22 October 1998. "Though sizable, that number pales next to the about 107,000 Los Angeles students who were in formal bilingual classes before voters last June approved Prop. 227. Many of the students who are enrolled in English 'immersion' classes actually get substantial help in their native languages." Do you believe that the debate over whether bilingual education is good or bad is finished? Are the issues as simple as either side would have us believe?

10. What is more important for the success of students: credentialed teachers or English-only classes?

11. Does it matter in what language a student learns mathematics?

12. What is the strongest argument made for bilingual education? What is the weakest argument?

13. What is the strongest argument made against bilingual education? What is the weakest argument?

14. A common assertion is that European immigrants did not have bilingual education; they all wanted to learn English. True or false? Why or why not?

15. Study the photo on page 56. What impression do you believe Unz wanted to make? Why do you believe Latinos would object to the photo?

## NOTES

1. Rosalie Pedalino Porter, "The Case against Bilingual Education: Why Even Latino Parents Are Rejecting a Program Designed for Their Children's Benefit," *The*

*Atlantic Monthly* 281, no. 5 (May 1998): 28–39, http://www.theatlantic.com/issues/98may/biling.htm, accessed 24 July 2003.

2. Jean Stefanic and Richard Delgado, *No Mercy. How Conservative Think Tanks and Foundations Changed America's Agenda* (Philadelphia, Pa.: Temple University Press, 1996), 9–19.

3. Stephen Krashen, "Bilingual Education: Arguments for and (Bogus) Arguments Against," Georgetown University Roundtable on Languages and Linguistics, 6 May 1999, http://ourworld.compuserve.com/homepages/jwcrawford/Krashen3.htm, accessed 24 July 2003.

4. Ibid.

5. María L. La Ganga, "Bilingual Ed Initiative Wins Easily," *Los Angeles Times,* 3 June 1998.

6. Amy Pyle, Patrick J. McDonnell, and Hector Tobar, "Latino Voter Participation Doubled Since '94 Primary," *Los Angeles Times,* 4 June 1998.

7. "Notebook," *The New Republic* 12 November 2001, 10ff.

8. "Habla Inglés, Por Favor: Ron Unz Has Battled Bilingual Ed out West. Now He Takes on the Nation's Largest School District—New York," *Newsweek,* 12 March 2001, 64; Roberto Rodríguez, "California Has Another Proposition. (Ron Unz Initiative to Ban Bilingual Instruction)," *Black Issues in Higher Education* 14, no. 23 (January 1998): 11ff.

9. Ron Unz, "California and the End of White America," *Commentary* 108, no. 4 (November 1999): 17ff.

10. Gregory Rodríguez, "English Lesson in California: In the Face of a Ballot Challenge, Support for Bilingual Education Is Wavering," *The Nation* 266, no. 14 (April 1998): 15 (4); Rodolfo F. Acuña and Gregory Rodríguez, "Who Killed Bilingual Education? (Pro and Con Arguments Concerning What Led to the End of Bilingual Education in California)," *The Nation* 266 (23): 2 (29 June 1998).

11. "History of Bilingual Education," *Rethinking Schools Online: An Urban Educational Journal* 12, no. 3 (spring 1998), http://www.rethinkingschools.org/special_reports/bilingual/langhst.shtml, accessed 24 July 2003.

12. Julie Leininger Pycior, *LBJ and Mexican Americans: The Paradox of Power* (Austin: University of Texas Press, 1997), 183–187; Rodolfo Acuña, *Occupied America: A History of Chicanos* 4th ed. (New York: Addison, Wesley Longman, 2000) 333–34, 454–56.

13. *Lau v. Nichols,* no. 72–6520, Supreme Court of the United States, 414 U.S. 563; 94 S. Ct. 786; 39 L. Ed. 2d 1; 1974 U.S. LEXIS 151, 10 December 1973, Argued, 21 January 1974, Decided.

14. "History of Bilingual Education," *Rethinking Schools Online: An Urban Educational Journal* 12, no. 3 (spring 1998), http://www.rethinkingschools.org/special_reports/bilingual/langhst.shtml, accessed 24 July 2003.

15. Stefanic and Delgado, 3.

16. Clara E. Rodríguez, *Puerto Ricans; Born in the U.S.A.* (Boulder: Westview Press, 1991), 140.

17. Ibid., 29.

18. Ibid., 30.

19. Julian Guthrie, "Bilingual-Education Showdown; California Board Is Considering Modifications of Prop. 227 Law," *The San Francisco Chronicle,* 2 March 2002.

20. Duke Helfand, "The Bilingual Schooling Battle Flares Anew; Education: Au-

thor of Prop. 227 Accuses State Board of Weighing New Rules that Would Nullify the Law," *Los Angeles Times,* 20 February 2002; Georgie Anne Geyer, "Even Liberals See Failures of Bilingual Education," *The Denver Post,* 14 January 2001.

21. "Eighteen Calif. School Districts Sued; Shoddy Classrooms, Textbook Shortages, Teacher Quality Cited," *The Washington Post,* 13 December 2000.

22. Nanette Asimov, "One in 7 of State's Teachers Uncredentialed; Poorest Children Stuck with the Least Qualified," *The San Francisco Chronicle,* 12 December 2001. Nanette Asimov, "One in 7 California Teachers Unqualified; Programs Designed to Lure Credentialed Instructors," *San Francisco Chronicle,* 7 December 2000. Nanette Asimov can be reached at nasimov@sfchronicle.com. See http://www.cftl.org, accessed 24 July 2003.

23. A summary from Peter Duignan, "Bilingual Education: A Critique," *Hoover Institution.* http://www-hoover.stanford.edu/publications/he/22/22a.html, accessed 24 July 2003.

## SELECTED WORKS

Bilingual Education, University of Texas, http://www.edb.utexas.edu/coe/depts/CI/bilingue/be-def.html. Accessed 24 July 2003.

Bilingual Education Web sites, http://www.ecsu.ctstateu.edu/depts/edu/textbooks/bilingual.html. Accessed 24 July 2003.

California Dept of Education English Learners Language and Culture in Education, http://www.cde.ca.gov/el/. Accessed 24 July 2003.

Chávez, Linda. "Congress and Bilingual Education." 26 June 2001, http://www.townhall.com/columnists/lindachavez/lc20010626.shtml. Accessed 24 July 2003.

Duignan, Peter. "Bilingual Education: A Critique," *Hoover Institution,* http://www.hoover.stanford.edu/publications/he/22/22a.html. Accessed 24 July 2003.

ERIC Clearinghouse on Languages and Linguistics, http://www.cal.org/ericcll/digest/subject.html. Accessed 24 July 2003.

Krashen, Stephen. "Bilingual Education: Arguments for and (Bogus) Arguments against," Georgetown University Roundtable on Languages and Linguistics, 6 May 1999, http://ourworld.compuserve.com/homepages/jwcrawford/krashen3.htm. Accessed 24 July 2003.

Language and Education Links, NCELA (National Clearinghouse for English Language Acquisition and Language Instruction Educational Programs), http://www.ncbe.gwu.edu/links/biesl/. Accessed 24 July 2003.

"Let's Teach English to All of America's Children and End Bilingual Education Nationwide." English for Children, http://www.onenation.org/. Accessed 24 July 2003.

NCELA (National Clearinghouse for English Language Acquisition and Language Instruction Educational Programs). "Reflections and Success Stories," http://www.ncela.gwu.edu/success/. Accessed 24 July 2003.

Porter, Rosalie Pedalino. "The Case against Bilingual Education: Why Even Latino parents Are Rejecting a Program Designed for Their Children's Benefit." *The Atlantic Monthly* 281, no. 5 (1998): 28–39. Atlantic Online, May 1998, http://www.theatlantic.com/issues/98may/biling.htm. Accessed 24 July 2003.

Portraits of Success. National Association for Bilingual Education (NABE), http://
    www.lab.brown.edu/public/NABE/portraits.taf. Accessed 24 July 2003.

Rodríguez, Clara E. *Puerto Ricans. Born in the U.S.A.* Boulder, Colo.: Westview Press,
    1991.

Rodríguez, Richard. *Hunger of Memory: The Education of Richard Rodríguez.* New
    York: Bantam Books; reissue edition, 1983.

Stefanic, Jean, and Richard Delgado. *No Mercy. How Conservative Think Tanks and
    Foundations Changed America's Agenda.* Philadelphia, Pa.: Temple University
    Press, 1996.

Unz, Ron. "California and the End of White America," *Commentary* vol. 108, no. 4
    (1999): 17ff.

Voice of Citizens Together, http://www.americanpatrol.com/. Accessed 24 July 2003.

# 4

## OPEN BORDERS

### BACKGROUND

Immigration affects all U.S. Latinos, even Puerto Ricans, who are U.S. citizens. The truth be told, Puerto Ricans are targets of American racist nativism directed at Latino immigrants. Since the early 1970s, anti-immigrant organizations and politicians have fanned nativist fears in reaction to the heavy migration of people from Mexico, Central America, and Asia. The rise of immigration swelled the ranks of organizations devoted to immigration control. The Internet helped this growth, and entire Web pages warn about the impending silent invasion of American soil by criminal aliens. Much of the literature is inflammatory and plays on American angst, such as that of Matthew Campbell, who writes, "The year is 2100. America is in ferment. The second civil war has ended in defeat for English-speaking whites, encircled in their heartland in the Midwest. The southwestern states of California, Arizona, New Mexico and Texas have broken away from the union to form provinces in the new, Hispanic country of Aztlan. Unlikely as this vision of the future may seem, the break-up of the United States within the next 100 years is regarded by some people as an entirely plausible consequence of a new wave of immigration."[1]

Former presidential candidate Pat Buchanan is among those who proposed a political solution to the alien invasion, promising during the 2000 presidential campaign to "stop this massive illegal immigration cold. Period. Paragraph. I'll build that security fence and we'll close it, we'll say 'Listen Jose, you're not coming in.'" Buchanan, a fiery speaker, continues with the following: "All I'm saying is that our levels of immigration now in the last 30 years have been enormous. It's almost over a million legal immigrants a year, and half a million illegals who come here and stay. And you're rapidly changing the nature of the entire country; we speak 300 languages. Unless we do something and make sure the things that unite us are elevated—like language and history and all the rest of it—we're gonna lose our country, my friend."[2]

Many Latinos resent this tough rhetoric and find themselves under siege. For instance, the term *illegal alien* is offensive to them because it conjures up the image of criminals and aliens from outer space invading the United States. They say the word *illegal* criminalizes poor people, who want the same thing all Americans do, which is adequate food, shelter, and clothing, and that the word *alien* dehumanizes them and encourages violence toward them. Latinos prefer the term *undocumented worker* or at the very least *unauthorized immigrants*. The Latinos' reaction to nativist attacks varies from ignoring them to militantly confronting their statements. Among the disparate Latino groups, Mexican Americans are the loudest voices, largely because Mexicans are the largest of the Latino groups and most affected. Mexican Americans also have the greatest number of elected officials and the largest national network. Within the Mexican American community, there are divisions on how to deal with nativists, ranging from those who call themselves Chicanos, to the more moderate groups. And, even among those calling themselves Chicanos, there are many strategies and tactics. For example, many share the sentiment that "[t]he borders crossed us . . . ," which merely means, "we're here and we ain't going away. Moreover, we are indigenous to the land."

As mentioned previously, care must be taken not to generalize about the pro-immigrant groups. For example, the Mexica Nation, a nationalist group, believes that as indigenous people, Chicanos form a nation, and declares, "[w]e do hereby declare the following manifesto in order to free our people from the descendants of Europeans (Anglo-American, Latinos-Hispanics, Euro-Mexicans and other 'whites') who have illegally and stubbornly remained on our land through their deceit, the enslavement of our people, racial rape, and the cultural castration of our people. They have fortified their position as trespassers and thieves by destroying our identity, history, heritage and independent Anahuac [the Aztecas were part of this linguistic group] Indigenous thought."[3]

The sentiment that the United States illegally seized more than half Mexico's land is shared by many Mexican Americans who do not necessarily agree with the Mexican nation. They are not calling for independence but are demanding just treatment for immigrants and the recognition that Mexicans have just as much, if not more, right to be in the United States as Europeans do. These groups lobby for laws, make arguments to counter the nativist propaganda generated by anti-immigrant groups, and establish organizations to protect the rights of the foreign-born. The Catholic church has played a leading role in this school of thought. Indeed, Cardinal Roger Mahony of Los Angeles has said, "The divisive rhetoric of the immigration debate is harmful in itself. It plays upon fears and emotions, it affirms the racism and prejudices deeply ingrained in the hearts and minds of people. But when individuals seek to further embody this rhetoric in social policy, then the evil of this rhetoric becomes institutionalized. It is given life. It is what we call social sin."[4]

The negative reaction of Americans to immigrants is a product of its history. Nativism is nothing new. It is the response of mainstream Americans to the successive waves of immigrants coming into the country from Europe, Asia, and Latin America. During the colonial period, the British formed colonies along the tidewater of the Atlantic Ocean, thinking of themselves as native while ignoring that the Indians were the natives and that the African was part of the migration process. Later, Scotch-Irish immigrants arrived and were forced into the backwoods, the Western frontier region. With this immigration wave came Germans and more imported African slaves. About 500,000 African Americans lived in the colonies by the time of the American Revolution.

The transformation of the economy during the first part of the nineteenth century brought the second wave of immigration in the 1820s; immigrants were pulled by the lure of jobs and pushed by conditions in their own countries. From 1820–60, Europeans came from Great Britain, Ireland, and western Germany with a few from Norway, Sweden, and the Netherlands. Many of these immigrants were Catholic, and the White Anglo-Saxon Protestants (WASPs) rejected them. Anti-immigrant riots broke out in cities such as Philadelphia and New York and spread throughout the Northeast. In this context, the Texas filibuster (1836) and Mexican American War (1848) added to the growing nationalism among Americans and reinforced anti-foreign and anti-Catholic sentiments. In the 1850s, anti-immigrant voters formed the Native American Party, also known as the Know Nothing Party, which called for the exclusion of immigrants and advocated anti-immigrant policies. After the Civil War, spurred by the building of the railroad and technological innovations such as electricity, more Irish, Germans, Poles, Italians, Jews, and other central and southern Europeans were pulled into the country. The uprooted immigrants struggled against poverty and discrimination in cities.

The first immigrants officially excluded were the Chinese. The Chinese Exclusion Acts of 1882, 1892, and 1902, and the Gentlemen's Agreements with Japan of 1900 and 1907 reduced and then eliminated the Japanese as immigrants. Until 1895, most immigrants came from northern or western Europe. After this point, most immigrants came from southern or eastern Europe, primarily from Austria, Hungary, Italy, and Russia. This change made many Americans nervous since the new immigrants were darker, spoke foreign languages, had different customs, and were Catholic and Jewish.

Convinced that immigrants were responsible for crime, violence, and industrial strife and that they could not easily assimilate them into American society, Congress passed the Literacy Act of 1917, largely to keep European immigrants out of the country. Congress aimed the 1921 Immigration Act that followed at immigrants from southern and central Europe and established an annual quota of 3 percent of each nationality based on the 1910 census. Only 375,000 immigrants could be admitted annually. Great Britain, Ireland, and Germany received more than 70 percent of this quota, which they rarely filled. The purpose was to preserve the American racial mix, which was predominately northern European. In 1924 Congress passed another act, setting the limit at 2 percent for each nationality based on the 1890 census, when the percentage of southern and eastern Europeans was much lower. The law limited the number of immigrants to the United States to 165,000 annually. The act discriminated against immigrants from southern and eastern Europe and barred Asians completely.

The Immigration Act of 1924 did not limit Mexicans or other Latin Americans. Agricultural interests needed Mexican labor and many U.S. corporations were interested in promoting Pan-American trade. U.S. Rep. Martin Madden of Chicago, chair of the House Appropriations Committee, complained by stating, "The bill opens the doors for perhaps the worst element that comes into the United States—the Mexican *peon*. . . . [It] opens the door wide and unrestricted to the most undesirable people who come under the flag." Sen. Matthew M. Neeley of West Virginia charged, "On the basis of merit, Mexico is the last country we should grant a special favor or extend a peculiar privilege. . . . The immigrants from many of the countries of Europe have more in common with us than the Mexicanos have."[5]

Many Mexicans had been in the American Southwest since before the American takeover. Others entered the United States throughout the nineteenth century for political and economic reasons. As the Southwest industrialized at the turn of the century, thousands of Mexicans were pulled north. Conditions in Mexico also pushed Mexicans northward. U.S. and European capitalists invested in railroads, mines, agriculture, and other industries that transformed the Mexican economy and society and led to a mass exodus from farm work. Labor contractors went into Mexico and recruited uprooted Mexican workers to come to what had become the American Southwest. The demand for Mexican labor increased as U.S. policy restricted Asians and Europeans from entering the country and as agriculture, the railroads, mining, and manufacturing became more dependent on Mexican labor. Meanwhile, the building of a railroad that connected Mexico with the United States transformed Mexico's economy, uprooting many Mexicans from farms and pushing them north in search of work.[6] The incessant demand for labor and the shortage of workers created by the restriction of European immigration also led to the migration of African Americans from the South to the factories of the Northeast and Midwest.

The dependence on Mexican labor did not shield Mexican workers from discrimination, however. In early 1921 the bottom fell out of the economy, and Mexicans became the scapegoats for the failure of the U.S. economy. American authorities shipped thousands back to Mexico. This set the stage for the Great Depression of the 1930s, when deportation and repatriation programs sent an estimated one million Mexicans back to Mexico.[7]

Meanwhile, between 1915 and 1930, some 50,000 Puerto Ricans migrated to the United States. Another wave followed between 1940 and 1969, and an additional 800,000 Puerto Ricans migrated, principally to the New York City area. The demand for labor strengthened the pull of Puerto Ricans to the United States. This new wave went to New York but also migrated to rural areas where they worked as farm workers.

The Jones Act (1917) made Puerto Ricans citizens of the United States. Puerto Rican migration to the mainland coincided with the decline of European immigration. Americanization programs attempted to remake Puerto Ricans, who became even more determined to preserve their identity and strengthen bonds with their homeland. Some suggest that part of that glue that held the community together was Puerto Rican *salsa* (dance) and the dance clubs.

World War II accelerated Mexican and Puerto Rican migration because of the abundance of jobs in the United States. The Mexican *bracero* program brought several million contract laborers to the United States from Mexico from 1942–64. Other Mexicans came both with or without documents. Puerto Ricans also were encouraged to migrate, not only to New York City but to Chicago and even to the tanneries of Milwaukee. Americans did not meet these waves of Latinos with open arms, and the U.S. government, in response to a wave of nativism, shipped more than a million Mexicans back to Mexico annually from 1953–55 in what they called "Operation Wetback." Nativism followed a pattern, worsening in times of economic stress, when nativist sentiment made the immigrant the scapegoat for the nation's economic problems.

Congress passed the Immigration Act of 1965 during the civil rights era of the 1960s and, more significantly, in times of relative prosperity. For the first time, Congress put Latin Americans under a quota, and it allowed Asians to immigrate to the United States. Policy changed from basing immigration on national origins to admitting immigrants based on family preferences. In addition, the improvement of the European economy contributed to a slowing down of European immigration. For example, from 1930 to 1960, about 80 percent of U.S. immigrants came from European countries or Canada, but by 1977 to 1979, only 16 percent came from Europe and Canada, with Asia and Latin America accounting for about 40 percent each. The new act was indifferent to ethnic origin and gave attention to family ties and the reunification of families.

As Americans saw more darker-skinned immigrants in the streets, panic spread among Euroamericans that the country was becoming darker.[8] Congress responded by putting caps on legal Mexican migration.[9] This led to the rise of nativist groups who promoted the notion that illegal aliens were invading the country. The intensity of the attack led to the formation of pro-immigrant defense groups that responded that the immigrant was neither a criminal, that is, illegal, nor were they Martians (aliens). Latino immigrants were human and consequently were simply undocumented workers.

Meanwhile, Cuban immigration had picked up sharply during the 1950s because of political conditions in Cuba. For decades Cubans had fled tyranny in their country. After 1959 many fled Castro's revolution. Many in this wave were from wealthy families and were well educated. The United States granted them asylum and assisted qualified applicants in finding homes, finding jobs, and paying them health benefits and stipends. Most of the later waves of Cuban immigrants were relatives of the first group or were poor people looking for work. About 125,000 *Marielitos* came in the 1980s. Cuban Americans called themselves *Marielitos* because the Cuban government put them aboard boats at the Cuban port of Mariel and sent them to Miami. The Marielitos included many unskilled workers, criminals, and mentally ill people. They also included many Cubans of African ancestry who were hard-working people.[10]

Simultaneously, beginning in the early 1970s, internal crises pushed Central Americans and South Americans to the United States. The CIA-sponsored military overthrow of constitutionally elected Chilean President Salvador Allende in 1923 brought Chilean refugees to the United States. Over the last 10 years civil war forced many Colombians to flee their homes.[11] In 1979, Nicaraguans overthrew dictator Anastacio Somoza, which set off a series of revolutions in Central America. The wars pushed political refugees from El Salvador and Guatemala into the United States. In the 1980s the world saw increased military repression and rural counterinsurgency warfare programs supported by the United States. The result was numerous massacres; forced displacement; assassinations of political, religious, labor, student, and peasant leaders; and the disappearance of thousands. By the mid-1980s, about 300,000 Salvadorans and 50,000 Guatemalans lived in Los Angeles alone.[12]

The United States refused to recognize those fleeing El Salvador and Guatemala as political refugees. On the other hand, the United States recognized Nicaraguan refugees fleeing the revolution that overthrew Somoza, maintaining that the Salvadoran and Guatemalan insurgencies were communist inspired. Thousands of Salvadorans and Guatemalans who entered the United States without documents filed for political asylum and were routinely denied. U.S. churches, immigration lawyers, and activists won a class-action suit against the Immigration and Naturalization Service (INS) for discrimination. The government settled the suit in 1990, when the INS granted temporary protective status for these refugees, allowing them to work in the United States but leaving them with an uncertain legal future. In 1997 Congress attempted to resolve the issue and passed the 1997 Nicaraguan Adjustment and Central American Relief Act (NACARA). NACARA gave preference to Nicaraguan and Cuban refugees, who received a blanket amnesty and the right to apply for permanent residency because they were supposedly anti-Marxist.

In the late 1990s, Salvadorans and Guatemalans won the right to go before an immigration judge to prove, on a case-by-case basis, that returning to their countries would cause them to suffer extreme hardship. Previously these refugees faced costly legal battles with no guarantee that the United States would accept their petition. Under new rules, the U.S. government now presumes that returning these refugees would itself pose an extreme hardship for them. An INS official rather than a judge hears the cases. The Salvadoran and Guatemalan communities in the United States have political and refugee organizations and have integrated into the Protestant and Catholic refugee relief network. North American groups, such as the Committee in Solidarity with the People of El Salvador (CISPES),[13] formed along with human rights organizations, such as CARECEN (the Central American Refugee Center) and El Rescate, but simultaneously reached out to solidarity committees, politicians, and community and neighborhood associations.[14]

The first years of the new millennium found the question of immigration unanswered. Because of the relative prosperity, however, most Americans did not have strong feelings about the issue. The two militant sectors, those vehemently for and against immigration, remained adamant in their positions. The issue is one that lies beneath the surface and will become an issue when there is a downturn in the economy.

Volunteers with the organization Water/Winter Stations leave emergency supplies of water for undocumented immigrants who cross the U.S.-Mexico border. Since 1994 when the United States began to tighten the border to undocumented immigrants with Operation Gatekeeper, many immigrants have chosen to risk traveling through the desert. (AP/Wide World Photos)

## SHOULD THERE BE OPEN BORDERS?

### For

Open the borders! Keeping people out of the United States at a time when the so-called free market is going global is ridiculous. Further, Americans cannot condone the violence that is taking place at the U.S.-Mexican border, much of it caused by the U.S. Border Patrol. Anti-immigrant sentiment has created a large-scale industry of unscrupulous *coyotes,* smugglers of undocumented immigrants into the United States, that transports human cargo over often as many as five borders. Some Arizona ranchers are playing vigilante on the border while the government stands by and does nothing.

Even *Business Week,* a conservative magazine, points out that the graying of many European nations will reach the critical stage by the year 2050 when, for example, the median age in Spain will reach 55. *Business Week* posits that European nations will at that point be forced to import workers because of the old age of their populations. The current economic recession in Japan is partly attributed to the aging of the nation and the lack of expansion in its production. In contrast, the United States has grown because it takes in a million immigrants annually. The article says immigration "is one key reason economic growth has averaged 3.7 percent a year for the past decade."[15] Consequently, many nations are reconsidering their immigration policies.

The fact is that immigration creates new jobs and makes expansion possible. Almost the entire country suffered a severe recession during the 1980s due to deindustrialization. Los Angeles was the exception. Undocumented workers subsidized the garment and electronics industries, creating jobs for better-paid workers. Immigrants buy goods as well as sell goods, so the number of jobs expands as the number of workers expand. When immigrants send their children to school, immigrants create jobs and keep schools open in areas where there are not enough white children to fill them.

Immigrants contribute to the system by paying local, state, and federal income taxes and indirect taxes like sales taxes. Most data also show that most immigrants work; they are not on welfare. When immigrants and their families use emergency medical facilities, it is not because they are not working, but because they don't have medical insurance, and this is because employers refuse to pay for the cost of social production as in other industrialized countries, where employers pay for medical insurance. Indeed, undocumented workers pay taxes and often get nothing in return. An example is Social Security, to which they make contributions and rarely collect pensions.

The undocumented worker is also younger than the general population and is paying for the retirement of the aging baby boomers. By the year 2030, people 65 and over will increase from 34 million to 69 million. Latinos will make up a disproportionate share of active workers. These baby boomers will live longer than any other generation and thus collect more, paid for largely by minorities. Today the elderly population, not the undocumented, is straining Medicare.[16] The fact is that the United States and Europe lack population, and they have to attract immigration to remain economically strong and prosperous. Americans are not having babies in great enough numbers for population growth, so it makes sense to integrate these immigrants and educate them for the future of the country.

Hate always draws a crowd. People believe the worst, and politicians exaggerate the truth to get votes. More important, hate makes money, and there are racist organizations, too. The Federation for American Immigration Reform (FAIR) received $1.1 million from the Pioneer Fund between 1982 and 1992. The latter foundation funds literature that attempts to prove the genetic inferiority of nonwhite people. FAIR has an annual budget of around $5 million, and has some 40 other foundations contributing money to the anti-immigrant cause. It also receives money from individual donors who want to preserve their vision of America.

Only the most disingenuous person would deny that people want to close the border because they want to keep dark-skinned people out. Until September 11, 2001, the border patrol almost ignored the Canadian border. The nativist did not worry about white Canadians coming over the border. Cardinal Roger Mahony has labeled anti-immigrant drives as a "social sin." Comparing the statements of Pat Buchanan and Glenn Spencer to those of U.S. Latino militants is also dishonest, since the latter do not have national forums and do not attract funds. They run shoestring operations.

Where one stands on immigration depends on one's politics. The Public Policy Institute of California (PPIC) Statewide Survey in January 2000 showed Democrats (61 percent) and independent voters (58 percent) have mostly positive views of immigrants. Republicans are more divided on the benefits and costs of immigration (49 percent to 40 percent). Three in four Latinos see immigrants as a benefit, compared with nearly half of Euroamericans.[17] Significantly it is the Latinos, who the competition for jobs and living space most affects, that are the most positive about immigrants.

### Against

Most Americans today are against immigration, whether authorized or unauthorized. Author Peter Brimelow, an immigrant from Britain himself, writes in his book *Alien Nation* that the United States is in danger of becoming an alien nation, invaded by millions of brown-skinned immigrants from Latin America and Asia.[18] According to Brimelow, this is going to change the color code of America.

The United States cannot afford to take in any more people. Immigrants do not come alone. They bring their families with them, and taxpayers have to pay for them. There are an estimated 1 million children of illegal aliens in our schools, which cost taxpayers more than 5 billion dollars to educate. Because they do not know English and have been poorly educated in their own countries, we have to pay for special programs.[19] The fact is that Latinos have too many children. Today more Latino infants are born in California than white infants. Because they have no medical insurance, they put a strain on U.S. medical facilities. Americans are just too generous. Think about it: a person born in the United States is automatically a citizen no matter what the mother's citizenship status is. The United States is one of the few nations still granting automatic citizenship at birth. The United Kingdom and Australia repealed this policy in the 1980s after experiencing abuses similar to those happening in the United States. The immigration situation has gotten out of hand. The size of the undocumented worker population is close to 5 million.[20]

Tolerance of illegal immigrants promotes disrespect for the rule of law. U.S. laws giving citizenship to children born in the United States regardless of the legal status of the parents gives illegal aliens license to break laws and qualify for welfare.[21] Allowing illegal aliens to enter the United States also goes against a sense of American fairness. Why should immigrants who are here illegally get preference over 3.6 million people who are waiting to be admitted as legal immigrants to the country? Some applicants have been on that list for eighteen years.

Latin Americans are different from Americans. Latinos speak different languages, they look different, and they will change the customs and traditions that have made this country strong. Instead of pandering to criminals, the United States should toughen the enforcement of its laws. Instead of giving amnesty to lawbreakers, it should change the 1965 Immigration Act and revert to national origins. Americans should promote the immigration of people who share its customs, culture, and speak English.

## QUESTIONS

1. Jeff Pearlman, "At Full Blast: Shooting Outrageously from the Lip, Braves Closer John Rocker Bangs Away at His Favorite Targets: The Mets, Their Fans, Their City and Just about Everyone in It." 23 December 1999, http://sports illustrated.cnn.com/features/cover/news/1999/12/22/rocker/, accessed 2 August 2003. See also, "Rocker Apologizes for Sports Illustrated Remarks," Cnn.Com, 20 June 2000, http://www.cnn.com/2000/us/06/29/rockerroll, accessed 2 August 2003. Former Atlanta Braves pitcher John Rocker is quoted as saying, "It's [New York] the most hectic, nerve-racking city. Imagine having to take the [Number] 7 train to the ballpark, looking like you're [riding through] Beirut next to some kid with purple hair next to some queer with AIDS right next to some dude who just got out of jail for the fourth time right next to some 20-year-old mom with four kids. It's depressing. . . . The biggest thing I don't like about New York are the foreigners. I'm not a very big fan of foreigners. You can walk an entire block in Times Square and not hear anybody speaking English. Asians and Koreans and Vietnamese and Indians and Russians and Spanish people and everything up there. How the hell did they get in this country?" Why would John Rocker's remarks be considered offensive? Do you believe that some or many people agree with him?

2. Look up the word *Aztlan*. Generally, the meanings vary and reflect the political ideology and biases of the speaker. What the word initially meant was the legendary place from where the Azteca originated. Chicano activists mostly interpreted it as saying that Chicanos were indigenous to the Americas, and that if

Anglo Americans did not want Mexicans in the Southwest, it was the European who should return from where they came. Today, the extreme right misinterprets the term to mean that Chicanos want to take back Occupied Mexico. Do these definitions conflict or agree with the Kick Them Outers? What impact would the notion of Aztlan color have on the notion of a border?

3. Study the different waves of immigrants to the United States. How were they similar and how did they differ? Why in the case of U.S. Latinos does the border take on a different meaning than in the case of European immigrants?

4. Compare the 1921, 1924, and 1965 Immigration Acts. What is the difference between national origins and family preferences? There is a movement to return the United States to national origins. How would this affect the tensions at the border? Why would this change be supported by nativists?

5. What is the difference between a political and an economic refugee? Are Puerto Ricans immigrants? Why do some Mexicans not consider themselves immigrants? Does the United States play a role in creating the conditions for migration to the country?

6. Read Paul F. Clifford, "Origins of Salsa the Puerto Rican Influence." (Available at http://www.geocities.com/sd_au/articles/sdhsalsapr.htm, accessed 26 July 2003.) The author claims, "Salsa has origins in Cuban music but credit for its worldwide popularity belongs to the Puerto Ricans of New York!" Salsa's roots are firmly based in the Afro-Spanish musical traditions of Cuba. Many artists came from El Barrio (in upper Manhattan, not the Bronx). The term *salsa*, much like the term *jazz*, is simply a word used to describe a fusion of different rhythms. It was invented at the end of the 1960s to market Latino music and, thanks to New York Puerto Ricans, has gained a following throughout the Latino and non-Latino world. The conclusion is that salsa has helped mainland Puerto Ricans keep their identity, and it is forging an identity with other U.S. Latino groups. Do you agree? How could this music also irritate nativists?

7. Read Tom Davis, "Immigrants Are Good for the Neighborhood," *Washington Post*, 12 March 2000. (Available at http://www.adti.net/html_files/imm/wp_neighborhood.html, accessed 26 July 2003.) According to Congressman Davis, how does his neighborhood benefit from immigration?

8. Terrorism has been tied to undocumented workers and their families. Do you agree or disagree? Why or why not?

9. In "Open Borders," the argument is made that immigrant bashing is profit-driven. Support or oppose this argument. Is the motive the same in regards to those wishing to return to Aztlan? Analyze the arguments against the policy of "Open Borders." Which of the arguments do you find most compelling? Why? What evidence do you have for your conclusion?

10. A solution to increased immigration is to tighten U.S. borders. On the Arizona/Mexico Border, ranchers have taken this matter in their own hands and are patrolling the borders themselves, picking up those they consider unauthorized. Why do actions such as these bother pro-immigrant advocates? Why are they cheered by nativists? What do you think?

11. Do you agree with Cardinal Mahony that immigrant bashing is a social sin? Why or why not?

12. Patrick J. Buchanan, "Let the 'Ashcroft Raids' Begin," 9 November 2001, ties unauthorized immigration to terrorism. Is this responsible? Http://www. theamericancause.org/patlettheashcroft.htm, accessed 26 July 2003.

13. Go to an Internet search engine. Type in "Latino and immigration and good." Select two articles and list how society benefits from immigration.

14. Make a chart listing the best arguments for and against immigration. What arguments in your view are most convincing?

15. Why do you think that nativism is stronger during recessions and depressions than in times of prosperity?

16. Why do immigrants come to the United States?

## NOTES

1. Matthew Campbell, "Hispanic Influx Threatens to Change Face of America," 9 July 2000, http://www.americanpatrol.com/RECONQUISTA/LondonTimes Recon000709.html, accessed 24 July 2003.

2. Pat Buchanan, Reform Party Presidential Candidate, 2000, http://www. geocities.com/Colosseum/Midfield/3110/quotes.html, accessed 24 July 2003.

3. Excerpt of Mexica Manifesto, http://www.mexica-movement.org/, accessed 24 July 2003.

4. Cardinal Roger Mahony, quoted in Dianne Klein, "Curbs on Illegal Immigration Are 'Social Sin,' Mahony Says," *Los Angeles Times,* 11 December 1993.

5. Quoted in Job West Neal, "The Policy of the United States toward Immigration from Mexico" (master's thesis, University of Texas at Austin, 1941), 113.

6. See Rodolfo Acuña, *Occupied America: A History of Chicanos,* 4th ed. (New York: Addison Wesley Longman, 2000).

7. Francisco E. Balderama and Raymond Rodríguez, *Decade of Betrayal: Mexican Repatriation in the 1930s* (Albuquerque, N. Mex.: University of New Mexico Press, 1995).

8. Rodolfo F. Acuña, *Anything but Mexican: Chicanos in Contemporary Los Angeles* (London: Verso, 1996), 114.

9. Julián Samora and Richard A. Lamanna, "Mexican Americans In A Midwest Metropolis: A Study of East Chicago," in *Forging a Community: The Latino Experience in Northwest, Indiana, 1919–1975,* ed. James B. Lane and Edward J. Escobar (Chicago: Cattails Press, 1987), 230; Leo R. Chávez, *Shadowed Lives: Undocumented Immigration in American Society* (San Diego: Harcourt Brace Jovanovich College Publishers, 1992), 15.

10. "Cuban Immigration into Dade County, Florida," Metro-Dade County Planning Department Research Division, 6 January 1985. Reprinted in *La Colonia Cubana,* 2 August 2003, http://www.liceocubano.com/Eng/Circular/Edicion_II/ Aporte3.asp, accessed 2 August 2003; "Cuban Immigration to the United States," *Cubans—Their History and Culture,* Refugee Fact Sheet No. 12, http://www. culturalorientation.net/cubans/IMMI.htm, accessed 2 August 2003.

11. Margalit Edelman, "Colombia's Explosive Refugee Crisis," *The Providence Journal Bulletin,* 8 July 1999, http://www.adti.net/html_files/imm/Colombia%27s_ Explosive_Refugee_Crisis.html, accessed 24 July 2003.

12. *Los Angeles Times,* 12 May 1986; Anjalo Sundaram and George Gelber, eds., *A*

*Decade of War: El Salvador Confronts the Future* (New York: Monthly Review Press, 1991); Ralph Lee Woodward, Jr. *Central America: A Nation Divided,* 2d ed. (New York: Oxford University Press, 1985).

13. Charles Nicodemus, "FBI Agents Get Training about Rights; Decree Ends 'Spying' Case Here," *Chicago Sun-Times,* 15 December 1997. The FBI's admitted misconduct during its probe of CISPES. CISPES sued in 1988.

14. H. Aquiles Magaña, "Salvadorans and Organizational Development in the U.S. Since the 1980s," Unpublished. Magaña is a professor in Central American Studies at California State University at Northridge.

15. Stephen Baker, "The Coming Battle for Immigrants," *Business Week,* 26 August 2002, 138–40.

16. Alexander T. Tabarrok, "Bring on the Bounty Hunters," Independent Institute, http://www.independent.org/tii/news/tabarrok_bounty.html, accessed 24 July 2003.

17. Mark Baldassare and Cheryl Katz, "2000 Orange County Annual Survey: Immigration and Race Issue," Department of Urban and Regional Planning, School of Social Ecology, University of California Irvine, http://data.lib.uci.edu/ocas/2000/report/00immigration.html, accessed 24 July 2003.

18. Peter Brimelow, *Alien Nation: Common Sense about America's Immigration Disaster* (New York: Random House, 1995); Patrick J. Buchanan, *The Death of the West: How Dying Populations and Immigrant Invasions Imperil Our Country and Civilization* (New York: Thomas Dunne Books, 2002). Some groups such as the Federation of American Immigration Reform have distanced themselves from Buchanan. "Pat Buchanan—Equal Opportunity Maligner FAIR Report: Pat Buchanan in His Own Words," FAIR: Fairness and Accuracy in Reporting, 26 February 1996, http://www.fair.org/current/buchanan-bigot.html, accessed 2 August 2003. This organization should not be confused with FAIR: The Federation of American Immigration Reform; Jim Naureckas and Janine Jackson, "It's the Mexicans, Stupid, the Phony Populism of Pat Buchanan," (May/June 1996), http://www.fair.org/extra/9605/buchanan.html, accessed 24 July 2003.

19. The Federation for American Immigration Reform, August 1997, http://www.fairus.org/html/04139708.htm, accessed 24 July 2003. Political Research Associates, "Pulling up the Ladder: the Anti-Immigrant Backlash," http://www.publiceye.org/magazine/v09n2/immigran.html, accessed 24 July 2003.

20. The Federation for American Immigration Reform, August 1997, http://www.fairus.org/html/04139708.htm, accessed 24 July 2003.

21. Ibid.

## SELECTED WORKS

Acuña, Rodolfo F. *Anything but Mexican: Chicanos in Contemporary Los Angeles.* London: Verso, 1996.

Balderama, Francisco E., and Raymond Rodríguez. *Decade of Betrayal: Mexican Repatriation in the 1930s.* Albuquerque, N. Mex.: University of New Mexico Press, 1995.

"A Brief History of Immigration: From the Discovery and Settlement of the United States to the Destructive Flood of Immigration Today." Americans for Immigration Control: A Brief History of Immigration. Http://www.immigrationcontrol.com/short_history.htm. Accessed 24 July 2003.

Brimelow, Peter. *Alien Nation: Common Sense about America's Immigration Disaster.* New York: Random House, 1995.

Buchanan, Patrick J. *The Death of the West: How Dying Populations and Immigrant Invasions Imperil Our Country and Civilization.* New York: Thomas Dunne Books, 2002.

Davis, Tom. "Immigrants Are Good for the Neighborhood." *Washington Post,* 12 March 2000. Http://www.adti.net/html_files/imm/wp_neighborhood.html. Accessed 24 July 2003.

Gutiérrez, David G. *Walls and Mirrors: Mexican Americans, Mexican Immigrants, and the Politics of Ethnicity.* Berkeley, Calif.: University of California Press, 1995.

"Heightened Militarization at the U.S./Mexico Border Is Death Knell for Many (July 2000)." Central America/Mexico Report, http://www.rtfcam.org/report/volume_20/No_3/article_2.htm. Accessed 24 July 2003.

Immigration and the United States–Four Periods of . . . Essay on Cuban immigration, http://www.americanhistory.about.com/cs/immigration/. Accessed 24 July 2003.

Immigration Control: A Brief History of Immigration, http://www.immigration control.com/short_history.htm. Accessed 24 July 2003.

Klein, Dianne. "Curbs on Illegal Immigration Are 'Social Sin,' Mahony Says." *Los Angeles Times,* 11 December 1993.

Martin, Philip, and Elizabeth Midgley. "Immigration to the United States." *Population Bulletin* 54, no. 2 (June 1999). Http://www.prb.org/Content/Navigation Menu/PRB/AboutPRB/Population_Bulletin2/Immigration_to_the United_States.htm. Accessed 2 August 2003.

Peters, Philip. "The Alexis de Tocqueville Institution: Immigration . . . Central American Refugee Compromise: Supporting Democracy in Central America, Restoring Fairness to U.S. Immigration Law." Http://www.adti.net/gw-immigration.html.

Tabarrok, Alexander T. "Bring on the Bounty Hunters," Independent Institute. Http://www.independent.org/tii/news/tabarrok_bounty.html. Accessed 24 July 2003.

# 5

## AFFIRMATIVE ACTION

### BACKGROUND

Affirmative action comes down to the issue of equality and the role that government should play in bringing about equal protection for those who do not have equal access. For example, society has come to accept handicap parking and handicap access to public places as part of citizens' public lives. Often, businesspeople have to spend money to bring about this access. Movie theaters and restaurants give senior citizens' discounts, and civil service gives veterans ten points on civil service examinations because they served in the armed forces. Federal, state, and local governments require some public organizations to give religious holidays to religious groups. Are these examples of preferential treatment? Do they differ from affirmative action?

Historically, education has been the main highway to the middle class for immigrants and minorities. In recent years, because of the transformation of the U.S. economy with factories that once paid union-scale salaries moving to third-world countries, this has changed. Today, the main options for workers are low-paying service sector and low-paying factory jobs. This change has clogged the education highway. This transformation of the economy has had social consequences; today it is getting harder to get into prestigious universities where students have better opportunities to get admitted to graduate programs and professional schools. Without this access social mobility is cut to a snail's pace, and it prolongs social inequality.

There is the misconception that affirmative action is a creature of the 1960s. However, it has been part of the civil rights tradition of this country as far back as World War II when African Americans and Latinos complained about equal access to government employment. President Franklin Roosevelt issued Executive Order 8802, which forbade discrimination against workers in defense industries. He established the Federal Employment Practices Commission, which was supposed to ensure compliance. But, even though blacks and Latinos fought in the war, the policy was avoided, and employers discriminated against people of color.

After the war, minorities fared even worse discrimination as industries gave white males preference in jobs. Because of a lack of education, many minorities were ineligible to take advantage of the G.I. Bill to help them go to college, and housing developers denied G.I. loans for homes to Latinos in integrated areas. Meanwhile, consciousness of their rights increased among blacks and Latinos. Decisions such as *Mendes v. Westminster School District* (1946) and *Brown v. the Board of Education* (1954) ended de jure segregation, yet unequal access persisted.

In 1961 President John F. Kennedy issued Executive Order 10925 in which he instructed federal contractors to take "affirmative action to ensure that applicants are treated equally without regard to race, color, religion, sex, or national origin." Simultaneously he also created the Committee on Equal Employment Opportunity.[1]

In 1965, President Lyndon Johnson signed the historic Civil Rights Act, which prohibited employment discrimination by employers who had more than fifteen workers. The law also established the Equal Employment Opportunity Commission (EEOC). The next year, President Johnson issued Executive Order 11246, requiring all government contractors and subcontractors to expand job opportunities for minorities. Johnson created the Office of Federal Contract Compliance in the Department of Labor to monitor compliance, and in 1967 he amended Executive Order 11246 to include women and required a good faith effort to give minorities and women equal opportunities.

Democrats were not the only ones who saw the need for affirmative action. President Richard Nixon in 1969 issued the Philadelphia Order authorizing flexible goals and timetables to correct "under utilization" of minorities by federal contractors. The next year, Order No. 4 expanded the plan to include non-construction federal contractors; this order was also revised to include women. That same year, Nixon issued Executive Order 11625, which ordered comprehensive plans and specific programs for a national Minority Business Enterprise Constructing program, and, just before he left office in 1973, he issued a "Memorandum—Permissible Goals and Timetables in State and Local Government Employment Practices."[2] Throughout this history of trying to bring about equality, federal authorities included institutions of higher learning because they are among the largest beneficiaries of government contracts, and because lawmakers considered colleges and universities as the key to equality.

Throughout this civil rights history, a sector of American society opposed equity or affirmative action programs. However, the 1960s were a time of economic prosperity and low unemployment, and saying no to affirmative action was difficult while a war was going on and when minorities were dying disproportionately in that war. Racial discontent and urban rebellions also played a role in convincing many Americans that something had to be done about discrimination and inequality. Affirmative action was a part of the proposed solution.

The mood of the country quickly changed after the 1973 recession, and upward mobility tightened for white males. Previous generations always had faith that their children would own their homes and have it better than their parents. As mentioned, corporations eliminated industrial jobs that had once been the stepping stone of European ethnics into the middle class. Other changes occurred, such as a restructuring of the middle-class American family. During the 1950s, most households were supported by a single wage earner. In the 1970s, working or not working was no longer an option for women; they had to work if they were to maintain a middle-class lifestyle. In the crunch, fewer Americans could afford to own a home on a husband's salary alone.

Simultaneously, institutions of higher learning, spurred by affirmative action, began actively to recruit minorities. The competition was felt in graduate and professional schools and the more prestigious private and public institutions. This threatened many white families and encouraged a backlash to the 1960s. Even Nixon, who saw the need for affirmative action, began to backtrack on enforcement. Moreover, Nixon laid the groundwork for the policy's demise by his federal courts nominees, who had a conservative view of affirmative action. The federal judges and the justices appointed by Gerald Ford, Ronald Reagan, and George Bush, Sr., deconstructed the 1960s and the policy of educational equality through affirmative action.

Opposition to affirmative action or, as conservatives interpreted it, preferential treatment of minorities entering college came from an unexpected source. Jewish American organizations, historically at the vanguard of social change, opposed affirmative action programs because they set quotas. In the past, quotas *limited* the number of Jews admitted into prestigious universities and graduate and professional schools. These Jewish organizations said they did not oppose the admission of minorities but opposed quotas for achieving equality. In other cases, angry white men believed they were being discriminated against, calling affirmative action reverse discrimination.

Within less than a decade, the white backlash gained sufficient ground to challenge special programs using race to admit a specific number of minority applicants for integrating the medical and other professions. Opponents framed their argument in terms of a tension existing between equality and equity, and they argued that the special admission of Latinos and African Americans was lowering the quality of education and subverting the American ideal of individualism. The argument was that if individuals worked hard enough, they could achieve anything they wanted. This was America, and if Latinos and blacks were not doing as well, it was because they were not working hard enough. Why should deserving and better-prepared white students suffer because of past injustices?

By the second half of the 1970s, the courts began siding with those challenging the constitutionality of special admission programs. The courts held that although these programs were serving compelling state interests, they denied due process to white males.[3] The debate came to a head in 1976, when the California Supreme Court held that the University of California at Davis' special admissions program was unlawful and enjoined the university from considering the race of any applicant. The court ordered Allan Bakke's admission.

Bakke, 36, a white male, applied to the Davis Medical School in 1973 and 1974. In both years, the medical school considered him under the general admission's program, and Bakke received an interview. Despite a strong benchmark score of 468 out of 500, the medical school rejected Bakke. His application had come late in the year, and no applicants with scores below 470 in the general admissions process were accepted. At the time, four special admissions slots were left unfilled for which Bakke was not considered. His faculty interviewer found Bakke "rather limited in his approach" to the problems of the medical profession and found disturbing Bakke's "very definite opinions which he based more on his personal viewpoints than upon a study of the total problem."[4]

The second time around, UC Davis again rejected Bakke's application. In both years, applicants were admitted under the special program with grade point averages, MCAT scores, and benchmark scores lower than Bakke's. After the second rejection, Bakke sued in the Superior Court of California, seeking mandatory, injunctive, and declaratory relief compelling his admission to the medical school, claiming UC Davis excluded him because of his race, violating his rights under the Equal Protection Clause of the Fourteenth Amendment, the California Constitution, and Title VI of the Civil Rights Act of 1964. The California Supreme Court agreed with the trial court.[5] (Also pertinent at the time was that medical schools regularly rejected applicants in their 30s as being too old.)

Two years later, the U.S. Supreme Court in part affirmed the California Supreme Court. The high court held that Davis could use race as a variable but not as the sole criterion for admission.[6] The justices used the now infamous dictum that the courts had to work toward a color-blind society. Justice Thurgood Marshall, the only African American Supreme Court Justice, wrote a stinging rebuttal:

I do not agree that petitioner's admissions program violates the Constitution. For it must be remembered that, during most of the past 200 years, the Constitution as interpreted by this Court did not prohibit the most ingenious and pervasive forms of discrimination against the Negro. Now, when a State acts to remedy the effects of that legacy of discrimination, I cannot believe that this same Constitution stands as a barrier.

Justice Marshall then historically dissected the history of discrimination against blacks:

We consider the underlying fallacy of the plaintiff's argument to consist in the assumption that the enforced separation of the two races stamps the colored race with a badge of inferiority. If this be so, it is not by reason of anything found in the act, but solely because the colored race chooses to put that construction upon it. The relationship between those figures and the history of unequal treatment afforded to the Negro cannot be denied. At every point from birth to death the impact of the past is reflected in the still disfavored position of the Negro. . . . In light of the sorry history of discrimination and its devastating impact on the lives of Negroes, bringing the Negro into the mainstream of American life should be a state interest of the highest order. To fail to do so is to ensure that America will forever remain a divided society.

Justice Marshall continued his scathing attack on the majority opinion:

I do not believe that the Fourteenth Amendment requires us to accept that fate. Neither its history nor our past cases lend any support to the conclusion that a university may not remedy the cumulative effects of society's discrimination by giving consideration to race in an effort to increase the number and percentage of Negro doctors. . . . While I applaud the judgment of the Court that a university may consider race in its admissions process, it is more than a little ironic that, after several hundred years of class-based discrimination against Negroes, the Court is unwilling to hold that a class-based remedy for that discrimination is permissible. In declining to so hold, today's judgment ignores the fact that for several hundred years Negroes have been discriminated against, not as individuals, but rather solely because of the color of their skins. It is unnecessary in 20th-century America to have individual Negroes demonstrate that they have been victims of racial discrimination; the racism of our society has been so pervasive that none, regardless of wealth or position, has managed to escape its impact. . . . The dream of America as the great melting pot has not been realized for the Negro; because of his skin color he never even made it into the pot.

(Although Congress passed the 14th Amendment to protect the due process of blacks from the state, courts during the nineteenth century rarely applied it in favor of blacks. Instead, they interpreted the word *citizen* to read *person* and ruled that corporations were persons and that the states could not overly regulate them.)

Critics accused the court of judicial activism, which is when justices make laws not specifically based either on the Constitution, on laws passed by Congress, or on case precedent. The dissent saw the color-blind argument as pretextual. Justice Harry Blackmun wrote that "in order to get beyond race, you must first take account of race," pointing out that although Congress passed the 14th Amendment to remedy the Constitution's legalization of racism, it was used historically to limit the integration of blacks and others. Instead of working toward a color-blind society, it helped create racial inequality, favoring the interests of whites.[7] The dissent also questioned whether Congress ever intended to prohibit the voluntary use of racial preferences to assist minorities to achieve equality. They accused the court of replacing a commitment to equality with a policy of denial and evasion. They also believed the court was manipulating the truth through the use of metaphors that distorted the reality of racism and inequality.

The court cases legitimized the political struggle of the right, which was part of the culture war that raged in American society during the last two decades of the twentieth century. As the Supreme Court and the mood of the country became more conservative, a persistent whittling away of the principle of affirmative action occurred. Meanwhile, conservative think tanks and foundations actively reconstructed the definition of race and equality.

On November 5, 1996, in California, anti-affirmative action interests succeeded in putting Proposition 209, opposing affirmative action, on the ballot. John H. Bunzel—a past president of San Jose State University, a former member of the U.S. Commission on Civil Rights, and a senior research fellow at Stanford's conservative Hoover Institution—argued that equality was the antithesis of merit. During the debate over Proposition 209, Bunzel said the people wanted government-sponsored affirmative-action programs outlawed:

It is precisely this kind of moral simplicity, however, that makes Proposition 209 so troublesome. The proposition's backers asserted the superiority of pure principle. They asked, 'Doesn't everyone agree that we want a colorblind and equal-opportunity society?'

The use of race to overcome past and present racism has resulted in 'excesses' and has frequently violated the promise of equal protection to all citizens. It seems fair to say that Proposition 209 is as blunt an instrument in confronting these 'excesses' as affirmative action has often been in using race to overcome racism.[8]

The heat of the discourse spawned dozens of books carrying the simple message that white males were being discriminated against. The anti-affirmative action voices portrayed themselves as the defenders of fairness and champions of a color-blind society, concluding that if the people want a color-blind society, society has to have color-blind policies. This discourse angered many minorities, who strongly objected to the portrayal of Latinos and blacks being unqualified. The hyperbole over affirmative action divided Americans.

Voters passed Proposition 209, the so-called California Civil Rights Initiative, by a 54 to 46 percent margin. Some 73 percent of African Americans and 70 percent of Latinos voted against Proposition 209. Asian Americans also voted against it, although only by 56 percent. White males voted for 209 by a 66 percent margin and white females by 58 percent. In California, three-fourths of the voters were white. This vote climaxed but did not end a bitter debate over how to reach equality of opportunity in the United States. The attitude of voters had changed dramatically since the 1960s when middle-class Euroamericans defied their parents to protest for free speech, civil rights, and the end of the Vietnam War.

The Bakke decision was the first in a long string of cases that led to *Hopwood v. Texas* in 1996, in which the appellate court found: "the University of Texas School of Law may not use race as a factor in deciding which applicants to admit in order to achieve a diverse student body. . . . The use of race, in and of itself, to choose students simply achieves a student body that looks different. Such a criterion is no more rational on its own terms than would be choices based upon the physical size or blood type of applicants."[9] Further, the court held "that any consideration of race or ethnicity by the law school for the purpose of achieving a diverse student body is not a compelling interest under the Fourteenth Amendment."

The University of Texas admittedly had higher test score standards (199) for resident whites and non-preferred minorities. Mexican Americans and blacks needed a score of 189. For denial, a score for non-minorities was 192; for denial the cut off for blacks and Mexican Americans was 179. Resident white applicants had a mean GPA of 3.53 and an LSAT of 164. Mexican Americans scored 3.27 and 158 and blacks scored 3.25 and 157 respectively. The category of "other minority" achieved a 3.56 and 160. In 1992, the entering class included 41 blacks and 55 Mexican Americans, 8 percent and 10.7 percent of the class respectively.

The question to consider is, do tests really gauge potential? Does a compelling societal interest trump scores? For example, does the education and income of a student's father affect test scores? Does what school the student attended play a factor? Finally, do law review classes make a difference? Wealthy students often take numerous review classes, retaking the exam several times. Private tutoring for graduate school exams can cost upward of $6,000. Is this fair? Proponents of affirmative action also argue that the question of GPA is problematic. How much difference is there between a 3.27 and a 3.56? How does having to work 30 to 40 hours a week affect GPA? It could be argued that a 3.27 from Harvard would mean more than a 3.53 from a state university, that is, if one does not consider that at Harvard the student can drop a class on the day of the final examination, whereas a California state university does not permit a student to drop a class after the third week of instruction, which usually is before students have had the opportunity to take their midterms.

Besides wanting to make society more equal by bringing Latinos, blacks, and women into the mainstream, another goal of affirmative action was to serve under-served areas better. For example, medical schools give applicants from rural areas preferential admissions because of the lack of doctors in isolated rural areas. In minority communities in California in 1975, one Euro-American lawyer practiced for every 530 Euroamericans, one Asian for 1,750 Asians; the ratio for blacks was 1 to 3,441; for Latinos, 1 to 9,482; and for Native Americans, 1 to 50,000. In primary care medicine, one white doctor practiced for every 990 whites; the ratio for blacks was 1 to 4,028; for Native Americans, 1 to 7,539; and for Latinos, 1 to 21,245.[10] Bakke supporters argued that an oversupply of professionals existed and that service did not depend on the professional's ethnic or racial background. Admittedly, there is little research in this area. However, no one can deny the need for doctors in black and Latino areas, and the probability is higher that black and Latino doctors (and other black and Latino professionals) will work with the poor and with clients of their color more readily.[11]

## SHOULD LATINOS HAVE PREFERRED ADMISSIONS AT COLLEGES AND UNIVERSITIES?

### For

President Lyndon Johnson believed that we could not bring about social and political equality without achieving economic equality. Further, affirmative action has made a significant difference for Latinos. Even President Nixon supported affirmative action as a vehicle for ending inequality and discrimination and moving Latinos into the middle class. In the 1990s, 10.6 percent of Latinos had a bachelor's degree or higher compared with 28.1 percent of non-Hispanic whites. Before affirmative action programs, less than 4 percent of Latinos were professionals. Most reputable studies also show that affirmative action programs closed the gap between rich and poor, yet because many of these programs have been diluted, the gap has widened in recent years.

Conservatives have politicized the debate over affirmative action to take the focus away from the overall crisis in public education. As minority enrollment has increased, so has the per capita expenditures per student. California, which in the 1950s spent more per student than any other state except New York, ranks among the lowest today. Tuition at California state universities has risen from $100 annually in 1970 to nearly $2,000. Because of the growth in population, competition for admission has increased, and higher education is no longer guaranteed. Meanwhile, elite schools have tightened their admission requirements. Even if no minorities were admitted to premier universities, the number of slots for white males would be negligible. Moreover, minorities who are being admitted are in the top 5 to 10 percent of their graduating classes.

Minorities should not be singled out for receiving preferential admissions. They only make up a small part of the admissions pool. Universities routinely lower admission standards for legacies to the children of alumni. For example, special admission was not an issue when George W. Bush was admitted to Yale, when former Vice President Dan Quayle received preferential admission into law school, or when Vice President Dick Cheney twice flunked out of Yale University. Indeed, George W. Bush was not admitted to the University of Texas Law School, but he was admitted to Harvard's School of Business as a special admit. Athletes are also admitted to prestigious institutions though they often fall well below admission standards. However, the assumption is that Latinos and blacks are not qualified and that the legacy admits are qualified.

According to Alex Liebman, a student at Yale University, "At Princeton University in the early 1990s, fully 25% of the student body were varsity athletes."[12] The children of alumni at Harvard University in 1991 were three times more likely to be accepted than other students who applied. Harvard University admits about 20 percent of its entering class based on the criterion that the student is the son or daughter of an alumnus or donor. Sixty-six percent of applicants accepted at the University of Pennsylvania were children of alumni. At Notre Dame, 25 percent of its first-year class was reserved for the children of alumni. In other words, the sons and daughters of the rich inherit privilege in the United States, but no one talks about this preferential treatment.

Preferential treatment is an unacceptable argument. Today, there are handicap ramps, and some people would call this preferential treatment. Yet, would it be fair not to have them? Criticism of affirmative action usually boils down to what in Spanish is called *chisme*, which means rumors or gossip. Affirmative action has not had a negative impact on white workers. Seniority systems protect white workers, and in time of recession, minority workers—

the last hired—are the first fired.[13] Older union members routinely get special favors for their sons to join the union.

Affirmative action has worked. The Labor Department reports that affirmative action has helped 5 million minority members and 6 million white and minority women move up in the workforce. People believe what they want to believe. Most of the public wants to believe that minorities are getting special help when in reality they are not. For example, union members widely accept that non-whites get preferential treatment when it comes to education overall. But the reality is white schools have better facilities and better qualified teachers and counselors. They have more advanced placement classes. More minority students are apt to hold jobs than white students while in high school and in college, which affects their school performance.

Even with this glaring inequality, affirmative action is not about doing away with standards. This is not about selecting unqualified candidates. Whites' averages on test scores are higher, and that is why there is a push for better public schools in minority areas. But, to set the record straight, many minority applicants have higher grades and scores than their white counterparts. Many who supposedly get preferential treatment have as high, equivalent, or higher scores than legacy admittees, despite the privileged education of the latter. Also, many do not consider that most middle-class whites and Asians have through the years taken special Kumon-like tutorial math classes, which presently have an enrollment of more than 2.9 million children. Kumon Math and Reading Centers offer an after-school supplemental education program.[14] Most Latinos cannot take these classes because of the cost.

While most minority students do not take SAT prep classes, most of the white middle-class and Asian students do. The Princeton Review advertises "better scores, better schools" and guarantees the outcome. Their advertising brochure brags, "Our SAT students improve an average of 140 points, and the top 25% improve by a whopping 256 points! When you take our SAT classroom course, we guarantee your SAT score will improve by at least 100 points, or we'll work with you again for up to a year, FREE."[15] The tuition ranges from $99 to $699 for online courses; classroom classes cost more, and the student can take private tutoring classes that run into the thousands of dollars.[16] These benefits add to the advantages of better high schools and counseling.

The work of Dr. Patricia Gándara of the University of California at Davis clearly shows the benefit of good schooling and documents that Latinos who attend integrated schools do much better than those in segregated environments. Indeed, peer group conversations influenced their decision to pursue higher education more than their school counselors. Gándara noted that, "Many pegged their own performance against the standard set by particular

Oakland teacher during a demonstration outside of a meeting of University of California regents in San Francisco, 2001, as part of civil rights affirmative action organization. (AP/Wide World Photos)

white, Asian, or Jewish students. They believed that if they were competing favorably against these students, they were probably pretty capable." The subjects of her study "all came from families in which neither parent completed high school or held a job higher than skilled labor; the average father finished grade four, and most were sons and daughters of farm workers and other unskilled laborers. Most began school with Spanish as their primary language, yet all completed doctoral-level educations from the country's most prestigious institutions."[17] Gándara's studies show that the parents cared and the students achieved because of programs such as affirmative action. It was a form of encouragement and created a culture of learning. Affirmative action has had a tremendous impact on Latinos, creating a small but expanding middle class.

What Latinos want is a better educated populace where people of all colors are participating in society. Latinos want equality with white America. Latinos can no longer rely on well-paying blue-collar jobs, so Latinos have to go to college if they are going to make it into the middle class. Since the 1960s

Latinos have made tremendous strides because affirmative action has given them opportunity to succeed and fail occasionally. If society doesn't want preferential admissions, then they should be cut for everyone, rich and poor. Why should race be the only variable excluded from preferences? Eliminate the legacy admits. Eliminate the SAT, LSAT, and all testing where a student can pay to get a better score. Stop playing politics and start concentrating on educating more people in college instead of eliminating them.

### Against

Why should white males pay for the sins of their parents and grandparents? According to Professor Carl Cohen, affirmative action is unethical because "the sacrifice of fundamental individual rights cannot be justified by the desire to advance the well-being of any ethnic group."[18] The Fourteenth Amendment of the Constitution says that no state "shall deny to any person within its jurisdiction the equal protection of the laws." Clearly affirmative action is depriving white males of equal protection under the law. They are not to blame for the fact that minorities have been discriminated against or have less skills than they do. Why should affirmative action penalize white males for what happened before they were born?[19]

American society tries to be fair. How else can society measure skills other than giving exams? Tests are administered for firefighters, police, and civil service employment, so why not for college admission? The SAT is not any more biased than other exams. It measures knowledge, and it just happens that whites and Asians score near the top, Latinos in the middle, and blacks near the bottom. Perhaps it could be said that the reason for this is economic background, but the fact remains that whites and Asians have superior skills, so why penalize them? Moreover, it is also a fact that the families of Asian and white students make them study more.

Quality is sacrificed when institutions grant less-skilled minorities admission based on the color of their skin. It drags the more advanced students down and promotes mediocrity. All people have special gifts. African Americans, for example, are better basketball players, Mexicans play the guitar better than whites, and Asians are better in mathematics. Just because conditions at urban public schools are often terrible, is that any reason to defund suburban white schools? To suggest that the economic injustices must be corrected is communistic. The sad fact is that if all the wealth in this country were suddenly redistributed, the same people would end up with the money because it is a survival of the fittest.

John H. Bunzel of the Hoover Institution at Stanford University argues that "the university must remain equally committed to maintaining high professional standards in its faculty hiring . . . the university could never adopt a double standard of evaluation. That would be demeaning and condescending." Bunzel challenges and destroys the argument that affirmative action is justified because it brings about equality. Bunzel says, "I had always hoped that the true goal of affirmative action would become an 'equality of actual opportunities' for all individuals so that the best possible person could be fairly found for every opening."[20] What Bunzel and others are saying is that universities should not sacrifice quality to bring about equity. Universities should admit students according to merit. Logically, unqualified students should want to better their skills instead of getting preferential treatment. That is why there are community colleges.

Unfortunately, liberals and minorities believe government owes them a living and now believe that discriminating against white males is fair. In 1963, King said that he dreamed of a day when his children would "not be judged by the color of their skin but by the content of their character." King only asked that government permit blacks an equal chance to succeed. King called for "equality before the law," not preferential treatment.[21] The United States can achieve equality only by removing all references to race, and in that way society will become color-blind. The issue should not be race or class; it should be that the United States is still the land of opportunity for all.

## QUESTIONS

1. What does the Fourteenth Amendment have to do with preferred admissions at colleges or universities? Could it be interpreted differently?

2. What is race equality? Do all economic classes in America have the same opportunity? Should family income be considered preferential treatment? Why or why not?

3. Would it be reasonable to admit law or medical students *strictly* based on their admission tests? What does the Bakke decision say? What does the Hopwood case hold? If you were a lawyer, could you make an argument for abolishing legacy admits? What would that argument be?

4. If one wanted to compare grade point average, should students be admitted solely based on GPA? What are the arguments for and against? Should the university or college that a student graduates from be taken into account?

5. What does Proposition 209 state? Would it permit preferences according to one's religion? Would it ban legacy admissions or athletic scholarships? Does it profile race?

6. David B. Wilkins, "The Affirmative Action President's Dilemma," *Chicago Tribune*, 7 February 2001 (also available at http://www.commondreams.org. views01/0207-05.htm, accessed 26 July 2003), writes, "It is common knowledge that President Bush was not much of a student. Although the facts of his

lack of academic distinction—at Phillips Academy in Andover, Mass., Yale University and Harvard Business School—are well known, few people have stopped to ask a seemingly obvious question: How did someone with mediocre grades get admitted to two of this nation's most prestigious universities? With respect to Yale, the answer is plain. George W. Bush was admitted to Yale because his father, George Herbert Walker Bush, and his grandfather, Prescott Bush, were prominent alumni." Did President Bush get preferential treatment? How and why is his case different from that of minorities? Should there be legacy admissions? Do you believe that it is fair to discuss legacy admissions?

7. Does color blindness promote racial neutrality? Its critics say it encourages racial discrimination and the attitude that Latinos and blacks are acceptable if they stay in their place. Will this rationalization narrow or widen opportunities? Why do proponents of affirmative action say that we must recognize that there has been an accumulated advantage from a legacy of societal discrimination? Do you agree or disagree and why?

8. Why is there so much resentment to so-called preferential admissions of Latinos and blacks and not against legacy admissions? Why is there no resentment to the preferential admission of the sons and daughters of a donor or alumni of the university? Is it un-American to talk about economic preferences? Why?

9. Go to an Internet search engine. Type "affirmative action and Latino and immigrants." What are some opinions expressed by the listings? James S. Robb, "The Most Bizarre Affirmative Action Abuse Yet," *National Review*, 6 November 1995, says that immigrants are the beneficiaries of affirmative action and that this was never the intent. He calls this an abuse. What do you think? (Also available at http://home.netcom.com/~jimrobb/NR-article.html, accessed 26 July 2003.)

10. It has been said that the real beneficiaries of affirmative action were women, who have made considerable strides under affirmative action programs. Why aren't white men as threatened by them? Read Sally Pipes and Eugene Volokaii, "Women Need Not Fear the Civil Rights Initiative CCRI: Its Language Strengthens Rather than Weakens Laws against Sex Discrimination," *Los Angeles Times*, 24 January 1996. Why were the proponents of Proposition 209 catering to women?

11. Summarize the argument for the preferential admission of Latinos. What could you add to the argument?

12. Summarize the argument against the preferential admission of Latinos. What could you add to the argument?

13. Go to the Internet and type "The Wealth Gap Challenges American Ideals" into a search engine. Some authors argue that the debate over affirmative action diverts attention from the growing economic divide in the United States. Do you agree? Why or why not?

14. Are tests biased? What do they measure and do they not measure?

15. Are Latinos asking that unqualified Latinos be admitted to higher institutions such as medical school?

## NOTES

1. Americans for a Fair Chance; "The History of Affirmative Action Policies," Washington, D.C., (July 2000), www.inmotionmagazine.com/aahist.html, accessed 24 July 2003.

2. Dean J. Kotlowski; "Richard Nixon and Origins of Affirmative Action," *The Historian,* (Spring 1998), http://www.findarticles.com/cf_o/m2082/w3_v60/20649393/pl/ article.jhtml, accessed 24 July 2003. Nixon was not the first to implement affirmative action; however, he was the first to set quotas.

3. Opinion of Justice Lewis Powell, *Regents of the University of California v. Bakke,* 438 U.S. 265 (1978), http://www.civnet.org/resources/teach/basic/part6/41.htm, accessed 24 July 2003.

4. Goodwin Liu, "The Myth and Math of Affirmative Action," washingtonpost.com, 14 April 2002, http://www.washingtonpost.com/ac2/wp-dyn/A41620-2002Apr12?language=printer, accessed 2 August 2003.

5. *University of California Regents v. Bakke,* 438 Supreme Court of the United States, U.S. 265, 76–811 (1978). 12 October 1977, Argued, 28 June 1978, Decided. http://caselaw.lp.findlaw.com/scripts/getcase.pl?court=US&vol=438&invol=265, accessed 24 July 2003.

6. Ibid.

7. Rodolfo F. Acuña, *Sometimes There Is No Other Side: Chicanos and the Myth of Equality* (Notre Dame, Ind.: Notre Dame University Press, 1998), chapter 1.

8. John H. Bunzel, "The Nation; Post-Proposition 209; The Question Remains: What Role for Race?" *Los Angeles Times,* 8 December 1996.

9. *Hopwood v. Texas,* 78 F.3d 932, 962 (5th Cir. 1996), http://www.law.utexas.edu/ hopwood, accessed 24 July 2003.

10. Celeste Durant, "California Bar Exam—Pain and Trauma Twice a Year," *Los Angeles Times,* 27 August 1978; Robert Montoya, "Minority Health Professional Development: An Issue of Freedom of Choice for Young Anglo Health Professionals" (paper presented at the annual convention of the American Medical Student Association, Atlanta, Ga., March 1978), 4.

11. "The Need for Minority Doctors," 90.3 WCPN (northeast Ohio), aired 20 September 2002, http://www.wcpn.org/news/2002/07-09/0920minority_doctors. html, accessed 2 August 2003; Ceci Connolly, "Report Says Minorities Get Lower-Quality Health Care: Moral Implications of Widespread Pattern Noted," *Washington Post,* 21 March 2002. Available at Health Professional Network, http://www. healthpronet.org/prog_resources/news_041502a.html, accessed 2 August 2003.

12. Alex Liebman, "How'd That Guy Get in, Anyway?" *Argos* 1, no. 2 (summer 1998), http://www.gofast.org/argos-summer-1998/article3.htm, accessed 24 July 2003.

13. S. Plous, "Ten Myths about Affirmative Action," http://www.understanding prejudice.org/readroom/articles/affirm.htm, accessed 24 July 2003.

14. KUMON, http://www.kumon.com/home.

15. The Princeton Review, http://www.review.com/integrated/templates/defaultrh/ testprep.cfm?TPRPAGE=61&TYPE=SAT, accessed 24 July 2003.

16. Ibid.

17. Patricia Gándara, "Choosing Higher Education: Educationally Ambitious Chi-

canos and the Path to Social Mobility," *Education Policy Analysis Archives* 2, no. 8 (16 May 1994), http://epaa.asu.edu/epaa/v2n8.html, accessed 24 July 2003.

18. Carl Cohen, *Naked Racial Preference: The Case against Affirmative Action* (Boston: Madison Books, 1995), 96–7.

19. Ibid.

20. John H. Bunzel, "Essays in Public Policy: Affirmative Action in Higher Education: A Dilemma of Conflicting Principles," Hoover Institution, http://www.hoover.stanford.edu /publications/epp/89/89b.html, accessed 24 July 2003; John H. Bunzel, "Affirmative Action in Higher Education: A Dilemma of Conflicting Principles," Essays in Public Policy Hoover Institution, 1996, http://www-hoover.stanford.edu/publications/epp/89/89a.html, accessed 2 August 2003.

21. Lucas Morel, "Prop. 209: Relearning the Lesson of Human Equality Editorial," Ashbrook Center, September 1997, http://www.ashbrook.org/publicat /oped/morel/97/prop209.html, accessed 24 July 2003.

## SELECTED WORKS

Acuña, Rodolfo F. *Sometimes There Is No Other Side: Chicanos and the Myth of Equality.* Notre Dame, Ind.: Notre Dame University Press, 1998.

The American Association for Affirmative Action, http://www.affirmativeaction.org/. Accessed 24 July 2003.

Bell, Derrick. *And We Are Not Saved: The Elusive Quest for Racial Justice.* New York: Basic Books, 1987.

Bunzel, John H. "The Nation; Post-Proposition 209; The Question Remains: What Role for Race?" *Los Angeles Times,* 8 December 1996.

Calleros, Russell. "Keeping Our Foot in the Door: The Case FOR Affirmative Action and AGAINST Prop. 209." *Kennedy School Citizen (1996–1997),* Harvard University, http://hcs.harvard.edu/~concilio/Prop209.html. Accessed 24 July 2003.

Cohen, Carl. *Naked Racial Preference: The Case against Affirmative Action.* Boston: Madison Books, 1995.

Delgado, Richard. *The Rodrigo Chronicles: Conversations about America and Race.* New York: New York University Press, 1995.

Gándara, Patricia. "Choosing Higher Education: Educationally Ambitious Chicanos and the Path to Social Mobility," *Education Policy Analysis Archives* 2, no. 8 (1994), http://epaa.asu.edu/epaa/v2n8.html. Accessed 24 July 2003.

Henry, William. *In Defense of Elitism.* New York: Anchor, 1994.

Kull, Andrew. *The Color Blind Constitution.* Cambridge: Harvard University Press, 1992.

Liebman, Alex. "How'd That Guy Get in, Anyway?" *Argos* 1, no. 2 (1998), http://www.gofast.org/argos-summer-1998/article3.htm. Accessed 24 July 2003.

Plous, S. "Ten Myths about Affirmative Action," http://www.understanding prejudice.org/readroom/articles/affirm.htm. Accessed 24 July 2003.

Sabo, Martin Olav. "Income Gap Home Page," http://www.house.gov/sabo/ie.htm. Accessed 24 July 2003.

West, Cornell. *Race Matters.* New York: Vintage, 1994.

# 6

## INTERRACIAL DATING AND MARRIAGE

### BACKGROUND

Interracial dating has been part of the American experience from the beginning of the country's history. However, it has only been until recently that it has become commonplace and then only in certain parts of the country. In the early twentieth century, Anglo Americans killed a Mexican youth for walking a white girl home in Texas. Legal and social taboos also existed against relationships between Anglo Americans and Africans and Indians. Moreover, considerable tension existed among the Italians, Irish, and Jews, who often lived next to one other but did not date one another, and when they did, there were problems. For example, many Jewish immigrants did not want their daughters and sons to marry Protestants or Catholics because Jews believed intermarriage would lessen their children's ties to their religion. Catholics and Protestants often felt the same way about each other and about Jews. If and when these groups dated or intermarried, they preferred that it was with a member of the majority society. Going out with or marrying a White Anglo-Saxon Protestant (WASP) was an indication that the immigrant was moving up in status, becoming more Americanized or assimilated.[1]

During the nineteenth century, Mexicans intermarried with Anglo Americans. However, intermarriage was limited to the elites, with cohabiting rarer among the poor. As white women entered the Southwest, this fragile relationship ended, and white families frowned upon race intermixing with Mexicans. Many Mexicans also reacted defensively and discouraged interracial dating. This early contact laid the basis for later attitudes such as, "It's all right if my son goes out with a *gringa* (a white girl), but I wouldn't want him to marry her because *gringas* don't know our culture, and the first time they get mad at each other she is going to call him 'a dirty Mexican.'" Until World War II in California and other western states, legislatures legally prohibited Asians from forming dating relationships with whites, especially Filipinos, who often came to the States as bachelors *(solos)* and could be imprisoned for dating white women.[2]

Part of the reason interracial dating between Latinos and whites was not common was because Latino neighborhoods *(colonias)* usually were segregated. The few Nicaraguans and Guatemalans who entered the country usually assimilated or integrated into the pre-existing Mexican or another Latino *colonia*. Among Latinos themselves, skin color often governed dating practices. Often, lighter-skinned Mexicans tended to date lighter-skinned people of their own nationality. Lighter-skinned Cubans and Puerto Ricans also discouraged dating darker-skinned people of the same nationality. The attitude was "I don't want my daughter to go around with a dark Cuban. We're Cuban but we're more Spanish. That's the way life is. Dating leads to marriage and the children suffer." Dating was considered a prelude to marriage, so parents frowned upon dating outside the culture or race.

Popular culture reinforced the taboos on interracial relationships. Several movies point out the pitfalls of interracial dating or intermarriage, such as the classic *Giant* (1956) based on the Edna Ferber novel. George Stevens won the Academy Award for best director for *Giant*. The film starred Elizabeth Taylor, Rock Hudson, James Dean, and Dennis Hopper. Hopper played Jordan Benedict III, who was married to a Mexican woman, which in the 1950s was forbidden love in West Texas. *Giant* begins in the early 1920s, ends in the early 1950s, and portrays the racist and sexist culture of West Texas then.[3]

The musical *West Side Story* (1961) is the story of a Puerto Rican teenage girl and a white boy who fall in love. The film is an updated *Romeo and Juliet* story set in the streets of New York City in the 1960s. María and Tony are caught in the midst a feud between two gangs, one Puerto Rican and the other Anglo. María's brother, Bernardo, is the head of the Sharks (the Puerto Rican gang) and Tony leads the Jets (the Anglo gang). Both gangs arrange the time, place, and weapons for a gang fight, or rumble as they called it. At a dance, María and Tony meet and fall in love at first sight, but one is Puerto Rican and the other white. The Jets and the Sharks symbolize the two races. At a crucial point in the story, Tony says to María, "We'll be all right. I know it." María responds, "It is not us. It is everything around us."[4]

The fight is inevitable, and Tony kills María's brother. She is ready to forgive Tony and even ready to elope with him. María sends Anita, her best friend, to give Tony a message, but Anita runs into the Jets, who hassle her. Frustrated, she says María is dead. In grief, Tony runs through the streets of New York, screaming for the killer to take his life, which happens.[5]

Latinos criticized the casting of Natalie Wood for the role of María. She was a white actress playing a Puerto Rican. Her voice was dubbed in the songs, and her Puerto Rican accent was not authentic. Most of the cast also was white. The most credible actor was Rita Moreno, a Puerto Rican, who played María's best friend, Anita.

A third movie that deals with forbidden love is *Lone Star* (1996), which takes place in South Texas near the Mexican border. The sheriff, Sam Deeds, son of the late legendary lawman Buddy Deeds, investigates a murder. During the investigation, Sam's hostile relationship with his father unravels. The viewer learns that Sam has always loved Pilar (played by Elizabeth Peña), a Mexican single mother, but was kept from dating her. Sam always believed that the reason was racial. Pilar teaches high school history with a critical perspective, showing the negatives and positives of Texas society. Pilar wrestles with her feelings for Sam and copes with her teenage son. Pilar's mother, Mercedes (played by Miriam Colón), runs a Mexican restaurant. The film constantly shifts to the past, exploring the lives of Sam's father and Pilar's mother.[6] Throughout the film, the theme is one of forbidden love. Sam discovers why so many people loved Buddy, and he also discovers that Buddy was also Pilar's father.

Antipathy to interracial dating was common even in the 1960s. During this time, the European ethnics began to lose their identities. The third and fourth generations prospered and often moved into the suburbs. Integration with other ethnic groups broke down resistance to inter-ethnic dating. Also, as these groups became more mobile and moved West and to other parts of the country, ethnic solidarity broke down, and being Irish or Italian did not have the same meaning. U.S. Latinos, who were mostly Mexicans in the Southwest and Puerto Ricans in the East, generally lived in their own barrios. Mixing, as they called it, was confined to those living in Anglo neighborhoods. Interracial dating with blacks was taboo. In 1963, 59 percent of whites told interviewers from the Survey Research Service of the National Opinion Research Center that there should be "laws against marriages between Negroes and whites." By 1970, whites were split down the middle. Since 1972, support for such laws among whites has lessened.[7]

As Americans approached the end of the millennium, race relations improved or perhaps were just different. Youth appear to be more open than their parents and grandparents on the topic as suggested in a recent poll: "In January 1997, 70 percent of white teens, 86 percent of black teens and 83 percent of Hispanic teens told CBS News pollsters that they would date people of a different race. Two-thirds said their parents wouldn't be bothered by it . . . three quarters of white teens, 69 percent of black teens, and 74 percent of Hispanic teens said interracial dating would be 'no big deal.' Blacks were more likely than whites and Hispanics to say it 'sometimes causes problems.' Of those who had dated someone of another race, white students were more likely than black and students to say their parents minded. Only small proportions said their friends minded."[8] A Gallup poll that year supported these findings and suggested that "57 percent of U.S. teens who dated said they had gone out with a person from another race or ethnic group. That compares with 17 percent in 1980 (but that poll did not specifically include Hispanics.)"[9]

The pollsters cautioned that "teenage idealism does not always translate into adult behavior." Also, contradicting the optimism was a sharp upswing in the 1990s of reported hate crimes as well as a continuation of racially motivated violence. There were several widely publicized cases of black men being killed or beaten for associating with white women.[10] A 2000 poll conducted by Zogby America for Reuters asked more than 1,225 adults, "Would you approve of your son or daughter dating someone outside of your race?" Sixty-seven percent said they would approve of their child having an interracial relationship; more than 22 percent staunchly opposed it; 10 percent were not sure. More than 62 percent of the white respondents said they would approve of interracial dating by their son or daughter; 86.8 percent of blacks supported interracial dating, as did 79.9 percent of Latinos. Slightly more than 52 percent of Asian Americans supported interracial dating; 35 percent of Asian Americans said they would not approve; 26 percent of whites said they would disapprove; and 9 percent of Latinos said no.[11]

According to a national survey by *The Washington Post,* the Henry J. Kaiser Family Foundation, and Harvard University, the overwhelming majority of couples polled said they had introduced people of other races to their parents, that parents and family members accepted them, and they felt comfortable speaking openly about their relationships. Many students said they felt the children would benefit from having parents of different races. Even so, nearly half the black-white couples believed marrying someone of a different race makes marriage more difficult, with two-thirds of couples in black-white partnerships saying that at least one set of parents objected to marriage at the start. While whites generally were tolerant of interracial dating, 46 percent said that marrying someone of their own race was better. Interracial marriages among Latinos are indeed common. The best estimate is that there are around two million Latino-white couples, about 700,000 Asian-white couples, and about 450,000 black-white couples in the United States.[12]

Despite the optimism about interracial dating, color still plays a role. David

Harris, a University of Michigan sociologist, points out, "Let's say you're white and you're involved in a relationship with a Latina, but she doesn't have many indigenous Indian characteristics . . . people may say she's white like you, or Mediterranean, or they won't know what's going on. They fly under the radar." One woman told how her friends and family had no idea that her husband was Puerto Rican before they married. "A lot of people, when I say my husband is Hispanic, say they thought he was Italian . . . my parents love him dearly, but my father didn't know he was Puerto Rican until he liked him. I just didn't say anything. I think he assumed he was Italian."[13]

Polls are often deceiving. From reading them, one could deduce that the barriers to interracial dating and marriage have come tumbling down. For instance, a 2001 poll found that "about three-quarters of Latino families would warmly accept black people, who ranked somewhat below white people in their eyes. Among Asian families, 77 percent would welcome a new white member and 71 percent a Latino. Black people were somewhat less likely to be accepted, at 66 percent."[14]

However, anecdotal evidence contradicts, or at least questions, this optimism. As with the movies, land mines still exist in interracial relationships. The offspring of these unions are caught in limbo. Often the offspring must choose between what seem like two worlds. University of California at Davis Law Professor Kevin Johnson, an offspring of an interracial marriage, writes those mixed race individuals adjust to "the status of Whiteness" and expose "themselves to criticism from both Anglos and their own community." Johnson explains that the Latino's surname often plays a part in determining identity. Those with Spanish surnames have to either change their names or Anglicize them. In his case, the name Johnson partially hid his identity. As a child he never had to choose, because his mother's family wanted to assimilate and perpetuated the myth of their having Spanish ancestry. Ultimately, Johnson chose to pursue his Mexican American identity while his brother "with sandy blond hair and blue eyes, exercised his right to choose in a different way. He never identified as Mexican American." Johnson eventually married a Mexican American and chose to work with Latinos. "Many assume that I am White because of my surname and appearance and wonder how it is possible that a Latino could be named Johnson, how I could have children named Teresa, Tomas, and Elena, or why I am so interested in 'Latino' issues . . . mixed-race people have been marginalized when not ignored. The derogatory reference to 'half-breeds' exemplifies the marginalization. . . . Though animosity toward mixed-race people may be on the wane . . . [t]he rich diversity literally embodied by Multiracial people [has been] hidden from view, hidden from discourse, hidden from recognition and thus, invisible." Johnson concludes, "Mixed-background Latinos today may feel as if they fail to fit into either Anglo or Latino society and may be in a unique position to suffer subtle insults and other challenges to their identity."[15]

Are young Americans color blind, and is the United States becoming a melting pot? The fact is that much of the interracial dating is limited to the middle class.[16] For example, logically there would be limited contact between Latino and white students in many Los Angeles Unified Schools, where high schools such as Roosevelt and Garfield are upward of 96 percent Latino.[17] A Mumford Institute study conducted at Latino schools shows that school segregation has increased among Latinos in Los Angeles. In 1989 the average Latino was attending a school 53 percent Latino, whereas 10 years later it was 57 percent Latino. Latinos overall appear to live in isolation from whites with most urban areas registering an isolation of more than 50 percent.[18] Today, in the Los Angeles–Long Beach area, for example, the residential isolation of Latinos is 63.16 percent, and the average Latino child is apt to attend a school that is 69.3 percent Latino. In the future, these schools will be even more segregated, as busing is stopped and more schools are built in Latino neighborhoods. Segregation is even more dramatic when one looks at a core of 10 Los Angeles high schools in the inner city that were more than 90 percent Latino in 1999. Add to this the segregation of Latinos in New York City and Chicago where the average Latino student attends a school that is 72.3 and 71.2 percent Latino respectively.[19] The logical assumption is that students at highly segregated schools are not candidates for interracial dating since there is little contact in elementary through secondary schools.

Assessments under controlled situations have yielded opposite results. Under one such controlled study, "Results showed that both men and women held negative attitudes toward interracial relationships, although Black students held more favorable attitudes than did White students. These findings also showed that the women were less accepting of interracial friendships and romantic relationships than the men were. Both Black and White students said that family perception of these interracial relationships would be negative."[20] Do these assumptions carry over to Latino-white or Latino-other relationships?

Mixed marriages have been increasing. This has not gone unnoticed by advertisers. Some demographers are calling this the beginning of the blend. "The number of married couples who are of different races or ethnic groups has doubled since 1980. And they tend to be upscale, well-educated, and young. . . . Fully two-thirds of all Hispanics who have attended some college or have a college degree cross group lines when they marry, and the interracial marriage rate is one in three for Hispanics in top income brackets."[21] William H. Frey, senior fellow of demographic studies at the Milken Institute in Santa

Monica and a professor at the State University of New York–Albany, says that with greater mixing, "racial or ethnic attitudes will soften, that identities will be less distinct, and that there will be an impact on attitudes in the communities surrounding these households. And this trend has real momentum behind it because it is so pronounced among young people."[22] There is a strong correlation among Latinos in interracial marriages to economic success and education. Latinos "with a college degree and a substantial income are more than five times as likely to out-marry than those who didn't finish high school or who live in poverty."[23] In sum, "between 1980 and 1990, the odds of interracial marriage increased by 9 percent for Hispanic men and 18 percent for Hispanic women."[24]

Significantly, most interracial marriages are between whites and racial minorities rather than between different racial minorities. The odds of Latinos intermarrying with whites are ten times higher than marrying African Americans or Asians. The same pattern is true for blacks and other minorities. They are more apt to marry a white person than they are to marry a Latino or Latina. Where Latinos live plays a huge role in this process. Economics, language, and residential distance are all factors. The data also suggest that native-born Latinos are more likely than immigrants to mix with whites. The fact that Latinos are more likely to intermarry with whites also infers that Latinos are assimilating much more rapidly into mainstream American society than either Asians or blacks. Nevertheless, assimilation among Latinos is much slower than among the European immigrants who were white. The bottom line is that economic class, skin hue, generation, location and type of schooling, and culture all play a role in interracial dating.

## SHOULD LATINOS DATE OR MARRY THOSE OF OTHER RACES?

### For

Tina Turner's song, "What's Love Got to Do with It?" is the perfect question to ask in regard to interracial dating. Love has everything to do with it. A person should be able to choose whom she or he wants to date, and if marriage is the outcome, so be it. Would anyone want to go back to the times when it was against the law to marry or date a person of another color? Society has come a long way since the late 1960s, when the courts held anti-miscegenation laws to be unconstitutional.

The *Washington Post* reported, "In 1992, for instance, the volunteer coordinator of Patrick J. Buchanan's Republican presidential campaign in New Jersey was removed after he compared mixed marriages to the cross-breeding of animals. And it was only three decades ago, in 1967, that the Supreme

Table 6.1
**Relative Odds for the Logistic Regression of Hispanics' Marriage to Whites for Hispanics by Sex on Selected Independent Variables, 1980 and 1990**

| Variables | Hispanics Marrying | |
|---|---|---|
| | White Women | White Men |
| **Educational Attainment for Hispanics** | | |
| Less than high school[a] | 1.00 | 1.00 |
| High school graduate | 2.29 [***] | 2.82 [***] |
| Some college | 3.99 [***] | 4.42 [***] |
| College graduate | 7.91 [***] | 9.35 [***] |
| **Educational differences** | | |
| Husband better educated | .69 [***] | 1.46 [***] |
| Same education | 1.00 | 1.00 |
| Wives better educated | 1.39 [***] | .51 [***] |
| **Nativity and years since immigration for Hispanics** | | |
| 5–15 years | .29 [***] | .30 [***] |
| More than 15 years | .70 [***] | .63 [***] |
| U.S. Born [a] | 1.00 | 1.00 |
| **Region** | | |
| Northeast | 1.31 [***] | 1.23 [***] |
| Midwest | 3.77 [***] | 3.45 [***] |
| South [a] | 1.00 | 1.00 |
| West | 1.56 [***] | 1.54 [***] |
| **Year** | | |
| 1980 [a] | 1.00 | 1.00 |
| 1990 | 1.09 [***] | 1.18 [***] |
| **N** | 36,538 | 35,731 |
| **-2 log-likelihood** | 4488 | 5225 |

[a] Reference category.
[*] P<0.10. [**] P<0.05. [***] P<0.01.

Court ruled anti-miscegenation laws unconstitutional, wiping those statutes off the books in Virginia and 15 other states. But the sentiments that undergirded those laws are increasingly giving way to interracial tolerance."[25]

Whether people like it or not, since 1960 interracial marriages have increased ten times over to 1.6 million. With the growth of the Latino middle class, it is natural that the number of Latino-white marriages will increase. Besides, most Latinos are no longer immigrants and thus have more in common with European Americans. Because of the 1960s and the media, ethnic stereotypes and taboos are not as bad as they were a generation ago. Race and ethnicity is not as prevailing an issue, as it was a hundred years ago.[26] For example, Jews no longer marry just Jews, Irish no longer marry just Irish, and Italians no longer marry just Italians.

Taboos on interracial dating and marriage keep Latinas relegated to an unequal status. These taboos limit their choices to marriages within a macho culture. Statistics show that Latinas are moving up economically at a higher rate than Latinos, who are holding them back. Although there are more females than males, after age 24 the male-female ratio declines.[27] Interracial dating leads to interracial marriages, which improves the culture because males are forced to compete and treat women better. Latino males have been interracially dating for years, and no one says it is wrong.

The dating game among Latinas and black females is part of the adjustment to the fact that there are not enough men.[28] In the 1990s, according to the U.S. Department of Labor, "[a]s with non-Hispanic white and black women, Cuban and Puerto Rican origin women outnumber their male counterparts. Only among persons of Mexican descent do males age 16 and over outnumber females—4.9 million as compared with 4.7 million."[29] Women have it harder than males, and they need someone to support them, so if they better themselves by dating interracially, why not? For instance, the U.S. Department of Labor says that the number of bachelors' and doctors' degrees awarded to Latinas more than doubled between 1977 and 1990. Before 1970, Latino parents would discourage their daughters from leaving home and attending college. However, these taboos are rarer, and there has been a steady rise in the number of Latinas enrolled in colleges. Again, according to the Department of Labor, "In undergraduate schools between 1980 and 1988, they [Latinas] increased their enrollment from 222,000 to 344,000; in graduate schools from 16,000 to 22,000; in professional school, they doubled from 2,000 to 4,000." Whom are they supposed to date and marry?[30]

In 1969, males composed 60 percent of the U.S. college population; in 1999 they made up 56 percent. In the California State University system, which has one of the largest concentrations of Latinos, women overall outnumber men 60 to 40. Some researchers suggest that this imbalance is caused by low-income African American and Latino youth who are not attending colleges in the same numbers as their female counterparts. National studies show that race and class play a determining role in the imbalance between females and males attending college. Among middle-class college students the ratio is 50 to 50, whereas among low-income students, 44 percent were men. Breaking down the low-income students racially, 46 percent were white men, 43 percent Latinos, and less than a third were African American. This is a growing problem, and in California more females are graduating from college than males.[31] Latinas did not create this problem, so why should they be expected to marry someone less educated than they are?

It is not as if Latinos are all the same and marry Latino mates who look alike. According to a *Washington Post* article, interracial marriage is eroding barriers: "In much of Latin America . . . marrying a person of lighter skin color is considered a move up the social ladder. Some Latinos invoke the phrase, *mejorando la raza*, improving the race, to signal their approval." Because of this, almost one-third of U.S.-born Latinos between the ages of 25 and 34 are married to non-Latino whites.[32] It is something Latino leaders are going to have to accept. When Latinos came to the United States, they accepted a new life. Sure there is discrimination, but all Americans should be working toward an ideal society, and interracial dating breaks down walls between people. Interracial dating and marriage make us more tolerant of each other. It breaks down racial barriers. Refusing to mix with other races helps perpetuate racism. Having a multiracial society enriches everyone. Diversity adds not only color, but also cultural diversity. The country will benefit from becoming more tolerant of others. For Latinos, being biracial and bicultural is part of their history.

### Against

According to a scholarly article in the *International Migration Review*, "Intermarriage is considered both a cause and one of the most important indicators of the assimilation of newcomers into the larger society . . . [and] high rates of intermarriage between groups can occur only when some form of social proximity of large numbers of people from different ethnic backgrounds has evolved into a common aspect of life. Social proximity may occur in residential and occupational settings, or in other formal or informal settings, such as routine aspects of social life."[33] Reflecting on this quotation, one must keep in mind that interracial relations exact a price.

Interracial dating in America is not the utopia the media polls paint. Race is still the name of the game in the United States. When Latinos and Latinas go to visit a person of another race, the parents will ask them their name.

When they tell them, they might ask, "What are you, where are you from?" As the *International Migration Review* article suggests, interracial dating and marriage is largely limited to middle-class Latinos. A case in point is that in El Paso, Texas, only 13.58 percent of Latinos are exposed to white neighbors; in Miami, it is 17.92 percent and in Los Angeles it is 16.97 percent.[34]

Generally, there is a failure on the part of scholars and the media to get beyond the polls. This is synthesized through the college experience and students. For many whites, dating Latinos becomes a beauty contest. White males choose Latinas they consider to be pretty in the Anglo sense. The Jennifer López or Salma Hayek look-alikes are in great demand, as Hollywood has emphasized lately. Today, Latinas and Asian women are in—they are trophies. As for white females, they choose Latino males who are upwardly mobile, who look more like them, or who are athletes. They dismiss the Latinos and Latinas who look or talk too *barrio*.

Yet it goes beyond dating. Interracial dating results in the mixing of the races. Unless mixed-race children reject one or the other of their ethnicities, they are caught between two worlds. It is not a peaceful meshing for many children, and the mixed-bloods get it from both sides. What club are you going to join? Which group are you going to choose? Who do you want to be?

Identity in the United States means survival—not so much a survival of ethnic identity but of ethnic solidarity in advocating for the interests of those left behind in the barrio, those of the poor and working classes. For example, there were differences between Jews. German Jews had their prejudices against Polish and other Jewish groups. However, Jews maintained and, in large part, kept their groups together. German Jews built organizations that pulled up the Slavic Jews and helped them with civil rights and social services. To varying degrees, the other ethnic groups, as recently as the 1950s, were not mixing with other groups and followed this pattern. It took until two or three generations after the 1921 and 1924 Immigration Acts for the descendants of the European immigrants to mix into the melting pot, and by that time the wave of European immigrants was gone. What makes Latinos different from the descendants of European immigrants is that their homeland is not an ocean away from the United States, so Latinos are not as likely to quickly, if ever, lose their language and culture.

Interracial dating and marriage become problematic when the most educated sectors of the community marry out of their race. It is not the first time in U.S. history that this has happened. In the Southwest, Anglo Americans regularly married Mexican women of the upper classes and even poorer women. This lasted as long as there was a shortage of white women, and after that it became taboo. The offspring for the most part had little affinity for the working classes or improving their lot. It can be argued that the best way to help Latinos at the lower end of the social scale is to keep them together as an ethnic or racial group and thereby bring up the entire group.

Dating is a relatively new phenomenon for all peoples. Mixing cultures is something that will happen whether society likes it or not. However, just like everything else in this country, there is a price to pay. There are things in Latino culture that Latinos should preserve.[35] It is not just a matter of assimilation. Knowing two languages and being bicultural enrich Latinos and the country. The bettering of the race is about keeping the group together and giving its people a feeling of responsibility for those less fortunate. The preservation of culture allows a bond with other Latinos who have not made it instead of abandoning them and perpetuating an underclass.

## QUESTIONS

1. If Catholics or Jews do not want their child to date a non-Catholic or a non-Jew, are they racist?

2. Watch the movie *West Side Story*. If race were not a factor, why would it matter if Natalie Wood played a Puerto Rican? Some Mexicans objected to the fact that Jennifer López, who is of Puerto Rican descent, played the title character in the movie *Selena*. Is this the same kind of criticism?

3. In *West Side Story*, what did María mean when she responded to Tony's statement, "We'll be all right. I know it," by saying, "It is not us. It is everything around us"?

4. Go to an Internet search engine. Type "Alice Robinson, Interracial dating sometimes difficult, but still rewarding." Download the article. If it is not available, type in "difficulties of interracial dating." What does the Robinson article say on the subject? If your search engine does not pull up this article, what do the other articles say about it? How is interracial dating sometimes difficult? How is it sometimes rewarding? Would it be fair to compare María and Tony's situation to today's world? How would the situations in *Giant* and *Lone Star* differ?

5. Gregory Rodríguez, in "Candidates' Racial Views Outdated," *Los Angeles Times*, 5 March 2000, writes that Milken Institute demographer William H. Frey has projected that only 10 states will be racially and ethnically diverse by 2025. While California, Arizona, Florida, Hawaii, Illinois, Nevada, New Jersey, New Mexico, New York, and Texas will become what Frey calls "melting-pot states," the 40 other states will remain mostly white. Does this article contradict Rodríguez's theme about assimilation? Why or why not? (If you wish to read further about Rodríguez or Frey, go to an Internet search engine and type "William H. Frey" or "Gregory Rodríguez.")

6. The polls overwhelmingly show that youth of all colors want to date interracially. What do you think about the polls? Are you as optimistic about interracial

dating? Looking at the fact that the sampling included about 300 Latinos out of some 1200 respondents, would you be cautious about overgeneralizing Latino attitudes? Why or why not?

7. Where is interracial dating and marriage most common for Latinos? Is this the same in the case of blacks? What pitfalls are evident?

8. In the case of Mexicans and Puerto Ricans, do they date interracially? What factors would affect this phenomenon? Explain these factors.

9. Given the colonial attitude of all Latino groups and the diversity of racial features within Latinos, which group would most prefer to date outside of its own group and why?

10. Are you racist if you do not want to date a member of another group? Should Latinos date members of other groups? Explain your position.

11. There are significantly more Latinas in college than Latinos. How would this affect the rate of interracial dating and interracial marriage? Read the *For* and *Against* arguments in this chapter. How would this ratio of Latinas to Latinos affect the each of these arguments?

12. Go to an Internet search engine. Type in "Latino male college graduation." According to the articles you find, why do Latino males not go to college at the same rate as Latinas? Is this the same for other groups?

13. Do children of interracial marriages have problems? Should this be a consideration in interracial dating? Why or why not?

14. Ultimately, who decides whether interracial dating is good or bad? Does the view of white society matter more than those of others? Would interracial marriage have been common during World War II? Why or why not?

15. Go to the Resource Guide and under the film section, list the films that might deal with interracial dating or marriage. Watch the films *La Familia* and *The Pérez Family*. Critique them. Based on these films, would Latino culture encourage mixing with other races?

## NOTES

1. Teresa Watanabe, "Gap in Census Leaves Need for Religious Data," *Los Angeles Times,* 27 April 2001, http://www.ajc.org/InTheMedia/RelatedArticles.asp?did=379, accessed 2 August 2003. Congress barred the Census Bureau in 1976 from compelling people to reveal their religious affiliations. The author asks the following:

Are American Jews marrying outside the faith at a rate of 52 percent? Ever since that statistic was reported in 1991, fears that Jews could be headed down a demographic path to disappearance have topped the American Jewish agenda. Yet some demographers estimate the intermarriage rate to be far lower. . . . Are Latinos abandoning traditional Christian denominations en masse for evangelical movements? Trying to define the number of evangelicals can be difficult. And pinpointing the number of Latinos, regarded as the evangelical world's fastest-growing segment, is even dicier because their immigration status and language barriers stymie accurate counting. . . . Another minefield is methodology, demonstrated by the Jewish intermarriage debate. When a Jewish population survey reported the 52 percent intermarriage rate in 1991, the reaction was furious. Suddenly, the issue of 'continuity' exploded. Orthodox Jews, with their traditional ways, large families and low intermarriage rates, produced a controversial chart claiming that only they would increase the number of Jews over time.

2. Hrishi Karthikeyan and Gabriel J. Chin, "Preserving Racial Identity: Population Patterns and the Application of Anti-Miscegenation Statutes to Asian Americans, 1910–1950," *Asian Law Journal* 9 (2002): 1–39, 14–19, http://academic.udayton.edu/race/01race/aspi02.htm, accessed 2 August 2003.

3. James Berardinelli, review of *Giant,* http://movie-reviews.colossus.net/movies/g/giant.html, accessed 25 July 2003.

4. *West Side Story* (the movie), 1961, http://course1.winona.msus.edu/pjohnson/h140/studentsf01/westsidestory, accessed 25 July 2003.

5. *West Side Story* (the musical), TheatreHistory.Com, http://www.theatrehistory.com/american/musical001.html, accessed 25 July 2003.

6. James Berardinelli, review of *Lone Star,* http://movie-reviews.colossus.net/movies/l/lone_star.html, accessed 25 July 2003.

7. Karlyn Bowman, "Pollsters Examine Race Relations in the Nation" *Archives, Roll Call,* 30 March 2000, http://www.rollcall.com/pages/columns/bowman/00/bowm0330.html, accessed 25 July 2003; Karlyn Bowman, "Polls Shed Light on Future of Race Relations," *American Enterprise Institute, Roll Call,* 9 July 2003, http://www.aei.org/news/newsID.17955,filter./news_detail.asp, accessed 25 July 2003.

8. Ibid.

9. Ann Scott Tyson, "Young Love Bridges Race Divide," *Christian Science Monitor,* 3 December 1997, http://www.search.csmonitor.com/durable/1997/12/03/us/us.4.html, accessed 25 July 2003.

10. Ibid. "More than Half of Teens Who Date Have Dated Interracially: Study," *Jet,* 24 November 1997, 32ff. "Fifty-seven % of teenagers who have been on dates have dated outside their race. Sixty % of African American teenagers who date, 47 percent of whites who date and 90 percent of Hispanic teenagers who date have dated someone from another race." Given the degree of segregation in places like Los Angeles especially among Mexicans and Central Americans, these figures could be open to discussion.

11. Karlyn Bowman, "Pollsters Examine Race Relations in the Nation," *Archives, Roll Call,* 30 March 2000, http://www.rollcall.com/pages/columns/bowman/00/bowm0330.html, accessed 25 July 2003.

12. Darryl Fears and Claudia Deane, "Biracial Couples Report Greater Tolerance: U.S. Survey Finds Acceptance Weakest among Whites," *The Washington Post,* 8 July 2001, http://www.post-gazette.com/headlines/20010708biracialnat2p2.asp, accessed 25 July 2003; Francine Russo, "When Love is Mixing it Up: More Couples are Finding Each Other across Racial Lines–And Finding Acceptance," *Time* 158 (22): np. (19 November 2001), http://www.time.com/time/archive/preview/from_redirect/0,10987,1101011119-184008,00.html, accessed 25 July 2003.

13. Ibid.

14. Ibid.

15. Kevin R. Johnson, "'Melting Pot' or 'Ring of Fire'? Assimilation and the Mexican American Experience." LatCrit: Latinas/os and the Law: A Joint Symposium by *California Law Review* and *La Raza Law Journal. California Law Review* 85, no. 5 (1997): 1259–313.

16. Sean-Shong Hwang, Kevin M. Fitzpatrick, and David Helms, "Class Differences in Racial Attitudes: A Divided Black America?" *Sociological Perspectives* 41, no. 2

(1998): 367ff. Various authors argue that black America is becoming increasingly divided along class lines. The same thesis can be pursued with U.S. Latinos. Therefore, distinctions on where a U.S. Latino lives is important. Just like not all blacks are alike, neither are all Latinos.

17. Marc S. Mentzer, "Minority Representation in Higher Education: The Impact of Population Heterogeneity." *Journal of Higher Education* 64, no. 4 (1993): 417ff. Most of the articles take a black-white point of reference. This academic or scholarly article makes distinctions in the way scholars count ethnic groups other than blacks.

18. John R. Logan, "Choosing Segregation: Racial Imbalance in American Public Schools, 1990–2000," Lewis Mumford Institute, 29 March 2002, 11–14, http://mumford1.dyndns.org/cen2000/SchoolPop/SPReport/page1.html, accessed 25 July 2003.

19. Ibid. The Mumford Report points out that Latinos are the group least affected by court orders. "Latino Residential Segregation: 1990–2000. Census 2000 Update (8/7/01)," IUPLR, http://www.nd.edu/~iuplr/cic/mumford_aug.html, accessed 25 July 2003.

20. Jon K. Mills, Jennifer Daly, Amy Longmore, and Gina Kilbride, "A Note on Family Acceptance Involving Interracial Friendships and Romantic Relationships," *The Journal of Psychology* 129, no. 3 (May 1995): 346ff.

21. Roberto Suro, "Mixed Doubles (Interethnic Marriages and Marketing Strategy.) (Statistical Data Included)," *American Demographics* 21 (November 1999): 56–62.

22. William H. Frey, quoted in Roberto Suro, "Mixed Doubles (Interethnic Marriages and Marketing Strategy.) (Statistical Data Included)," *American Demographics* 21 (November 1999): 56–62.

23. Roberto Suro, "Mixed Doubles. (Interethnic Marriages and Marketing Strategy.) (Statistical Data Included)," *American Demographics* 21 (November 1999): 56–62.

24. Roberto Suro, "Mixed Doubles (Interethnic Marriages and Marketing Strategy.) (Statistical Data Included)," *American Demographics* 21 (November 1999): 56–62; Quoted in Zhenchao Qian, "Who Intermarries? Education, Nativity, Region, and Interracial Marriage, 1980 and 1990 [*]. (Statistical Data Included)," *Journal of Comparative Family Studies* 30, no. 4 (fall 1999): 579ff. "Interracial marriage, however, occurs far less frequently than interethnic or interfaith marriage. As early as 1910, interethnic marriage was relatively common among whites, but marriage across racial lines was extremely rare, due in part to anti-miscegenation laws forbidding marriage between persons of different races. This legal barrier was not abolished nationwide until 1967. Since then, interracial marriages have increased dramatically, from 310,000 in 1970 to 651,000 in 1980 and to 1,161,000 in 1992 (U.S. Bureau of the Census, 1993). These marriages have increased from 0.7 percent of all marriages in 1970 to 2.2 percent in 1992."

25. Michael A. Fletcher, "Interracial Marriages Eroding Barriers," *Washington Post,* 28 December 1998, http://www.washingtonpost.com/wp-srv/national/daily/dec98/melt29.htm, accessed 25 July 2003.

26. Ibid.

27. Denise Smith and Renee E. Spraggins, *Gender: 2000.* U.S. Census, September 2001, http://www.census.gov/prod/2001pubs/c2kbr01-9.pdf, accessed 25 July 2003.

28. Paul Offner, "What's Love Got to Do with It? Why Oprah's Still Single. (Society

and Opportunities for African American People)," *Washington Monthly* 34, no. 3 (March 2002): 15ff.

29. U.S. Department of Labor. Women's Bureau. "Women of Hispanic Origin in the Labor Force." *Facts on Working Women,* April 2000, http://www.dol.gov/wb/wb _pubs/hispwom2.htm, accessed 25 July 2003.

30. Ibid. Women maintained one-fourth of all Hispanic families (1,302,000 out of 5,373,000). Sixty-eight percent of female-headed Hispanic families included children under age 18. Between 1983 and 1993, the number of families maintained by women has increased—65 percent for Hispanics, 32 percent for blacks; and 16 percent for whites.

31. Terri Hardy, "A Student Gender Gap Has Been Growing by the Year at Colleges around the State–and the Nation," *Sacramento Bee,* 2 September 2002.

32. Michael A. Fletcher, "Interracial Marriages Eroding Barriers," *Washington Post,* 28 December 1998, http://www.washingtonpost.com/wp-srv/national/daily/dec98/ melt29.htm, accessed 25 July 2003.

33. Greta A. Gilbertson, Joseph P. Fitzpatrick, and Lijun Yang, "Hispanic Intermarriage in New York City: New Evidence from 1991," *International Migration Review* 30, no. 2 (summer 1996): 445ff.

34. Inter-University Program for Latino Research, "Latino Residential Segregation: 1990–2000. Census Update (8/7/01)," http://www.nd.edu/~iuplr/cic/mumford_aug. html, accessed 25 July 2003.

35. Agustin Gurza, "Vowing to Love, Honor and Preserve Cultures," *Los Angeles Times,* 31 October 2000.

## SELECTED WORKS

Arias, Elizabeth. "Change in Nuptiality Patterns among Cuban Americans: Evidence of Cultural and Structural Assimilation?" *International Migration Review* 35, no. 2 (summer 2001): 525ff.

Booth, William. "America's Racial and Ethnic Divides One Nation, Indivisible: Is It History?" *Washington Post,* 22 February 1998. Http://www.washingtonpost. com/wp-srv/national/longterm/meltingpot/melt0222.htm. Accessed 25 July 2003.

Buchanan, Patrick and Ben Wattenberg, "Immigration: A Cause of the Clash of Civilizations . . . or a Solution to It?" *The American Enterprise* 13, no. 7 (March 2002): 18ff.

Fears, Darryl, and Claudia Deane. "Biracial Couples Report Greater Tolerance: U.S. Survey Finds Acceptance Weakest Among Whites." *The Washington Post,* 8 July 2001. Http://www.washingtonpost.com/ac2/wp-dyn/a19824-2001Jul4? language = printer. Accessed 25 July 2003.

Gurza, Agustin. "Vowing to Love, Honor, and Preserve Cultures," *Los Angeles Times,* 31 October 2000.

Hwang, Sean-Shong, Kevin M. Fitzpatrick, and David Helms. "Class Differences in Racial Attitudes: A Divided Black America?" *Sociological Perspectives* 41, no. 2 (summer 1998): 367ff.

"Increasingly Multicultural: Rethinking Integration," *The Boston Globe.* Http:// www.boston.com/globe/nation/packages/rethinking_integration/increasingly _multicultural.htm. Accessed 25 July 2003.

Inter-University Program for Latino Research. "Latino Residential Segregation: 1990–2000. Census Update (8/7/01)," http://www.nd.edu/~iuplr/cic/mumford_aug.html. Accessed 25 July 2003.

Johnson, Kevin R. "'Melting Pot' or 'Ring of Fire'? Assimilation and the Mexican American Experience." LatCrit: Latinas/os and the Law: A Joint Symposium by *California Law Review* and *La Raza Law Journal, California Law Review* 85, no. 5 (October 1997): 1259–313.

Logan, John R. "Choosing Segregation: Racial Imbalance in American Public Schools, 1990–2000," http://mumford1.dyndns.org/cen2000/SchoolPop/SPReport/page1.html. Accessed 25 July 2003.

Logan, John R. "How Race Counts for Hispanic Americans." Lewis Mumford Center for Comparative Urban and Regional Research. University at Albany, 14 July 2003. Http://mumford1.dyndns.org/cen2000/BlackLatinoReport/BlackLatino01.htm. Accessed 24 July 2003.

Mentzer, Marc S. "Minority Representation in Higher Education: The Impact of Population Heterogeneity." *Journal of Higher Education* 64, no. 4 (July–August 1993): 417ff.

Offner, Paul. "What's Love Got to Do with It? Why Oprah's Still Single. (Society and Opportunities for African American People)." *Washington Monthly* 34, no. 3 (March 2002): 15ff.

Qian, Zhenchao. "Who Intermarries? Education, Nativity, Region, and Interracial Marriage, 1980 and 1990 (Statistical Data Included)." *Journal of Comparative Family Studies* 30, no. 4 (autumn 1999): 579ff.

Russo, Francine. "When Love Is Mixing It Up: More Couples Are Finding Each Other across Racial Lines—and Finding Acceptance." *Time* 19 November 2001.

Smith, Denise, and Renee E. Spraggins. *Gender: 2000.* U.S. Census, September 2001. Http://www.census.gov/prod/2001pubs/c2kbr01-9.pdf. Accessed 25 July 2003.

Suro, Roberto. "Mixed Doubles. (Interethnic Marriages and Marketing Strategy.) (Statistical Data Included)." *American Demographics,* November 1999.

Tyson, Ann Scott. "Young Love Bridges Race Divide," *Christian Science Monitor,* 3 December 1997.

U.S. Department of Labor. Women's Bureau. "Women of Hispanic Origin in the Labor Force." *Facts on Working Women,* April 2000, "WOMEN OF HISPANIC ORIGIN IN THE LABOR FORCE," *U.S. Dept. of Labor, Women's Bureau,* April 2000, http://www.dol.gov/wb/wb_pubs/hispwom2.htm. Accessed 25 July 2003.

# 7

## FUNDING EDUCATION AND HEALTH CARE FOR UNDOCUMENTED IMMIGRANTS

### BACKGROUND

Education and health care are basic human rights that most modern nations take for granted. However, today there is a debate in the United States as to whether this country can or should pay for health-care services of unauthorized workers and their families or for the education of their children. Driving this debate are the shift of the costs of health care and education to the middle class and the downturn of the economy in the 1980s and early 1990s. A logical discussion of this issue has been further complicated by the rising cost of health care, especially the cost of hospitalization, and by the fact so many public school students are Latinos.

The health care issue is especially volatile because it hits at the heart of the nation's public policy of encouraging a healthy society. Americans have historically rejected solutions such as universal health-care programs and have followed the lead of the American Medical Association in defeating such proposals, which many physicians label "socialistic."[1] Despite this aversion to universal health insurance, many American cities care about the health of their residents and have established health clinics that dispense free inoculations and pre-natal care to the poor as well as county hospitals that cater to poor patients. In recent years, these facilities have increasingly serviced immigrants, who compose a disproportionate number of medically uninsured workers. Unfortunately, because of budget constraints, many of these facilities have been closed.

The first president to propose a prepaid health insurance plan was Harry S

Truman who, in November of 1945 in a special message to Congress, proposed a comprehensive, prepaid medical insurance plan for all people through the Social Security system. Congress turned down the proposal. In the early 1960s a national survey showed that only 56 percent of those 65 years of age or older had health insurance, which prompted President John F. Kennedy to push for health insurance for the aged. In 1965, President Lyndon B. Johnson signed a bill to provide health insurance for the elderly and the poor, establishing both Medicare and Medicaid. Medicare was placed under the Social Security Administration (SSA), and Medicaid assisted state Medicaid programs. Over the years, Congress has narrowed the eligibility of health insurance recipients largely to social security beneficiaries. Efforts to widen these programs have been resisted by the middle class, who comprise the overwhelming majority of Americans. This portion of America is the sector most likely to have health insurance and want to maintain a freedom of choice in their health care coverage, which, in many cases, is an illusion since cost ultimately determines this freedom.

During the late 1980s, Congress advertised Health Maintenance Organizations (HMOs) as a solution to the dilemma. Henry Kaiser, during World War II, founded the nation's first HMO, now Kaiser Permanente, to keep the shipyard workers healthy. The basic goal was to have employers or workers pay for these low-cost health plans. However, over the years the costs of insurance have skyrocketed, and employers have refused to pay for the cost of social production, leaving many people without health care. This problem is especially acute among the working poor.

In the mid-1990s in California, Latinos were almost twice as likely to be without health insurance; this was true even though 87 percent of uninsured Latinos were from families with at least one wage earner.[2] Latinos lacked health insurance, not because they were not working, but because their employers did not pay for health insurance. Latinos generally worked for agriculture, small retail, service businesses, or light industry. These are sectors of the economy in which fewer workers have employer-paid health insurance. Almost 40 percent of non-elderly Latinos were completely uninsured compared with 23 percent of all non-elderly Californians. It was shown that fewer than 20 percent of the Los Angeles Latino population of more than three million were unauthorized immigrants. Studies also showed that "about 17 percent of poor Latino adult immigrants reported receiving public assistance in 1989, compared to 65 percent of poor blacks, 50 percent of poor U.S.-born Latinos, 49 percent of poor Asians, and 42 percent of poor non-Latino whites. The average Latino immigrant household income in 1989 of $29,989 was lower than that reported for other groups: $52,375 for non-Latino whites, $49,042 for Asians, $43,777 for U.S.-born Latinos, and $32,813 for black households."[3]

For Latinos the issue of extending health care to these families was personal. Many non-insured students were children who attended schools with their children. What was to be done when those children became ill? Still there was the question of who should pay for the service. As more Americans became concerned with the growing Latino population, the health care issue became embroiled with the question of the undocumented worker. Nativist groups became more vocal in blaming the health crisis on the immigrant. For example, the Federation of American Immigration Reform (FAIR) said 43 percent of non-citizens under 65 had no health insurance in El Paso County, which borders Juárez, Chihuahua, Mexico, resulting in the incidence of tuberculosis being twice the U.S. rate and the rate of dysentery several times higher in El Paso than throughout the rest of the United States. FAIR blamed Mexican and Central American immigrants who lacked medical care, and according to FAIR, these uninsured immigrants are a severe risk to the health and well-being of people on both sides of the border.[4]

Human rights activists argue that all workers and their families have the right to good health care. These activists point out that the goal is to have healthy, productive democratic citizens. Human rights activists posited that the average immigrant pays $1,300 or more a year in taxes.[5] These activists respond that the real issue is that the working poor cannot afford health insurance and that they receive public health-care assistance because the cost of health care is too high. Thus, the issue is not that they are undocumented but the cost of health insurance.

The different currents may actually stalemate a resolution of the health care issue because their purposes often cancel each other out. First, should society continue the public policy of having a healthy and democratic society? Secondly, who should pay for these services, which are admittedly getting out of hand? Third, would society resolve the problem of the lack of health-care insurance for the poor if all undocumented residents would go away?

Public education for the children of undocumented parents is similar to the health care issue. Public policy from the beginnings of this nation's history has been to offer free public school education to all residents. Education is the foundation of a democratic society. In 1982, the U.S. Supreme Court in *Plyer v. Doe* ruled in a 5–4 decision that education is guaranteed to all children and that denying education was unconstitutional. An education was thus a fundamental right, and the denial of a public education was racist. The ruling of the court relied on the Fourteenth Amendment and its equal protection clause according to *Plyer*, and that "a state law that impinges upon a substantive right or liberty created or conferred by the Constitution is, of course, presumptively invalid, whether or not the law's purpose or effect is to create any classifications." Thus, "Children denied an education are placed at a permanent and insurmountable competitive disadvantage, for an uneducated child is denied even the opportunity to achieve." In *Plyer,* one of the Justices wrote, "It is difficult to understand precisely what the State hopes to achieve by promoting the creation and perpetuation of a subclass of illiterates within our boundaries, surely adding to the problems and costs of unemployment."[6] The *Plyer* case, however, did not end the debate, and the narrowness of the decision encouraged public challenges.

Health-care services and schooling for undocumented immigrants set the context for California Proposition 187, the so-called Save our State initiative in November of 1994, denying publicly funded social services to undocumented California residents. According to then-Governor Pete Wilson, working taxpayers were emigrating out of California because of the increasing demands for expensive government services by poor people and immigrants. Wilson alleged an imbalance between the number of taxpayers and tax receivers and that the imbalance was jeopardizing California's ability to maintain funding levels for state programs. The growth of the tax receiver group

Member of an anti-immigration group in California, called Voice of Citizens Together holds a sign asking that pre-natal care be denied to undocumented immigrants, Glendale, California, 1996. (AP/Wide World Photos)

was driven by an increase in the number of school-age children resulting from immigration and a recent surge in the Latino birthrate. Governor Wilson proposed to deny citizenship status and public education to the children of undocumented immigrants.[7] Because of *Plyer*, the issue of free public education in grades K-12 was not written into the initiative. However, undocumented students would be denied the status of residents for the purpose of admission into California public universities and colleges.

The debate surrounding the denial of undocumented residents of California public health-care services and a publicly supported higher education was divisive. The question was not whether public education was the right of every citizen, rather the question was whether Californians could afford to give free health services and advanced schooling to unauthorized immigrants. The proponents of Proposition 187 said giving these services cost taxpayers and rewarded unauthorized immigrants for breaking the law, that there is a legal way to get into the United States, and everyone should abide by those rules. Those against Proposition 187 said it was just good policy to have everyone in the community in good health and well educated.

More often the debate revolved around immigration policy rather than health care or education policy. A recurrent theme was that the Immigration Reform and Control Act of 1986 had granted amnesty and green cards to roughly 600,000 undocumented California workers. Another theme was that Mexicans and other Latinos were coming to the United States to have infants that they could not afford to have and send to school in their countries. In other words, that Latinos were entering the United States for welfare.[8] Critics thus blamed immigrants for the runaway costs of medical care or for the high cost of higher education.

The position of the Catholic church on Proposition 187 was unequivocal. Before the election, Cardinal Roger Mahony said the measure would undermine "clear moral principles," stopping just shy of calling it a mortal sin. He said that Proposition 187 would tear families apart.[9] Victory of the proposition would be a blow to the moral authority of the Catholic church. However, white Catholics voted 58 percent to 42 percent for Proposition 187. On November 8, 1994, California overwhelmingly passed Proposition 187. Only the San Francisco Bay Area voted against it, by 70 percent.[10] Los Angeles voted for Proposition 187 by a 12 percent margin. Statewide exit polls showed Latinos opposing the proposition 77 percent to 23 percent.[11] Many priests recognized that there was racial bias associated with Proposition 187.[12] Many of the Protestant churches remained silent on the issue.[13]

The debate over education and health care for undocumented residents has temporarily subsided; first because of the growth of the Latino voting bloc, which voted heavily Democratic in subsequent elections. By the end of the 1990s Latino-elected officials controlled the Democratic Party Caucus in the California Assembly, and Republicans in California realized that Republican candidates needed a portion of the Latino vote to win statewide elections.

Second, while white Americans still had the vote to pass measures such as Proposition 187, political awareness was growing among Latinos, perhaps due in part to the 12 Los Angeles radio stations that broadcast in Spanish—overall there are 9.74 million radio listeners and 81 stations in greater Los Angeles. In addition, two of the 10 non-cable television channels are Spanish language in a designated market area that encompasses Los Angeles County and all of Orange, San Bernardino, and Ventura counties as well as parts of Kern, Riverside, and San Diego counties. Los Angeles-based Univision network's KMEX Channel 34 boasts higher ratings for its 6 P.M. and 11 P.M. newscasts than its English-language competitors. Southern California's Spanish language daily, *La Opinión,* has a circulation of nearly 140,000.

Lastly, the debate over education and health care for undocumented residents has temporarily subsided because of an upturn in the economy, which calmed nativism for the time being.

## SHOULD TAXPAYERS FUND THE EDUCATION AND HEALTH CARE OF UNDOCUMENTED IMMIGRANTS AND THEIR FAMILIES?

### For

The issue of whether to pay for the health care and education of undocumented workers and their family members has been politicized and distorted. Setting aside the question of immigration, what society needs is to pay greater attention to the debate over health care and education rather than be distracted by the unfounded arguments that the immigrant is deteriorating either of these systems. The sad fact is that health care has always been problematic in the United States, and the once-vaunted educational superstructure has been badly underfunded since the 1960s. This is tragic especially since every industrialized country has some form of universal medical insurance. For example, in 1883, German Chancellor Otto Von Bismarck introduced the German compulsory health insurance program.

The immigrant in general and the undocumented person in particular are the people who many Americans want to scapegoat. They are not inclined to educate Latinos because that would mean empowering them. When attending a meeting of state school boards in the late 1970s, Julian Nava, a former U.S. ambassador to Mexico under President Jimmy Carter, was asked by a

San Joaquin Valley school board member, "Dr. Nava, you don't want to educate Mexicans. Who then would pick our crops?"[14]

The preferential treatment of Cuban refugees by the federal authorities was an intelligent approach to the health care problem. It stands in stark contrast not only to how Latino immigrants have been treated, but to how Latinos who are U.S. citizens have been treated as well. The Cuban Refugee Program gave more than $1.2 billion of direct financial assistance to recently arrived Cuban American immigrants. Public programs provided more assistance. The health services were tailored to the Cuban American's needs; the policy was not one of sink-or-swim or go home. As a consequence, Cuban Americans in Miami participate in the economic life of the city. The same sort of support was given to refugees from the former Soviet Union.[15]

Selected Asian groups from Laos, Vietnam, and Cambodia have received similar aid. The Office of Refugee Resettlement of the U.S. Department of Health and Human Services actively supported these groups. Aside from this, the U.S. State Department reimburses refugee agencies $630 for each refugee they resettle. Many refugees were eligible for assistance under Aid to Families with Dependent Children or Supplemental Security Income. Low-income refugees were eligible for Medicaid.

In today's transnational economy, it is wrongheaded to believe that labor, especially Latino labor, will not come into the United States. The only way to end Latinos' migration into the United States would be to bring Mexican wages in Mexico on par with those in this country, and that is not going to happen in the near future. The policies of the World Bank and the International Monetary Fund demand high unemployment, low-wage labor, and the dismantling of social welfare programs in those countries.[16] In addition, the simple fact is that the white population is not growing, and, as is the case with other industrialized powers, the United States needs to import workers. These workers, like all American workers, need social services such as quality health care and good education systems. In this country corporations and millionaires have been given a free ride and are not required to pay for the cost of social production. The health-care system as it is presently constructed subsidizes these corporations, so the undocumented and the working poor are left without medical care. Their only recourse is to use emergency medical facilities, which are high maintenance. Instead of denying health care, the present system should be reformed to provide compulsory health care for all Americans. Society will be a healthier place for all.

Admittedly public education is in trouble, but it is also underfunded. Americans must remember that students create jobs for teachers; without students, there would be no teaching jobs and the economy would suffer. It is not the immigrants' fault that white students abandoned the public school system. White students did this in response to orders to integrate schools, and because some were racist toward blacks, they moved into private schools. So-called taxpayer revolts cut funding from the schools, which is why they deteriorated.

It is time to rebuild education, and no student should be held back. Education is a fundamental right. To deny education directly contradicts the Supreme Court ruling in the case of *Plyer v. Texas.* The job now for parents and educators is to motivate students to better themselves. Immigrant children, regardless of their status, are not going to succeed in elementary through secondary school if they know that despite their education their road will likely still lead them to menial, low-paying jobs. In addition, higher education should be tuition-free and open to all. A better educated workforce is needed to really take off in this age of technology.

In Texas, the entry of undocumented residents into state university systems has been facilitated by allowing them to pay in-state resident tuition. In June 2001, similar measures were proposed in California and Wisconsin. The Texas law chose to treat unauthorized immigrants who had graduated from a Texas secondary school (or who had obtained a GED) after at least three years of study in the local school system as eligible for in-state college tuition. The Texas legislators recognized that the children were brought into the country by their parents, and that for all intent and purposes this is their country. Should undocumented students be punished for the alleged sins of the parents and condemned to the margins of society?[17] Finally, there is no credible evidence that immigrants come to the United States only seeking health, education, or welfare. They make it the old-fashioned way; they work.

### Against

It is a fact that some 44 million people do not have health insurance. It is also a fact that the high cost of health coverage is causing many companies to drop their coverage. A major reason for this rise is the use of emergency care by immigrants who do not have medical insurance. Recently arrived immigrants and their young children account for most of the growth in the uninsured population. The problem will get worse, and an estimated 5 million to 6 million people will be added to the ranks of the uninsured over the next 10 years.[18] The solution to this problem is to withhold medical care from immigrants and their children, saving the taxpayers' money.

It is time for Americans to take care of their own people. About one-third of immigrants and their young children have no insurance, a rate two and half times more than native-born Americans.[19] Immigrant families account for 26 percent of the uninsured, yet they make up only 13 percent of the nation's total population. Should the taxpayers be forced to pay for their health care?

Americans are being blackmailed. Americans either pay for their health care or their own health becomes jeopardized due to the large costs of insuring the poor. In 1997, Congress created the State Children's Health Insurance Program (SCHIP) at an annual cost of $4 billion to care for about 1 million poor children. Despite the good intentions of Congress, SCHIP is going broke. In the last few years, immigration has increased the number of uninsured children in the United States by 700,000, nullifying most of the gains made under SCHIP. There is simply not enough money to go around, and foreigners are taking what is there from U.S. citizens.[20]

Why are so many immigrant families uninsured? Most immigrants have little or no education. Consequently, immigrants are not compatible with the United States' information-driven economy, which means that immigrants often work at jobs that do not provide health insurance. The immigrants' low pay makes it difficult for them to purchase insurance on their own, and their employers do not have sufficient profits to provide health care. Many public hospitals around the country are going broke because they are forced to serve uninsured immigrants. Congressman Charlie Norwood (GA-Republican) says that the total cost to taxpayers of treating the uninsured is perhaps $30 billion a year and this does not include $150 billion spent on Medicaid, which is being drained by illegal aliens.[21]

All Americans should be concerned about the growth of the uninsured population. Congress must adopt a sensible immigration policy and stop rewarding illegal aliens for breaking the law. In the meantime, the state must end the use of health facilities by illegal immigrants to cut the incentives for coming to this country.[22]

The cost of education has also skyrocketed while society is getting less for its dollar. Two million (40 percent) illegal aliens live in California alone. Seventeen percent of all K-12 students in California are illegal aliens. This costs California $1.6 billion annually.[23] The cost of public education for illegal immigrants in California is a minimum of $1.7 billion; in New York, $634 million; in Florida, $424 million; and in Texas, $419 million a year. Taxpayers do not owe these illegal immigrants an education. They are not Americans. They were not born here. And they are driving loyal Americans out of the schools.[24]

If it were up to many Americans, they would deny the children of illegal immigrants their elementary through secondary education, and they would use the money to improve the schools for Americans. However, the federal courts say this is unconstitutional. The public is not getting a good return for its investment. Immigrants have the lowest test scores and the highest drop-out rate of any societal group. At the very least, Americans should not be paying to send illegal aliens to colleges. Because they are not academically prepared, tax dollars expended on higher education for illegal aliens to prepare them for professional jobs is wasted. Why should state governments repeat the wrongheaded policies of the national government and attract illegal alien families to move to those states? Let the states spend their money on their own.[25]

## QUESTIONS

1. What role do statistics play in mobilizing people to one side or another? What methods do people use?

2. What is the public policy in regards to public health care and education? What are the arguments of the forces favoring health care and educational services to undocumented immigrants? What are the arguments of the forces against giving them services? Do they differentiate between authorized and unauthorized immigrants?

3. Why is there a health-care crisis? What evidence is there that immigrants caused it? Why do they not have health insurance? Is the lack of medical insurance a problem primarily for unauthorized workers?

4. Do you agree with the following statement: All immigrants come to the United States for social benefits such as health care and education. Why or why not?

5. What are the facts in *Plyer v. Doe*? Based on the "Equal Protection Clause" of the Fourteenth Amendment to the Constitution, it is unconstitutional to deny an undocumented student a primary education. Do you agree? Why or why not?

6. What was Proposition 187? Why did Latino voters resent it so much? Why has former-Governor Pete Wilson become an anti-Latino symbol? Is this attitude justified or not?

7. How do immigrants subsidize corporations?

8. Why was the treatment of the Cubans, the Soviets, and other selected refugees called an intelligent and humane policy? Why would other Latinos be resentful at not being treated in the same way?

9. Read the letter from an unnamed medical doctor to the Federation of American Immigration Reform, "Immigration from a Medical Point of View," http://www.fairus.org/html/09109109.htm. Accessed 26 July 2003. What is the point stated? Do you agree? Why or why not?

10. Go to an Internet search engine. Type "Susan Carroll, 'Dreams deferred: Living in the nation's shadows extracts a cost from those here illegally—and a cost from society,' *Tucson Citizen*, 5 September 2001." Http://www.tucsoncitizen.com/local/archive/01/immig01/9_5_01border.html. Accessed 26 July 2003. Why would the report of the Center for Immigration Studies be controversial? How does the U.S. government benefit from undocumented work-

ers' payments of Social Security and federal taxes? What other taxes do they pay?

11. Try to find David E. Hayes-Bautista, "To Win the War, Arm Americans with Education, Health Care, Liberty," *Pacific News Service,* 21 October 2001, on the Internet. Hayes-Bautista is the premier Latino health care expert. Research some of his other articles. How does this article contribute to the question at hand?

12. Try to find "Cardinal Roger Mahony, You Have Entertained Angels—Without Knowing it." (Or type "Mahony and immigration".) The Catholic church has consistently thrown its weight behind the humane treatment of the immigrant. From a religious perspective, summarize in one paragraph what Mahony's views would be on the question at hand.

13. What role will the growth of the U.S. Latino voting bloc have on the question of whether to give free medical care and education to undocumented residents?

14. Summarize the *For* position in this chapter. Should we make medical care and education available to unauthorized workers and their families?

15. Summarize the *Against* position in this chapter. The congressman makes the point that the issue should be debated dispassionately. Do you believe this is possible? Do you agree with his points? Why or why not?

16. Go to an Internet search engine and type "Federation of American Immigration Reform." What are the views of this organization on immigration?

17. The film *El Norte* (1983, directed by Gregory Nava) is available in most video stores. It is about a Guatemalan brother and sister fleeing Guatemala who finally arrive in Los Angeles without documents and the obstacles they encounter. What does the film say about why Central American immigrants come to the United States?

18. The film *Born in East L.A.* (1987, written and directed by Cheech Marin) is about a Chicano who doesn't know Spanish and is accidentally deported to Mexico without identification. He cannot convince U.S. authorities that he was born in the United States. What is the message of the film? Do you agree with its message? Why or why not?

19. *Fear and Learning at Hoover Elementary* (1997) is a documentary directed by Laura Angélica Simón. The documentary is about the impact of anti-immigrant legislation on Latino elementary school children. What was the impact of Proposition 187 on students?

20. The *For* and *Against* forces agree that there is a health-care crisis. How do they differ as to the causes and solutions to the crisis?

## NOTES

1. Conrad F. Mier, "Health Care: Reformed or Deformed?" *The Heartland Institute,* 2002, http://cfmresearch.tripod.com/healthcare/, accessed 25 July 2003. Also see A. Camarota and James R. Edwards Jr., "Uninsured Immigrants Burden the Health Care System," *Heartland Institute,* http://heartland.org/Article.cfm?art

ID = 456, accessed 25 July 2003. This article can also be found in a Google search. Type in "Universal health care socialistic."

2. "Latino Immigrants in LA, a Portrait from the 1990 Census," Alta California Policy Research Center, 1994; Patrick McDonnell, "Study Seeks to Debunk Stereotypes of Latinos," *Los Angeles Times,* 21 October 1994; Douglas Shuit, "Study Finds Latinos to be Group Most Lacking in Health Coverage," *Los Angeles Times,* 19 July 1994.

3. *Rural Migration News* 1, no. 1 (January 1995), http://migration.ucdavis.edu/rmn/Archive_RMN/jan_1995–10rmn.html, accessed 25 July 2003.

4. The Federation of American Immigration Reform, "Immigrants and Public Health: Why Immigration is a Health Care Concern," http://www.fairus.org/html/04149711.htm, accessed 25 July 2003.

5. "Unite against Racism: Defend the Immigrants among Us," Socialist Agenda, http://www.angelfire.com/tx/broadspectrum/index.socialism7.html, accessed 25 July 2003.

6. *Plyer v. Doe,* 457 U.S. 202 (1982), http://caselaw.lp.findlaw.com/scripts/getcase.pl?court = US&vol = 457&invol = 202, accessed 25 July 2003.

7. "Immigrants or Transnational Workers? The Settlement Process among Mexicans in Rural California," http://www.cirsinc.org/pub/alarcon.html, accessed 25 July 2003.

8. "Latino Baby Boom Powers Growth Spurt," *San Jose* (California) *Mercury News,* 11 August 2001.

9. Ted Rohrlich, "Mahony Says Prop. 187 Poses Threat to Moral Principles," *Los Angeles Times,* 9 October 1994; John Dart, "187 Shows Clergy's Weak Influence on Electorate," *Los Angeles Times,* 19 November 1994.

10. Howard Breuer, "Voters Approve Prop. 187, Lawsuits to Follow," *Daily News,* 9 November 1994; David Ferrell and Robert J. Lopez, "California Waits to See What Prop. 187 Will Really Mean," *Los Angeles Times,* 10 November 1994.

11. David E. Hayes-Bautista and Gregory Rodríguez, "A Rude Awakening for Latinos," *Los Angeles Times,* 11 November 1994; Patrick J. McDonnell, "State's Diversity Doesn't Reach Voting Booth," *Los Angeles Times,* 11 November 1994.

12. María Puente and Gale Holland, "Deep Vein of Anger in California / Prop. 187 Reinforcing Divisions," *USA Today,* 11 November 1994.

13. John Dart, "Prop. 187 May Show Clergy's Political Role Is Dwindling," *Los Angeles Times,* 20 November 1994.

14. Conversations with Julian Nava, Professor Emeritus at California State University at Northridge. Nava was the U.S. Ambassador to Mexico during the Jimmy Carter Administration.

15. United Jewish Communities, "Immigration and Support for Refugees," http://www.uja.org/content_display.html?ArticleID = 1629, accessed 25 July 2003; Tom Corfman and Helena Sundman, "Refugee Agencies Dodge Funding Crisis," http://www.chicagoreporter.com/1993/04–93/0493RefugeeAgenciesDodgeFundingCrisis.htm, accessed 25 July 2003.

16. Eric Mann and Kikanza Ramsey, "The Left Choice Is the Best Choice," http://www.thestrategycenter.org/AhoraNow/body_mannramsey_an1_part1.html, accessed 25 July 2003.

17. "Taxpayers Should Not Have to Subsidize College for Illegal Aliens," Federa-

tion of American Immigration Reform, http://www.fairus.org/html/04182108.htm, accessed 25 July 2003.

18. Congressman Charlie Norwood, "The Hidden Catalyst behind America's Rising Number of Uninsured," January 2001, http://www.house.gov/norwood/weekly 010101uninsured.htm, accessed 25 July 2003; Grace-Marie Arnett, "Health Reform Debate in Congress Takes a Free Market Turn," *Galen Institute,* 15 September 1999, http://www.galen.org/news/091599.html, accessed 25 July 2003.

19. Ibid.

20. Ibid.

21. Ibid.

22. Ibid.

23. Becky Smith, "Illegal Aliens: To Teach or Not to Teach," EDUC 420 (class syllabus), Professional Teacher and American School Mary Washington College, http://www.altenforst.de/faecher/englisch/immi/illegal.htm, accessed 25 July 2003.

24. Ibid.

25. "Taxpayers Should Not Have to Subsidize College for Illegal Aliens," Federation for American Immigration Reform, http://www.fairus.org/html/04182108.htm, accessed 3 August 2003; Becky Smith, "Illegal Aliens: To Teach or Not to Teach," EDUC 420 (class syllabus), Professional Teacher and American School Mary Washington College, http://www.altenforst.de/faecher/englisch/immi/illegal.htm, accessed 25 July 2003.

## SELECTED WORKS

Acuña, Rodolfo F. *Anything but Mexican: Chicanos in Contemporary Los Angeles.* London: Verso, 1996.

Armbruster, Ralph, Kim Geron, and Edna Bonacich. "The Assault on California's Latino Immigrants: The Politics of Proposition 187." *International Journal of Urban and Regional Research* 19, no. 4 (1995): 655ff.

Clement, Michael S. *Children at Health Risk.* Oxford: Blackwell Publishers, 2002.

Connell, Rich, and Nora Zamichow. "Fighting for Their Citizenship: About 37,000 in the U.S. Military Have Green Cards. A Fast Track to Naturalization Is the Goal for Many; Others Seek Education, Careers." *Los Angeles Times,* 1 April 2003.

Farr, Kathryn Ann, and Maria Wilson-Figueroa, "Talking about Health and Health Care: Experiences and Perspectives of Latina Women in a Farmworking Community," *Women & Health Spring* 25, no. 2 (1997): 23ff.

The Federation of American Immigration Reform (FAIR). "Immigrants and Public Health: Why Immigration is a Health Care Concern," http://www.fairus.org/html/04149711.htm. Accessed 25 July 2003.

———. "Taxpayers Should Not Have to Subsidize College for Illegal Aliens," http://www.fairus.org/html/04182108.htm. Accessed 25 July 2003.

Hernández, David Manuel. "Divided We Stand, United We Fall: Latinos and Immigration Policy." *Perspectives in Mexican American Studies Annual* 6 (1997): 80ff.

Kramer, Elizabeth J., ed. *Immigrant Women's Health: Problems and Solutions.* Indianapolis, Ind.: Jossey-Bass, 1999.

Lamberg, Lynne. "Nationwide Study of Health and Coping among Immigrant Children and Families. (Medical News and Perspectives.)" *AMA, The Journal of the American Medical Association* 276, no. 18 (13 November 1996): 1455ff.

Mejia, Victor. "Latinos Upset by Proposition 187 Mediation." *Hispanic* (July 1999), 10.

Michelson, Melissa R. "The Effect of National Mood on Mexican American Political Opinion." *Hispanic Journal of Behavioral Sciences* 23, no. 1 (2001): 57ff.

Newton, Lina Y. "Why Some Latinos Supported Proposition 187: Testing Economic Threat and Cultural Identity Hypotheses." *Social Science Quarterly* 81, no. 1 (2000): 180ff.

Stefanic, Jean, and Richard Delgado. *No Mercy: How Conservative Think Tanks and Foundations Changed America's Social Agenda*. Philadelphia: Temple University Press, 1996.

# 8

## AMNESTY PROGRAM

### BACKGROUND

According the *Merriam-Webster Dictionary*, *amnesty* comes from the Greek word amnēstia which means forgetfulness; this comes from amnēstos, forgotten which is from a- + mnasthai, to remember. Its popular meaning became "the act of an authority (as a government) by which pardon is granted to a large group of individuals." It seems simple, but like any other definition, the experiences of the individual construct the meaning of the term. The biases and political interests of the people influence this interpretation of its meaning.

Amnesty has taken on a new meaning in twenty-first-century America. While nativists still perpetuate anti-immigrant beliefs, fewer politicians exploit the issue because of the growth of the Latino population, the need to court the Latino vote, and avoid appearing anti-Latino. The potential of the Latino vote led to a tentative agreement between President George W. Bush and Mexican President Vicente Fox to work on an amnesty plan, which Bush delayed after the terrorist attacks of September 11, 2001. Meanwhile, Latino-elected officials have made immigration a priority issue and are pushing for comprehensive immigration reform legislation, which would give amnesty to millions of Latino immigrants without papers. The devil in the negotiations is the definition of what an amnesty is and whom the law will cover.

Working out an amnesty program is complex. For example, the Bush-Fox plan would have offered amnesty to an estimated 3.5 million undocumented Mexicans, provided they learned English, held jobs, and paid a fine. Most

Mexican American organizations opposed this bill because it would favor Mexico and thus divide the unity among U.S. Latino groups. The Bush-Fox plan would have also included a proposed guest worker program, similar to the *bracero* program by which Mexico sent contracted workers to the United States from 1942–64. U.S. Latino organizations oppose a guest worker program, pointing to tensions and flaws in European nations' guest worker programs, and the problems with the last *bracero* program.

Pro-immigrant groups, along with Mexican President Vicente Fox, prefer using the terms *regularization* and *readjustment of status* to the term *amnesty*.[1] They insist the unauthorized workers have broken no laws and thus have nothing for which to be forgiven. Amnesty is supported by the AFL-CIO and the U.S. Chamber of Commerce along with many religious groups. The League of United Latin American Citizens (LULAC) is one of the biggest supporters of a general amnesty program to legalize long-term immigrants in the United States. LULAC also wants Congress to reject efforts of nativists to curb authorized immigration or create a moratorium on authorized immigration.[2]

General amnesty would give undocumented workers who are physically in the United States the ability to apply for lawful permanent resident status. The applicant would have to be of good moral character and not have been convicted of a criminal offense. The applicant would also have to be continuously present in the United States for a specified time.[3]

The rationale behind amnesty is that U.S. immigration laws are being broken and need fixing. Proponents say that present immigration laws are being used to discriminate against undocumented workers and the Immigration and Naturalization Service is being used to suppress wages, encourage unsafe working conditions, and undermine union organizing. The amnesty law is supposed to regularize these wrongs.

Those opposing amnesty for undocumented workers argue that in reality the word means forgiveness because the illegal alien broke the law and the government is forgiving a crime *illegal aliens* have committed. They say that granting amnesty would disrupt order and lead to disrespect for the law.

Amnesty does not affect all U.S. Latino groups equally since not all Latinos are immigrants. Puerto Ricans are U.S. citizens, and Cubans enjoy preferential treatment as to immigration laws. U.S. immigration policies most directly affect Mexicans and Central Americans, who compose more than two-thirds of the U.S. Latino population and an even higher percentage of Latino immigrants. The attitude of Latinos toward amnesty varies, and while many Latinos resent the competition of immigrants for jobs and housing, Latinos tend to be more tolerant of these newcomers. The hyperbole used by many nativist organizations concerns many Latinos since the nativist organizations do not distinguish between unauthorized and authorized immigrants and U.S.-born and foreign-born Latinos.

Many U.S. Latino leaders claim nativist organizations frame the argument about amnesty in extreme terms. For example, Eric Owens, writing for the conservative *National Freedom Association,* states, "There is a movement growing in California and elsewhere in the nation of which—with help from the media—most Americans are entirely unaware—but enjoys the support of both the California and federal government. . . . This phenomenon has come to be known as the *reconquista* movement (Spanish for "reconquest"). It is highly organized and its main principal revolves around the recapture of the American Southwest by Mexican immigrants, both legal and illegal, and the overturning of the treaty of Guadeloupe [sic] Hidalgo, signed by the United States and Mexico." Owens and others claim that the separatist movement has a "high profile and [is] well-funded."[4] This hyperbole infers that U.S. Latinos have armed militias. While the statement seems absurd at first, many U.S. Latino groups fear that in the hysteria following the September 11, 2001, terrorist attacks, and the wars in Afghanistan and Iraq, the government will look at all immigrants as potential terrorists.

The Mexican government, which once was silent on the rights of undocumented Mexicans, has become more vocal. Besides not appreciating the word amnesty, Mexican officials object to the characterization of Mexican citizens as illegal aliens. Mexican officials join pro-immigrant groups in pointing out that decades of using the term *illegal alien* has criminalized and dehumanized peaceful and law-abiding people whose only sin is to want to work and eat like everyone else. The words send a message that immigrants are criminals from outer space.

Little room exists for exchange of ideas on the question of amnesty. In this debate, old arguments never die and remain personal. Nativists repeat the arguments made at the time of the passage of the 1986 Immigration Control and Reform Act, which allowed 3 million undocumented immigrants to become legal U.S. residents if unauthorized residents could prove they had entered the country before 1982 and had lived here continuously. Of the 3 million eligible unauthorized immigrants, 2.5 million applied and 2 million obtained permanent residence. Although many observers said that the program was highly successful in incorporating the applicants, there are still detractors.

Anti-amnesty voices usually refer to the U.S. Immigration Act of 1965 and claim that it discriminated against the Irish and other Europeans "by giving preference to applicants who had family members legally in the U.S. Since Europeans had not been moving in large numbers to America for many years, they were all but locked out."[5] Actually, the Irish and other European immigrants had more family members in the United States in 1965 than did Latin Americans and Asians. The reason the European immigrants did not take advantage of the law was because they did not want to emigrate. Nativists also allege that non-European, mostly Asians and Latin Americans, manipulated family preference to create a relative-to-relative chain, accounting for more than 90 percent of the annual influx of 600,000 immigrants. Consequently, they claim that fewer Europeans are eligible to immigrate to the United States. For example in 1987, the INS granted 601,516 people permanent U.S. residences; only 3,060 of them were Irish.[6]

The pro-regularization position goes far beyond the ordinary values of human compassion and fairness. Pro-Latino immigrant groups appeal to the United States' historic willingness to embrace new citizens, which has usually been the case, if not always. They ask what public purpose would be served by disrupting or ruining the lives of millions of otherwise hard-working, law-abiding people? What public purpose would be served by permanently ostracizing them in a legal limbo? The defenders of the undocumented immigrants allege that not giving amnesty to undocumented workers encourages an underground economy, which abuses the immigrant.

Some guess that of the 6 million undocumented immigrants in the United States, about 60 percent are Mexican. The remaining immigrants—who come from Canada, Ireland, Poland, and Russia—have overstayed their tourist, work, or student visas. Critics charge that enforcement officers ignore them because they are Caucasian looking. Pro-immigrant groups also argue that stiff penalties on immigrants enacted by the 1996 Immigration Reform Act have not significantly reduced the flow of undocumented workers. They strenuously protest the get-tough tactics and the portrayal of undocumented immigrants as invaders, pointing out that it has led to profiling those who look foreign or undocumented. These policies have consequences such as those on the Arizona-Sonora border where vigilantes operate freely and where hundreds of immigrants, mostly without criminal records, die or suffer physical harm. Further, the get-tough policies, according to pro-immigrant activists, encourage a thriving business of coyotes, or smugglers of human beings.[7]

Finally, the pro-amnesty forces argue amnesty would make it harder for unscrupulous employers to force undocumented workers to work for substandard wages. Because of their hunger, undocumented workers continue to be exploited and are afraid to complain to authorities. Giving these workers authorized status would help stop this exploitation.[8] Working conditions are poor in many factories or agricultural fields, the pay remains at minimum-wage level, and most undocumented workers are without health benefits. Although many undocumented U.S. Latinos join unions, organizing them is extremely difficult. The result of this is that undocumented workers work under conditions most Americans would not tolerate for themselves. Consequently, many unions, once the implacable foes of open immigration, are now supporting amnesty since enforcing working standards and tax laws would be easier if government policies regularized the workers' status.

By the late 1990s, the debate over amnesty had come to a head. Pro-immigrant forces became more aggressive in pressing for amnesty and increased immigration quotas for Latin Americans. In September 2000, almost 10,000 people marched under a drizzling rain in downtown Chicago in favor of a general amnesty for about 6 million unauthorized immigrants. The protestors carried signs that read "No human being is illegal" and "Living wages for all workers." Sebastian Tapia, 34, carried a big crucifix and told reporters, "There were no borders for Christ." The Roman Catholic church supported the marchers.[9] Service Employees International Union Local 880 also supported them as did U.S. Rep. Luis Gutiérrez (D-Chicago) who is of Puerto Rican ancestry.[10]

Much of the debate over regularizing immigration and granting amnesty revolves around the 1986 Immigration and Reform Act (IRCA) and what it did and did not do. Like every other law, IRCA has had its fluctuations. Conservatives applied persistent pressure to modify it; for instance, a 1996 act amended the immigration law, making the status of permanent residents more tenuous. The 1996 act stipulated that authorities could deport immigrants who committed felonies and certain misdemeanors in the United States. That same year Congress passed the 1996 Welfare Reform Act, which barred immigrants who were permanent residents from taking part in most social welfare programs.[11] Moreover, Congress set minimum household income levels for sponsors of immigrants, making sponsorship requirements difficult to fulfill for many families. An estimated 40 percent of Dominicans who migrated before 1996 would no longer be able to do so under the new law.[12]

What human rights activists fear is that in their zeal to bring about a compromise in a new amnesty law, many middle-of-the-road legislators will compromise by taking a get-tough stance and tightening up present immigration laws even further. What human rights activists most fear is a return to a national-origins quota system. For example, if Congress changed U.S. immigration policy by moving away from family reunification granted by the 1965 Immigration Act and reverted to the national-origins quota system, which gave preference to northern Europeans, the effect could be to eliminate or seriously limit the number of Latin Americans entering the United States. Other concerns are that moderates and liberals will go along with giving the Border Patrol more funds and authority. Human rights activists are concerned that Congress will broaden the deportation powers of the Immigration and Naturalization Service and allow the bureau to convict immigrants for lesser misdemeanors while simultaneously increasing criminal penalties for unauthorized residents, violating the human rights of the immigrant. Human rights groups are quite concerned about the legitimization of racial profiling.

Yet another issue that will take on added importance in the debate over amnesty is the international implications of the program. The question of remittances—money sent back to Mexico and Central America—is important to the economies of Latin American countries. But even remittances are controversial, with the anti-amnesty people saying that remittances are examples of how undocumented aliens are draining the U.S. economy by sending resources out of the country. On the other hand, defenders will say that the undocumented workers earned the money and have the right to send it anywhere they choose.

Remittances are vital to the economies of Mexico and Central America. Remittances from their nationals have stabilized the region; stopping them would bankrupt Mexico and Central America. Moreover, trade with Mexico and Central America has favored the United States, and much of the money returns to this country. Indeed, those making U.S. trade policy, aware of the growth potential of the region, have moved to strengthen that relationship. In addition, the stability of the region is vital to the interests of the United States. Many foreign experts say that if all unauthorized immigrants in the United States suddenly returned to their countries of origin, their arrival would severely destabilize the region.

To appreciate the importance of remittances to the stability of the region, the vital role Mexico plays in the region must be considered. Mexico is the second largest trading partner of the United States after Canada. Mexican exports to the United States grew at 19 percent annually after Congress passed NAFTA in 1994, compared with 10 percent before NAFTA. In 1998, U.S. exports to Mexico were up 90 percent, and U.S. imports from Mexico grew nearly 140 percent more than 1993 levels (see Table 8.1).

Despite the popular belief that the United States has generously given Mexico foreign aid, the total aid from the United States Agency for International Development (USAID) gave Mexico $10,877,000 for 1998.[13] (This does not count military aid that amounted to about 26 percent of Mexico's total foreign aid budget in the 1998 fiscal year.) According to the Heritage Foundation, Mexico received more than $15 million in assistance from the United States in the 1998 fiscal year.[14] By contrast, for the fiscal year ending on September 30, 1997, the United States gave Israel $6.72 billion: $6.194 billion in foreign aid allotment and $526 million from agencies such as the

Table 8.1
The United States and Mexico at a Glance

|  | United States | Mexico |
|---|---|---|
| Population (2000) | 284 million | 100 million |
| Population growth (2001 est.) | .9% per annum | 1.6% per annum |
| GDP (2001) | $9,255 billion (1999) | $865 billion (1999) |
| GDP per capita (2001) | $30,200 (1999) | $8,500 (1999) |
| Area | 3,536,278 sq mi | 756,066 sq mi |

*Source:* U.S. Embassy in Mexico, in http://www.usembassy-mexico.gov/eataglance1 .htm.

Department of Commerce, the U.S. Information Agency, and the Pentagon. Such assistance is sizeable for a nation of less than 5.9 million people. Egypt also receives more than $1 billion in assistance annually.[15] Mexico, with a population of 100 million, receives less than $15 million. In short, proponents of amnesty say they are not criticizing foreign aid, just the priorities. According to them, the United States historically has not had a coherent Latin American policy, and it has never had a policy such as the Marshall Plan that economically stabilized Europe for the Americas. The United States has not been generous in foreign aid to most countries of the world, especially third-world countries. In 2001 the United States spent a total of $15 billion on foreign aid, less than 1 percent of the government's $1.9 trillion budget.

In 2000, immigrants sent $23 billion abroad, which became a source of national income throughout Latin America. Mexican workers in the United States sent more than $8 billion to Mexico in 2000, which equals the revenues derived from tourism.[16] From relatives in the United States, the Mexican state of Zacatecas received $1 million per day, which is more than the state receives from its federal government. Mexican President Vicente Fox's campaign in defense of the Mexican expatriate is easier understood in the context of these remittances. Remittances have influenced the politics of other Latin American countries. In Haiti, Nicaragua, El Salvador, and the Dominican Republic, remittances are more than 10 percent of each country's GDP (Gross Domestic Product). The government of El Salvador encouraged Salvadoran citizens in the United States to apply for Temporary Protected Status (TPS.) In 2000, Salvadoran workers sent $1.7 billion in remittances, staving off a collapse of the nation's economy.[17] The advocates for an amnesty program point out that unlike foreign aid, remittances are fully paid by the immigrant workers.

Where most Americans stand on the amnesty debate is up in the air. The economic times are relatively good in contrast to the early 1990s. Historically, this has meant that fewer Americans are anti-immigrant in prosperous times compared with periods of economic stress. A 2000 University of Chicago survey "showed a steep drop in the number of Americans who favored cutting the number of immigrants—from 62 percent in 1994 to 40 percent in 2000." Yet the same survey also showed "a majority—53 percent—agreed that immigration tends to hurt national unity. While 73 percent said immigrants contributed new ideas to the country, 71 percent said they also contribute to higher crime rates."[18]

## SHOULD THERE BE ANOTHER AMNESTY PROGRAM?

### For

Nativists repeat the notion that amnesty encourages a disrespect for the law so often that many Americans believe this assertion without criticism. This is hypocritical since agribusiness interests break laws every day by violating the rights of undocumented workers, yet the public turns the other way. Every day, investigators from the California Occupational Safety and Health Administration (Cal-OHSA) find unsafe working conditions in U.S. factories. According to Cal-OSHA, industries such as apparel and agriculture are hard to regulate because so many workers are undocumented immigrants, and they are afraid to come forward.[19]

Even the Supreme Court has contributed to this charade. On March 27, 2002, the Supreme Court ruled five to four that the federal government may not compel employers to award back pay to undocumented immigrants whom an employer illegally fired for trying to join a labor union. The Supreme Court held that the National Labor Relations Board (NLRB) had avoided the national immigration law's purpose of preventing the hiring of undocumented immigrants when the lower court ordered Hoffman Plastic Compounds Inc. to pay almost $67,000 to José Castro, a Mexican undocumented worker fired for joining a union. Here, the Supreme Court offered employers immunity in violating the rights of undocumented workers and violating labor law. Due to this ruling, undocumented workers cannot join unions for fear of being fired, although the law specifically gives workers the right to join unions. A new amnesty law would give protection to these workers and end union busting.

Amnesty is needed, and makeshift measures like the guest worker program for workers from Mexico or Latin America are no solution, because they further exploit workers who do not gain an equity in society.[20] When the

United States had a guest worker program during and after World War II, there was gross violation of worker rights. Europe had guest worker programs, and they spawned racism in European countries. Americans mainly respect power, and the only power poor people have is the ballot box. Because undocumented workers do not have a vote, politicians and nativists target them.

The present immigration policy of the United States is based on family reunification. Even conservatives such as Utah Republican Senator Orrin Hatch and the conservative Heritage Foundation have supported the principle of family reunification. Many of those to whom Congress would grant amnesty are longtime residents of this country, and most have children who were born here. Immigrants are hard-working people, and for the most part they are younger than white Americans, so they will be productive workers for many years. Most research proves that fewer of them will seek public assistance than is the norm in the general population, and that many of them will become highly skilled professionals if given a chance.[21]

University of Maryland economist Julian Simon says, "Immigration is the same good bargain for Americans that it was 100 years ago—and even more so today because we can provide them even more opportunities to make their dreams come true and enrich our nation as a result. . . . The evidence is clear: Immigrants don't come here to take welfare, they come here to make jobs."[22] Unfortunately, well-funded hate groups distort the facts and malign hardworking people. People forget that as a group, undocumented Latinos represent one of the largest groups of workers killed at the Twin Towers on September 11, 2001. They forget that more than 37,000 non-citizen immigrants, many of whom had parents without documents, fought in the recent war in Iraq; some died for this country.[23]

Some white Americans cannot come to grips with the fact that most of those who will benefit from amnesty do not look like them. In Chicago alone, "[m]ore than 130,000 Chicago residents, mostly from Mexico, could become new citizens by December, and that could translate into increased political power for Latinos."[24] Immigrants are showing that they are assimilating politically, and hundreds of thousands have become citizens, and they are voting. This is going a long way in ending the historical discrimination that has marred this great nation.[25]

At one time the American Federation of Labor (AFL) was the greatest enemy of both unauthorized and authorized immigrants. The AFL has changed its stance and today supports amnesty. Undocumented workers are among the most faithful union members, and their presence creates jobs and expands the economy for higher paying jobs. Still, most Americans have a less favorable view of Latin American immigrants, which is in part based on biases toward their home countries. For instance, a September 6, 2001, Gallup Poll showed that Americans overwhelmingly opposed amnesty or citizenship to undocumented workers or their families. The data also suggest that much of the opposition is because the public believes Congress will grant amnesty or citizenship mainly to Mexicans. What is clear is that the public associates negative stereotypes of Mexico with immigration. Where does the public get these negative views of Mexicans?

The Gallup Poll showed that just 17 percent of Americans in 2001 had a very favorable view of Mexico, ranking well below the 51 percent who had a very favorable view of Canada, 43 percent with a favorable view of Australia, and 41 percent with a favorable view of Great Britain. Mexico was on par with Israel, Egypt, and Brazil.[26] Where do Americans get this view? The media has constructed much of the negative images of immigration from the war on drugs to the negative discourse over unsafe trucks operating on U.S. highways.[27]

Yet U.S. prosperity is tied to Latin America. Today, the United States exports much more to Latin America than the United States buys from it. In addition, at one time the United States did not have a quota on Latin American immigration because Americans claimed they had a common heritage with Latin Americans because Europe had colonized all of the Americas, and the United States took the lead in forming a Pan American Union. The United States has also intervened in the affairs of Latin American countries by overthrowing constitutionally elected presidents.

Ironically, Americans want Latin Americans to be grateful to them. Americans resent when Latin American countries elect communist or even socialist leaders. So why not help those countries help themselves? If every undocumented immigrant were to return home, it would bankrupt those countries. Remittances earned by the sweat of the undocumented workers keep their home lands afloat. A regularization of immigration would help those countries financially and contribute to the health of the region.

Finally, the argument that the immigration acts discriminate against the Irish and other Europeans is incorrect. For years U.S. immigration laws excluded Asians altogether, and no one complained. Today, there are literally hundreds of thousands if not millions of Irish, Poles, Canadians, and others who are in the United States on unauthorized status and are free to move about the country.[28] According to a San Diego newspaper, among an estimated 6 million unauthorized immigrants in the country, about 2 million have intentionally overstayed their visas.[29] An estimated 70,000 unauthorized Poles reside in the United States, including an estimated 40,000 who overstayed tourist and student visas. Before September 11, the United States did not try to stop undocumented immigration of Europeans. Scholars of immigration acknowledge that it was and is much more difficult to get a visitor's or student visa from a third-world country. For instance, crossing to the Canadian border was similar to entering a revolving door or crossing a state line before 9/11. The border patrol waved visitors through unless they appeared to be Latino or from a third-world country. Yet those crossing the Mexican-U.S. border have always been scrutinized.

The United States has granted a large number of visas to refugees from other countries because these refugees were supposedly fleeing tyranny. This country has been generous in admitting hundreds of thousands of Soviet Jews because of anti-Semitism in the former Soviet Union. All the refugees had to show was "a well-founded fear of persecution."[30] Soviet Jews in 1989 alone cost the U.S. government $350 million. Unlike Latino immigrants who are fleeing hunger, Soviet Jews, as refugees, are eligible for public assistance. The United States granted hundreds of thousands of Armenians special status also.[31] In 2000, there were more than 50,000 Armenians in Glendale, California, alone, which is great because they add to diversity of the region. The nativists are against the regularization of immigration because they believe that it will benefit darker-skinned people, changing the racial profile of the United States.

### Against

Amnesty is anything but fair, so what is it? It is the pardoning of criminals. It allows government officials to commit virtually every conceivable violation of U.S. immigration law, and it gives, according to the Federation for American Immigration Reform, "official forgiveness to everyone who violated the laws of the United States. Terms of the agreement under which they were admitted to the United States."[32] Congress has "designed amnesty to be 'fair' to lawbreakers at the expense of law-abiding immigrants and American citizens."[33]

Amnesty betrays the trust of the American people, who through voting and opinion polls have overwhelmingly opposed a liberalization of these laws.[34] Amnesty goes against the will of the American people who are frustrated because Latinos have no regard for immigration laws. A 2001 Scripps Howard poll showed that only 29 percent of the 1,000 Texans polled favored amnesty.[35] On September 6, 2001, the Fox News Channel asked, "Should we give amnesty to illegal Mexican immigrants?" Nine percent replied yes, and 91 percent replied no.[36] A democracy is the rule of the majority.

In 1986, Congress passed the first amnesty law, the Immigration Reform and Control Act (IRCA), which forgave the crimes of millions of illegal aliens. According to good sources, IRCA cost taxpayers $78.7 billion in benefits over 10 years.[37] Barely three years after the passage of IRCA, Congress allowed another 2.7 million illegal aliens into the country. The pretext was that they were working in agriculture and had been working there for four years or more. To make things worse, the law, based on the 1965 Immigration Act that promoted family reunification, legalized millions of their dependents. Color has nothing to do with the issue. Instead, the issue is that these people are uneducated and will be left behind in today's economy. Their financial disadvantages affect society as they do not earn enough money to buy car insurance.[38]

Granting amnesty is similar to pardoning federal prisoners, releasing them into society and then claiming there is no crime problem because the prisons are empty. Handing out amnesty sends the message to illegal aliens that breaking the law is OK and that coming into the United States and taking the country's welfare will result in Congress forgiving every one in time, even rewarding them. The result will be that America will have lost control of its borders.

The amnesty of illegal aliens also breaks down the assimilation of Latinos because they never forget Spanish and their foreign customs and traditions. These uneducated people will bring in more uneducated people who will drag down the quality of the schools. They will detract from the high-skills, high-wage economy the United States is aiming for in the twenty-first century.[39]

Amnesty is not only about Mexicans, but it is also about people from El Salvador, Nicaragua, and the rest of Latin America. In 1997, Congress passed a law giving most asylum-seeking Nicaraguans and Cubans permanent residency. Although the Nicaraguan Adjustment and Central American Relief Act did not give Salvadorans, Guatemalans, and Soviet bloc asylum seekers equal status with Nicaraguans and Cubans, it suspended their deportation. Under pre-1997 rules, if they had been here for seven years and could prove that deportation would result in a personal hardship to the asylum seeker, a permanent resident spouse, parent, or child, the INS granted asylum. Latino organizations were not even satisfied with this liberal policy. In December 2000, Clinton signed the Legal Immigration Family Equality Act, which made Salvadorans and Guatemalans eligible for permanent residency if they had applied for permanent residency or asylum before 1991 or 1990 (depending on the program), had remained in the U.S. for seven years, and were of good moral character. If they could prove deportation would cause extreme hardship, they would be admitted even if they had been previously deported. The INS made these liberal rules even more liberal and assumed a hardship, so the asylum seeker did not even have to go before a judge to prove his or her case. Instead, the INS officers heard the case. The United States has the most liberal immigration laws in the world.[40]

Mexican President Vicente Fox has the nerve to demand an amnesty for 3 million illegal Mexican immigrants, besides demanding hundreds of thousands of guest worker visas and benefits for illegal immigrants. Who elected Fox president of the United States?[41] Mexico is trying to retake the Southwest. To allow more Mexicans into the country would be detrimental. They, along with other Latinos, are already 13 percent of the nation.

## QUESTIONS

1. Are all undocumented residents Latinos? What stereotypes are there about Latinos?

2. Read the article by Ron Unz, "The End of White America: An Exchange" *One Nation,* November 1999. Available at http://www.findarticles.com/cf_1/m1061/4_108/57231207/p1/article.jhtml?term= + Racially + +mixed + +people + +Social + +aspects, accessed 26 July 2003. Where did you hear the name of this article before? Is the tone similar or different from that in the quotation at the beginning of the chapter? Would Unz be for or against amnesty?

3. Latino activists at first opposed the Immigration Reform and Control Act (IRCA) of 1986 because it included employer sanctions, that is, fining employers who employ undocumented workers. Latino activists opposed sanctions because it was a way of starving out the undocumented worker.[42] Discuss the reasons why Latino activists opposed sanctions. Why would anti-immigrant organizations support sanctions?

4. IRCA also allocated $1 billion a year for four years under the State Legislation Impact Assistance Grant for classes in English, U.S. history, and government, which were mandatory for all amnesty applicants. On March 1, 1989, an emergency funding bill assisted the resettlement of an unanticipated surge of 25,000 refugees from the Soviet Union. To pay for this program, it was proposed to take $200 million away from the funds allocated by Congress for the amnesty program.[43] How would taking away funds from the amnesty program cause tension between the different pro-immigrant groups?

5. Go to the Internet. Try to pull up "David Bacon, 'Labor's Push for New Amnesty for Immigrants,' *Pacific News Service,* 21 June 2000." Labor organizations historically opposed open immigration because it said that immigrants made union organization more difficult and drove down the wages of American workers. Based on the article, why do you believe labor organizations changed their policies? What was their resolution in supporting amnesty?

6. Read Greg Burton, "Amnesty Essay Striking Sparks," *The Salt Lake Tribune,* 9 September 2001, or go to an Internet search engine and type "Howard Stephenson and amnesty." Based on your reading, why did state Sen. Howard Stephenson's support of amnesty for unauthorized immigrants generate such a backlash? Stephenson wrote, "Surely we can find room for their children in our schools." His critics called him a traitor. One wrote, "If you support giving illegal Mexicans legal status you will not be re-elected. . . . This is not your

country to give away so be careful what you support and what you do." Is it possible to have a dispassionate discourse on the topic?

7. Study the range of organizations and individuals opposing amnesty. What does your research suggest about the debate over amnesty?

8. Once again explain the difference between national origins and family preference. Does the principle of amnesty further or detract from the present policy of family preference? How would it differ in the case of national origins? Which is more equitable and why?

9. Why did the American Federation of Labor at one time oppose immigration in general? Why has it changed its opinion?

10. Why are most U.S. Latinos, the overwhelming number of whom are either born in the United States or are authorized residents, in favor of amnesty? Discuss.

11. Why is the discussion of immigration bogged down on ideological lines? Why do you believe there are so many misconceptions?

12. Why would amnesty advocates bring up the case of foreign aid to the Middle East as an example of disparate treatment? What are remittances? Are these workers taking money away from Americans or in reality buying stability for the region?

13. Did the special status of Soviet Jews, Armenians, Cubans, and other immigrants help their assimilation into American society? Why or why not?

14. Is race an issue in the question of amnesty? Why or why not?

## NOTES

1. "Limited Amnesty for Immigrants," *Chicago Tribune*, 6 August 2001, http://chicagotribune.com/news/opinion/chi-0108060024aug06.story?coll=chi-newsopinion-utl, accessed 25 July 2003.

2. Adopted by the LULAC National Assembly on June 9, 2001, at the 72nd LULAC National Convention in Phoenix, Ariz. http://www.lulac.org/Issues/Platform.html, accessed 25 July 2003.

3. National Coalition for Dignity and Amnesty for Undocumented Immigrants, Letter to U.S. House of Representatives and U.S. Senate, "Support a General Unconditional Amnesty," Campaign for General Amnesty, 1999–2000, http://www.petitiononline.com/i1pacman/petition.html, accessed 3 August 2003.

4. Eric Owens, "Mexicans Want America's Southwest: A Growing Movement among Mexican Americans that is Antagonistic to All Other Americans Seeks to Take Back the Southwest from the United States," *The Spotlight*, 25 December 2000, http://www.denverspiritualcommunity.org/SPOTLIGHT/SPOTLIGHTNewsDec00.htm#anchor961599, accessed 25 July 2003.

5. Quoted in Ed Magnuson, "The Re-greening of America; a New Wave of Irish Immigrants is Showing Its Muscle," *Time* 133, no. 12 (20 March 1989): 30ff.

6. Quoted in Ed Magnuson, "The Re-greening of America; a New Wave of Irish Immigrants is Showing Its Muscle," *Time* 133, no. 12 (20 March 1989): 30ff; Antonio McDaniel, "The Dynamic Racial Composition of the United States: An American Dilemma Revisited," *Daedalus* 124, no. 1 (January 1995): 179ff.

7. José Palafox, "Border Blockades Spark Hate Crimes, Vigilantism," http://www.americas.org/News/Features/200009_Border/nativistattacks.asp, accessed 25 July 2003.

8. Molly Ivins, "Ups, Downs of Amnesty for Immigrants," *Abilene Reporter-News*, 23 July 2001; Molly Ivins, "Proposed Worker Amnesty Just Isn't Fair," *Ashland Daily Tidings* (Oregon), http://dailytidings.com/2001/news0723/opinion/dt_opinion-01.php, accessed 25 July 2003.

9. Ana Mendieta, "Protesters Rally to Get Amnesty for Immigrants," reprinted from *Chicago Sun Times*, 24 September 2000, available in SEIU Local 880 Newsletter, http://www.seiu880.org/inthenews_articles/protesters_rally.htm, accessed 25 July 2003.

10. Ana Mendieta, "Protesters Rally to Get Amnesty for Immigrants," reprinted from *Chicago Sun Times*, 24 September 2000, available in SEIU Local 880 Newsletter, http://www.seiu880.org/inthenews_articles/protesters_rally.htm, accessed 25 July 2003; "H.R.500. Sponsor: Rep Gutierrez, Luis V. (introduced 2/7/2001) Latest Major Action: 2/7/2001 Referred to House committee Title: To revise various provisions of the Immigration and Nationality Act. Summary as of: 2/7/2001," http://thomas.loc.gov/cgi-bin/bdquery/z?d107:HR00500:@@@D&summ2 = m&, accessed 25 July 2003; Mike Dorning, "Gutierrez Bill Proposes Immigration Amnesty," *Chicago Tribune*, 6 February 2001, http://www.tepeyac.org/amnistia/i_opinionpublica_6feb01.htm, accessed 25 July 2003.

11. Christine Marie Sierra, Teresa Carrillo, Louis DeSipio, and Michael Jones-Correa, "Latino Immigration and Citizenship," *PS: Political Science & Politics* 33, no. 3 (September 2000): 535ff.

12. Ibid.

13. "The US and Mexico at a Glance: Foreign Aid from USAID (in thousands of dollars)," U.S. Embassy in Mexcio, http://www.usembassy-mexico.gov/eataglance1.htm, accessed 3 August 2003.

14. Brett D. Schaefer, "Does U.S. Foreign Assistance Elicit Support for U.S. Policy? Not at the United Nations," *Policy Research and Analysis. The Heritage Foundation*, 22 October 1999, http://www.heritage.org/Research/InternationalOrganizations/BG1335.cfm, accessed 3 August 2003.

15. Kathy Kiely, "Importance of Foreign Aid Is Hitting Home," *USA Today*, 4 December 2001; U.S. Embassy in Mexico, "The US and Mexico at a Glance," http://www.usembassy-mexico.gov/eataglance1.htm, accessed 3 August 2003; Washington Report on the Middle-East, "U.S. Financial Aid to Israel: Figures, Facts, and Impact: Summary. Benefits to Israel of U.S. Aid Since 1949 (As of 1 November 1997)," http://www.wrmea.com/html/us_aid_to_israel.htm#Israel, accessed 3 August 2003.

16. Eric Brazil, "Sending Dollars to Latin America: Wiring Money Home—Cheaply, Credit Unions Cut Costs for Immigrants," *The San Francisco Chronicle*, 24 June 2001.

17. "The Salvadoran Banking System at the End of 2000," *Informabansa*, no. 21 (May 2001): 2.

18. Howard LaFranchi, "Support Grows for Immigration, but Reservations Linger," *Christian Science Monitor*, 14 August 2001, http://www.csmonitor.com/2001/0814/p2s2-uspo.html, accessed 25 July 2003.

19. Aurelio Rojas, "Growers Hire Illegals with Impunity; Workers Pay the Price for Lax INS Scrutiny of Farm Industry," *The San Francisco Chronicle*, 19 March 1996, http://www.sfgate.com/chronicle/special/immigration/, accessed 25 July 2003.

20. Ibid.

21. Jim Specht, "Recent Laws Bring Wave of Newcomers; Policy of Reuniting Families Shapes Decade-Long Influx," *Chicago Sun-Times,* 8 December 1996.

22. Ibid.

23. National Coalition for Dignity and Amnesty for Undocumented Immigrants, "Experts: Illegal Workers Pay Dividend," *New York Times,* 15 October 2000, http://www.dignityandamnesty.org/i_analisis_diversos_15oct00.htm, accessed 25 July 2003; Rich Connell and Nora Zamichow, "Fighting for Their Citizenship: About 37,000 in the U.S. Military Have Green Cards. A Fast Track to Naturalization Is the Goal for Many; Others Seek Education, Careers," *Los Angeles Times,* 1 April 2003.

24. Jorge Oclander, "New Citizens Could Power Latino Bloc," *Chicago Sun-Times,* 17 July 1994.

25. Ibid.

26. Lydia Saad, "Americans Clearly Oppose Amnesty for Illegal Mexican Immigrants; Poll Analyses: Few Favor Increasing Immigration More Generally," *Gallup News Service,* 6 September 2001, http://www.gallup.com/poll/releases/pr010906.asp, accessed 25 July 2003.

27. Ibid.

28. "No Visa-Free Travel to US for Central Europeans," *Migration News* 4, no. 9 (September 1997), http://migration.ucdavis.edu/mn/archive_mn/sep_1997–15mn.htm.

29. David Washburn and David Hasemyer, "Exploited Visas Making 'a Sieve' of U.S. Border," *The San Diego Union-Tribune,* 28 October 2001, in *U.S. Border Control,* http://www.usbc.org/info/everything2001/1001exploitedvisas.htm.

30. Stephen Chapman, "Which Refugees Deserve Our Help," *The Baton Rouge State Times,* 16 September 1989.

31. Susan Ferriss, "Census Data Reveal Wide Immigrant Diversity: Ex-Soviets among the Poorest," *The San Francisco Chronicle,* 23 September 1993.

32. Federation for American Immigration Reform, "Fairness to Americans and Legal Immigrants Requires Opposing Another Amnesty for Illegal Aliens," July 2000, http://www.fairus.org/html/07431007.htm, accessed 25 July 2003. FAIR consistently opposes any liberalization of the immigration laws.

33. Ibid.

34. Edward Hegstrom, "Poll Discerns Anti-Amnesty Sentiment: Just 29 percent of Texans Favor It for Illegal Immigrants," *Houston Chronicle,* 10 September 2001.

35. Ibid.

36. "Should We Give Amnesty to Illegal Mexican Immigrants?," Fox News Channel, 6 September 2001, http://www.americanpatrol.com/POLLS/Polls.html, accessed 25 July 2003.

37. David Simcox, "Measuring the Fallout: The Cost of the IRCA Amnesty After 10 Years," Center for Immigration Studies, May 1997, http://www.cis.org/articles/1997/back197.htm, accessed 5 August 2003; The Federation for American Immigration Reform, "Immigration 101: A Primer on Immigration and the Need to Reform," 2000, http://www.fairus.org/html/immigration101.pdf, accessed 3 August 2003.

38. Report on the Legalized Alien Population, Immigration and Naturalization Service, M-375, March 1992; Federation of American Immigration Reform, "Why Amnesty for Illegal Aliens Was—and Remains—a Bad Idea," May 1997, http://www.fairus.org/html/04134705.htm, accessed 25 July 2003.

39. Federation of American Immigration Reform, "Why Amnesty for Illegal Aliens Was—and Remains—a Bad Idea," May 1997, http://www.fairus.org/html/04134705.htm, accessed 25 July 2003.

40. Ibid.

41. Yeh Ling-Ling, "United States Must Reject Mexico's Amnesty Demands," *The Union Leader,* (Manchester, New Hampshire) 13 August 2001, VDARE.COM—http://www.vdare.com/francis/contra_gigot.htm, accessed 25 July 2003.

42. Leo R. Chávez, "The Power of the Imagined Community: The Settlement of Undocumented Mexicans and Central Americans in the United States," *American Anthropologist* 96, no 1: 52–73, 1994.

43. Margo De Ley, "Taking from Latinos to Assist Soviet Immigrants—an Affront to Fairness," *Los Angeles Times,* 19 March 1989; Nativo López, "To Friends of Immigrants, National Committee for Fair Immigration Reform, a Fact Sheet," 4 April 1989; Stephen Moore, "A Pro-Family, Pro-Growth Legal Immigration Policy for America," *Background. The Heritage Foundation,* no. 735, (November 1989): 1–7; Carlos Alberto Montaner, "Robando Cerebros," *La Opinión,* 4 January 1992.

## SELECTED WORKS

The American Civil Liberties Union, http://www.aclu.org/library/aaidcard.html, accessed 25 July 2003.

Boswell, Thomas, and James Curtis. *The Cuban-American Experience. Culture, Images and Perspectives.* Totaowa, N.J.: Rowman and Allanheld, 1984.

Cornelius, Wayne, with Yasuo Kuwahara. *The Role of Immigrant Labor in the U.S. and Japanese Economies: A Comparative Study of San Diego and Hamamatsu, Japan.* San Diego, Calif.: Center for U.S.-Mexican Studies, University of California, San Diego, 1998.

de la Garza, Rodolfo, Louis DeSipio, F. Chris Garcia, John Garcia, and Angelo Falcon. *Latino Voices: Mexican, Puerto Rican, and Cuban Perspectives on American Politics.* Boulder, Colo.: Westview, 1992.

Delgado, Hector L. *New Immigrants, Old Unions: Organizing Undocumented Workers in Los Angeles.* Philadelphia, Pa.: Temple University Press, 1993.

Díaz, Elvia. "Democrats Join Latinos in Fight on Immigration. Public Assistance in Jeopardy." *The Arizona Republic,* 9 July 2003.

"Hispanic/Latinos in the Afghanistan and Iraq War 2002–03: Casualties," http://www.rose-hulman.edu/~delacova/latinos-war.htm. Accessed 25 July 2003.

Kiely, Kathy. "Importance of Foreign Aid Is Hitting Home." *USA Today,* 4 December 2001.

LaFranchi, Howard. "Support Grows for Immigration, but Reservations Linger." *Christian Science Monitor,* 14 August 2001. Http://www.csmonitor.com/2001/0814/p2s2-uspo.htm. Accessed 25 July 2003.

Ling-Ling, Yeh. "United States Must Reject Mexico's Amnesty Demands." *The Union Leader,* 13 August 2001, http://www.vdare.com/francis/contra_gigot.htm. Accessed 25 July 2003.

Muller, Thomas. *California's Newest Immigrants: A Summary.* Washington, D.C.: Urban Institute Press, 1984.

Saad, Lydia. "Americans Clearly Oppose Amnesty for Illegal Mexican Immigrants. Poll Analyses: Few Favor Increasing Immigration More Generally." *Gallup*

*News Service*, 6 September 2001. Http://www.gallup.com/poll/releases/pr010906.asp. Accessed 25 July 2003.

"The Salvadoran Banking System at the End of 2000." *Informabansa*, no. 21 (May 2001).

Sierra, Christine Marie, Teresa Carrillo, Louis DeSipio, and Michael Jones-Correa. "Latino Immigration and Citizenship." *PS: Political Science & Politics* 33, no. 3 (2000): 535ff.

Tomas Rivera Policy Institute. "Latino Electorate Continues to Speak out on Issues: Tomas Rivera Policy Institute." *La Opinion*, 6 February 1997. Http://www.azteca.net/aztec/immigrat/trc_poll.html. Accessed 25 July 2003.

# 9

# U.S. MILITARY AND POLITICAL PRESENCE IN CUBA

## BACKGROUND

Whether the United States violates the sovereignty of Cuba with its economic embargo of the island and its military presence in Guantánamo Bay is an important issue. It not only affects U.S. international relations but also causes tension between Cuban Americans and other U.S. Latinos. For instance, it has caused tensions with the Hispanic Congressional Caucus with Cuban American representatives insisting that members adopt an anti-Fidel Castro posture.

Critics of the United States view the stationing of U.S. troops in Guantánamo Bay Naval Base and its economic embargo as a flagrant violation of international law. According to critics, the maintenance of the base and economic embargo amount to a denial of the Cuban people's right to self-determination and sovereignty.[1] Others disagree and argue the United States should not pull its troops out of Cuba because the presence of U.S. forces on the island is vital to the interests of the United States and the region, and the presence proves the United States' commitment to human rights. The supporters of the U.S. presence say the embargo is important because the embargo weakens Fidel Castro and his communist regime while sending a message to the world that the United States does not approve of dictatorships.

## The History

The Cuban independence movement predated the Spanish American War, and the Spanish crown forced Cuban revolutionaries such as José Martí into exile in the 1880s. Many exiles spent time in the United States and returned to the island in 1895 when they began an armed struggle to gain independence from Spain. In 1898, relations between the United States and Spain worsened; pressured by American sugar growers in Cuba and a jingoistic press at home, the United States entered the war. Many reasons existed for this: Cuba is just 90 miles off the Florida coast, and Americans had always considered it within America's sphere of influence and vital to the security of the region. The peace treaty ending the war was between Spain and the United States, and the Cuban revolutionaries were not part of the negotiations. The terms of the Treaty of Paris gave the United States Guam and Puerto Rico and political control of the Philippines. Cuba was supposed to be an independent nation; however, Cuba was forced to incorporate the Platt Amendment into the Cuban constitution, which restricted Cuba's right to reach treaties with other nations and authorized the United States to intervene in Cuban affairs. The Platt Amendment also guaranteed the United States' right to lease property "in perpetuity" at Guantánamo Bay for building a U.S. naval base. Cubans at first refused to sign the U.S.-approved constitution but then signed the Constitution as a precondition for the United States' withdrawal from the island.[2]

American growers controlled Cuba's sugar economy, and there was widespread government corruption and disregard for the poor. Cubans made some progress by building railroads and seaports, and eliminating yellow fever.[3] The Cuban economy depended on the United States, which in turn supported dictators who favored American interests. During the Great Depression of the 1930s, Cuban students led protests to reform the state and Sgt. Fulgencio Batista, leader of the noncommissioned officers, became the military commander of the Cuban armed forces and the de facto head of state.[4]

U.S. President Franklin D. Roosevelt canceled the Platt Amendment in the 1930s but continued to rent Guantánamo Bay. In 1940, Batista was elected president of Cuba, and during World War II the sugar industry prospered. In 1944, Batista lost the presidential election and left for the United States. In 1952, Batista returned and led a coup d'etat and began a repressive and notoriously corrupt administration.

## The Embargo

Enter Fidel Castro, a young student activist, who led an unsuccessful attack on the Moncada Army Barracks in Santiago de Cuba on 26 July 1953. After a six month prison term, Castro went into exile in Mexico, organizing the 26th of July Movement. Joined by the Argentinean Ernesto "Che" Guevara in December of 1956, Castro, with fewer than 60 revolutionaries on the yacht *Granma*, landed in Oriente Province. Unsuccessful, the survivors fled to the Sierra Maestre Mountains, where the rebels waged a guerrilla war. After prolonged fighting, the revolutionaries entered Havana in January 1959 and took control of the government.

The new government vowed to end corruption, promote Cuban nationalism, and improve the lives of the poorer classes. Foreigners and large landowners owned much of the island, which was dependent on a single crop—sugar. The new government's emphasis on leveling society alienated much of the middle and upper classes and threatened U.S. corporations that had strong investments on land.[5] To lessen dependence on sugar, Castro concentrated on industrialization. Unable to get aid from the United States, Castro signed a treaty with the Soviet Union in 1960. The Soviet Union would give Cuba a massive amount of industrial equipment and technical assistance in return for sugar. Meanwhile, the Cuban government nationalized properties belonging to Americans, which included 36 large sugar mills, the national phone system, the national electrical system, all oil refineries, and all U.S.-owned banks. The United States retaliated with a trade embargo, placing sanctions on any country trading with Cuba.

In 1961 Castro announced that the revolution was a socialist revolution. He began a massive education and literacy campaign and poured resources into the health system. Meanwhile, relations with the United States worsened as the United States sponsored an ill-fated plan to invade Cuba at the Bay of Pigs using Cuban American volunteers. A year and a half later a crisis erupted over Russian nuclear missiles on Cuban soil. Led by the United States, all the Organization of American States (OAS) but Mexico broke diplomatic relations with Cuba. Meanwhile, there was a continuous exodus out of Cuba of former Batista supporters and members of the discontented middle class. This wave was in great part composed of *criollos* (descendants of Spaniards), who formed an exile colony in Miami. A second wave of emigrants left the island during the 1970s. This group included many who did not approve of socialism and/or the policies of the new government and its growing dependence on the Soviet Union. This wave also included middle-class Cubans who did not want to endure the poverty induced by the U.S. embargo, a general leveling of society, and reallocation of resources.

Meanwhile, the Cuban government made gains in the fields of education and health. Critics say Cuban education had always been better than in other Latin American republics. In 1899, Cuba registered only 16 percent of the school-age population in school, a figure that rose to 40 percent in 1902. By

1931, the literacy rate had reached 72 percent, but literacy never rose higher than that and was often limited to lighter-skinned Cubans. School enrollment rates did not rise above 60 percent. The revolutionary government sent nearly 300,000 children and adults into the countryside to teach literacy. By 1979, the literacy rates in Cuba rose above 90 percent, comparable to the rates in the United States and other developed countries.

Cuban public policy also promoted health care for every citizen, building free clinics throughout the country, even in rural areas. Life expectancy among Cuban men today is 74 years and 77 years among Cuban women. Infant mortality rates are about 12 per 1,000 births. Cuba has sent medical assistance to other third-world countries and has sent medical relief teams to countries struck by national disasters such as earthquakes. Critics allege that Castro squandered money by sending troops to Somalia and Angola to help revolutionaries, which further alienated the United States. On the other hand, many third-world and European countries applauded Cuba's support of revolutions.

Meanwhile, the economic embargo hurt Cuba and isolated the island from the United States. Plots to overthrow Castro unsettled the Cuban government, which tightened security. In April 1980, a crisis occurred when six Cuban dissenters drove to the Peruvian Embassy in Havana seeking asylum. Peruvians refused to turn over the dissenters to Cuban authorities. Encouraged by this, thousands of Cubans descended on the embassy asking for asylum. Castro opened the Mariel port, west of Havana, letting anyone who wanted to emigrate leave the island.[6] More than 120,000 undocumented Cubans arrived in Florida. But the arrival of so many Cubans unsettled Cuban Americans because many *Marielitos* had criminal records and allegedly many were mentally disturbed. The *Marielitos* also had darker skin and this bothered many nativists. In 1984, Cuba and the United States came to an agreement and set a quota of 20,000 Cubans whom the United States would allow to emigrate legally to the country annually. The agreement ended soon after when the United States established Radio Martí in 1985, which broadcast anti-Castro propaganda to the island. Both countries reinstated the agreement in 1987, and by 1998 only six countries sent more authorized immigrants to the United States than Cuba, and more Cubans arrive through authorized channels than by boat.[7] The Mariel and later arrivals tended to be mostly working class immigrants and large percentages were black or mulatto.

After 1991, deprived of aid from the Soviet Union and its bloc, the Cuban economy worsened. Meanwhile, the United States tightened the economic embargo. Foreign subsidiaries of American companies were forbidden to trade with Cuba, which worsened economic conditions on the island. Throughout this period, Guantánamo, which periodically has housed Cuban,

Haitian, and Dominican refugees, remained a point of irritation. In 2002 the United States housed Taliban and other suspected terrorists there.

## Cuban Americans

Throughout this history there has been controversy about what the policy of the United States should be. The Cuban Americans who made their home in Miami and other U.S. cities actively pursued a policy that the United States framed in Cold War terminology: democracy versus communism. For them, Castro was the problem, the symbol of communist oppression on the island, and the reason they could not return home. Cuban Americans formed special interest organizations like the Cuban American National Foundation (CANF), headed by the late Jorge Mas Canosa, who had links with conservative Republicans.[8] Cuban Americans were better educated than other U.S. Latinos and, although much smaller in number, enjoyed considerable influence in the U.S. Latino community. For example, only 5 percent of the U.S. Latino population lives in Miami, but Cuban Americans own 40 of the largest Latino-owned businesses in the country.[9] Cuban Americans own 30,000 total businesses, by far the highest rate of per capita ownership of U.S. businesses among Latinos.[10]

This economic power gave the Cuban American community an influence far greater than its numbers. For example, in February 1996, Cuban Russian-made fighters shot down two civilian planes, killing four Cuban Americans who were members of Brothers to the Rescue, a militant Miami-based anti-Castro group. Brothers to the Rescue were dropping anti-Castro literature over Havana just before the Cuban planes attacked. Cuba defended shooting down the planes because they violated Cuban air space. The United States supported the Cuban Americans, alleging that the downings occurred in international airspace.[11] Pro-Cuban American members of Congress pushed for a tightening of the embargo. Congress then passed the Helms-Burton Act, which denied visas to anyone who did business with anyone who currently held property that had been confiscated by the Castro government during the revolution. The act gave American citizens the right to file in domestic courts for financial compensation for the property they lost. Finally, the Helms-Burton Act restricted the movement of Cuban diplomats within the United States, closed off charter air routes to and from Cuba, and expanded Radio Martí.[12] Thirty-two members of the Organization of American States—every Latin American nation, but not the United States—supported a resolution labeling Helms-Burton as a violation of international law. Critics argued that this was a blatant violation of Cuba's sovereignty: first because the airplanes had violated Cuban airspace and second because it was intervening in the internal affairs of a sovereign nation and violated U.S. citizens' right to travel.

### Guantánamo Bay

Apart from the embargo, tensions arose because of Guantánamo and the incidents surrounding a boy named Elián González. Guantánamo is 45 square miles on Cuba's southeastern coast, and houses both military and civilian personnel. Ocean surrounds the naval base there on three sides, and on the fourth side, U.S. Marines guard the bay. The U.S. presence has been a thorn in the side of the Cuban government since well before Castro took power in Cuba. Pentagon documents suggest that the United States has probably stored nuclear weapons at Guantánamo since the 1962 Cuban missile crisis.

The U.S. Marines set up base at Guantánamo on June 6, 1898, at the beginning of Spanish-American War. In 1903, under pressure from the United States, Cuba leased Guantánamo for 2,000 gold coins a year, today valued at $4,085. The stated reasons were to protect Cuba and provide defense for the United States. Critics charge that the United States used the base to keep military personnel who would ensure that leaders friendly to the

The Cuban refugee camp at Guantánamo Bay Naval base is viewed from the Cuban side of the border. (AP/Wide World Photos)

United States maintained power. In 1934, the two countries renegotiated and stipulated that if the United States abandoned the fort, or through mutual consent, Guantánamo would revert to Cuba. Castro has complained that the base is an affront to Cuban sovereignty and has refused to take payment for the bay's rental. Critics charge a reason that the United States holds on to Guantánamo is to spy on Cuba. Another reason is that Guantánamo is strategically situated and is a base for anti-drug smuggling operations. Yet the question is whether the United States has a legal right to be there.

## The Case of Elián González

In November 1999, six-year-old Elián González was found clinging to an inner tube in the Atlantic Ocean off the coast of Florida. His mother and 10 other people drowned when their boat sank en route from Cuba to the United States. Elián was one of three survivors. For the next five months, Elián became a prize in a struggle between the Cuban exiles in Miami's Little Havana barrio and the people of Cuba. The Miami Cubans showered Elián with toys and gifts, and he became a TV superstar. A great-uncle, Lázaro González, and his daughter, Marisleysis González, led a campaign to keep Elián in the United States against the wishes of his father, Juan Miguel González, who traveled to the United States to reclaim his six-year-old son. When Elián's father and his Miami relatives could not come to an agreement, immigration officials resorted to a dawn raid on the Miami house on 22 April 2000, after which government authorities reunited Elián with his father in Washington, D.C.

Lázaro González and his family were supported by the anti-Castro Cuban exile groups, including the Free Cuba Foundation, the Cuban American National Foundation (CANF), and the refugee support group called Brothers to the Rescue. Protesters threatened to burn Miami if the U.S. government returned the boy they called "a little miracle" to Cuba. Members of the Congressional Black Caucus supported Juan Miguel González as did the National Council of Churches and various other religious groups. They said a father had the right to his son and that the United States would be violating Cuban sovereignty if it did not give Elián back to his father.

Meanwhile, the Latino community became divided over the Elián case. For some time Antonio González, president of the prestigious Willie C. Velasquez Institute of the Southwest Voter Registration Education Project, has been sending delegations to Cuba.[13] At the time of the incident, the Mexican government maintained relations with Cuba, which led to tensions between Mexicans in the United States and Cubans over attacks on the Mexican government. When the former chair of the Hispanic Congressional Caucus, Rep. Xavier Becerra, visited the island, Cuban members of the caucus resigned. Most Latinos felt that parental rights were utmost in the situation and that the boy belonged with his father. Coverage of the controversy dominated the front pages of Spanish-language newspapers, newscasts on Univision and Telemundo, and major mainstream news outlets across the country. Meanwhile, Cuban Americans pressured Latino groups to support them.[14] This lobbying was largely unsuccessful, although national groups such as Congressional Hispanic Caucus, the National Council of La Raza, and the Mexican American Legal Defense and Educational Fund (MALDEF) remained silent. Latino politicos avoided the issue with the exception of Rep. José E. Serrano (D-N.Y.), a Puerto Rican who said, "I'm very bitter and angry about this." The general Latino sentiment was that the United States had routinely deported Mexicans, Dominicans, Colombians, Africans, and others, so why should there be special treatment for Elián?[15] Further, "A Miami Herald poll . . . showed a sharp divide in South Florida over the Elián case, with more than 80 percent of Cuban Americans saying the child should remain in the United States and a similarly large share of whites and blacks saying the opposite. But non-Cuban Latinos were almost evenly split."[16] Little doubt exists that there were consequences from the Elián González case.

## SHOULD THE UNITED STATES MAINTAIN A MILITARY AND POLITICAL PRESENCE IN CUBA?

### For

The United States is bartering Cuban freedom away for trade concessions. Former President Bill Clinton signed a $78 billion agriculture spending bill that had an amendment that lifted the U.S. sanctions against the sale of food and medicine to Cuba. Who supported the bill? Liberal religious and humanitarian groups, the American Farm Bureau, and pharmaceutical companies who want to cash in on the new Cuba market.[17] Opposition to the embargo relates more to money than human rights. The embargo should not end until Cuba is free from Castro's tyranny.[18]

Cuban American exiles are loyal Americans who also love Cuba. Cuban Americans resent the dictatorship that oppresses Cuba. Cuban Americans support the embargo and do not believe it should be lifted. If anything, the embargo does not go far enough. The United States should launch a true blockade of the island.[19] If the embargo ends, Castro will have access to the World Bank, and the United States will subsidize his cruel and inefficient communist bureaucracy.

Most Cubans on the island do not support Castro. Cubans do not have a free press, and Castro jails dissidents. Castro squandered the $100 to $150 billion the Soviet bloc sent to Cuba on "Wars of Liberation" in Latin America and Africa, interfering with the sovereignty of other nations. Embargos work—witness the attempt to isolate South Africa and Haiti.[20]

Fidel Castro rules the island through intimidation and denies Cuba's citizens basic human rights such as freedom of speech and dissent. If the United States tolerates a dictatorship 90 miles from its shores, what credibility does it have as the leader of the free world? The embargo symbolizes the United States' intolerance of totalitarian dictatorship. It makes no sense to lift it; doing so would be immoral.[21]

The Cuban American National Foundation (CANF) has been maligned as a selfish and one-issue organization. CANF is a nonprofit organization established in Florida in 1981 to promote freedom. CANF supports a nonviolent transition in Cuba and promotes a market-based democracy such as the one in the United States. It believes in the rule of law and not dictatorships.

The focus is also taken away from the issues of communism when people focus on Cuban Americans as an ethnic lobbying group and on CANF and its influence on U.S. policy toward Cuba. The Brookings Institute, a think tank, has said that "Irish Americans lobbied 19th-century presidents to endorse Irish autonomy. . . . The truth is that ethnic groups weigh in on foreign policy matters only when conditions are right. Immigrants who came to the United States as political exiles (think Cubans) are much more likely to try to influence policy toward their ancestral homeland than those who came to find a better life."[22] So why single out Cuban Americans? During the Mexican Revolution, Mexican political refugees attempted to lobby for U.S. intervention. In more recent times, Jewish Americans have regularly lobbied for the interests of Israel. They have been very successful in lobbying Congress, so do their efforts take away from the validity of the issues? In the same way, it can be argued that Cuban Americans hate Castro for good reasons, and as Americans they have the right and even the duty to lobby for their interests.[23] The question of where the loyalties of the Cuban Americans lie misses the contributions that they make to U.S. foreign policy and that they are the most loyal and anticommunist group in the United States. Without their influence, Castro might have seduced Americans.[24]

Lastly, the United States legally leases Guantánamo Bay, and if the United States were to get out, it would be a tremendous victory for Castro. Guantánamo is essential to the security of the United States because it is of strategic importance to the region. Guantánamo should be kept because it is a beacon of freedom. The Caribbean is the underbelly of the United States, and the destiny of the free world is dependent on it. When the violation of sovereignty is discussed, it is a two-way street, and a nation has the right to promote its own interests. Guantánamo is isolated from the rest of the island and does not in any way interfere with the business of the Cuban government. However, its very existence helps the Cuban people morally and slows down the growth of the communist regime.

In addition, the Elián Gonzalez case has demonized the Cuban American community unfairly.[25] First, Cuban Americans do not all think alike. The case went beyond parental international custodial rights; Cuban Americans were defending the child's right as an individual to asylum. It objected to the U.S. government intervening by using the military to snatch the child from the home of his legal guardians here.[26] The media demonized Cuban Americans and took the focus away from the Castro dictatorship and to what the child would be returned. After all, his mother died to give him freedom. The media stereotyped Cuban Americans as irrational, and in doing so it took the focus away from the purpose of the demonstrations. The reality is that Americans are becoming apathetic toward communism, and Cuban Americans preserve the historical memory of what the loss of freedom means.[27]

### Against

Sanctions against Cuba have failed because the global community does not support them. Instead of serving to protect the Cuban people, sanctions are causing them to suffer more. Sanctions were successful against South Africa because the sanctions had moral authority. The Cuban embargo lacks moral authority. Further, in November of 1996, even Pope John Paul II asked for an end to the embargo.[28] Sanctions also failed to dislodge the military regime in Haiti, the poorest and most vulnerable country in Latin America.[29] Claiming that the United States is preventing medicine and food from entering Cuba all in the name of democracy is ridiculous and hypocritical. Nations such as Guatemala, China, Chile, and Indonesia have worse human rights records than Cuba but have received U.S. economic and political support despite their atrocities.[30]

As Philip Peters, who served in the State Department during the Reagan and Bush administrations, has written, "More than a decade after the fall of the Berlin Wall, Fidel Castro remains in charge in Havana, despising capitalism, taunting the Cuban-American community in Miami, theorizing about the evils of globalization, and keeping up with every imaginable statistic about Cuba. He has been in power for 41 years, outlasting U.S. strategies from the Bay of Pigs in the early 1960s to the tightened economic sanctions of the 1990s."[31] Peters maintains that Castro has remained in power because of U.S. foreign policy, which has given him an international forum and the sympathy of other nations, creating a David and Goliath scenario. Peters argues that it is in U.S. interests to open relations with Cuba. "Economic reforms in Cuba are still incipient, but small enterprise, foreign investment, incentive-based agriculture, and other changes have had important impacts: They helped the economy survive its post-Soviet crisis, and Cubans working in those sectors have gained experience with markets and augmented their earnings."[32] In other words, the United States should trade with Cuba not isolate Cuba.

Further, Peters says, "Cuban Americans have increasingly joined this discussion, as a younger generation of exiles values contact with the island and some first-generation exiles begin to question the effectiveness of the trade embargo. The Elián González crisis fueled doubts about the embargo when the young boy's plight captured American attention and weakened the pro-embargo hard-line position in public and congressional opinion . . . a policy that respects the rights of Americans to trade with, invest in, and travel to Cuba would more effectively serve U.S. interests in post-Soviet Cuba: defending human rights, helping the Cuban people, and connecting with the generation of Cubans that will govern that country in the early 21st century."[33] Americans should not make the mistake of assuming that all Cuban Americans are vehemently opposed to normalizing relations with Cuba. Many of the younger generation as well as the poorer Cubans arriving in the 1980s know that the policy hurts the poor. Even the Catholic church cannot condone the embargo and finds it ineffective and morally indefensible.[34]

The people of Cuba are entitled to self-determination. If Cubans do not want American troops on their soil, Americans shouldn't be there. The only reason that the United States is in Guantánamo is because of the Cuban lobby, led by CANF, which through political machinations has kept an unjust embargo alive and held onto Guantánamo. It is indisputable that the United States obtained the lease through coercion and has remained there although the lawful Cuban government has asked them to leave. It is also indisputable that the Cuban American National Foundation has used undemocratic means to attempt to overthrow the Cuban government.[35] Further proof of the extremism of the Cuban American lobby is the lobby's opportunism during the Elián González case, when the Cuban American lobby sought to deny his father parental rights and kept the child captive. If Cuba or any other country would have done this to an American citizen, the government would have labeled it a violation of our sovereignty, or worse still—terrorism.[36]

Second, in order for the United States to be the moral leader of the free world, it must be consistent. The United States funded the Bay of Pigs fiasco and assassination plots on Fidel Castro. Many people throughout the world believe that the United States conducted bacteriological warfare against Cuba. A mysterious strain of swine flu killed millions of pigs, ravaging the farm sector in Cuba. Also, between 1979 and 1981 there were destructive epidemics such as hemorrhagic conjunctivitis, dengue fever, sugarcane rust, and tobacco mold. A Cuban civilian airliner was blown up over Barbados in the mid-1970s. Because of the embargo, these accusations gain credibility and other countries believe them. Even if these accusations are untrue, there can be little doubt that the embargo has hurt Cuba, causing it to lose an estimated $60 billion.

To put it simply, much of the rest of the world does not look at Cuba the same way as the United States does. Cuba was unwavering in its support for the decolonization process in the 1970s and 1980s and has won support in the third world. Today Cuba has 2,000 physicians doing humanitarian work in third-world countries. There are 300 volunteer physicians in South Africa alone. Cuba has opened a Latin American university of medicine, the biggest of its kind in Latin America. Many of its students are from less developed Latin American countries. Cuban medical teams provided much needed emergency aid in the cyclone-ravaged Central American countries of Nicaragua and Honduras.[37]

Whom is the embargo hurting? Is it freeing Cubans? Is Castro causing all the present suffering in Cuba? Castro cannot be blamed entirely for the suffering, and Americans must look at the role of economic sanctions. Economic freedom is essential to socio-political freedom. Even if it is conceded that Castro is to blame, how do the sanctions hurt him? Does Castro have less access to medical supplies? Does Castro get less food? Is it rational to starve out a whole people because the United States does not agree with its leader? For 40 years the United States has tried this tactic, and it has not worked. It is up to the Cuban people to overthrow the government from within, and not for those outside Cuba to overthrow it.

It is not just the communists who are criticizing the United States for violating Cuba's sovereignty. Aaron Lukas, an analyst at the Cato Institute, says Cubans may not like Americans, but Cubans do not wish to harm Americans. About 80,000 U.S. citizens visit Cuba each year, and they are warmly received. There is proof that many Cuban Americans know the embargo hurts the people of Cuba because they send an estimated $800 million annually in remittances to relatives there, without which many Cubans would starve. This proves that the embargo has no moral authority.[38] People who lived under Castro have sent this money, and they may not like him, but they realize that their close relatives need the funds.

Instead of normalizing relations, the Helms-Burton Act of 1996 is intensifying political and economic tensions. Helms-Burton is an example of further interference with the sovereignty of the Cuban people. By denying U.S. citizens the right to travel or trade with Cuba, the U.S. government also infringes on the rights of its own citizens. It is ironic that Americans can travel to China but not to Cuba. Cuban leaders can rightfully appeal to the Cuban people to defend the revolution and blame Helms-Burton for the economic woes of Cuba. The Helms-Burton Act states that the United States can place sanctions against countries with investments in Cuba, yet Canada and Mexico are among the nations trading with Cuba. Many countries have rejected Helms-Burton as violating the principles of sovereignty.[39]

In addition, the United States has no business in Guantánamo Bay. The authority for this occupation is the Platt Amendment (1901), which was a direct assault by the United States against Cuba's national sovereignty.[40] The United States has a naval station with a fence, locked gate, and two mine-fields—one Cuban, one American—while simultaneously negotiating with Vietnam, North Korea, and China.[41] The United States stays in Guantánamo Bay although the Cuban government, which is a member of the United Nations, asks the United States to leave. In January 2002, the United States moved 300 Afghan prisoners to its naval base in Guantánamo Bay.

Lastly, the Elián González story was an outrageous example of how far the Cuban lobby will go in using a six-year old-child as a pawn.[42] Though the Cuban Revolution occurred more than 40 years ago and Cubans overthrew the bloody dictator Fulgencio Batista y Saldívar, the actions of a small group of obsessed individuals made the United States the laughingstock of the world community and endangered the rights of American children abroad. Americans should get out of Guantánamo Bay and end the embargo, and the Cold War should join other dead causes of history. Communism poses no threat to the United States, and if Americans are afraid of a small island with its tiny population, then Americans are in trouble.

## QUESTIONS

1. What does sovereignty mean? When does one nation-state have the right to violate another's sovereignty?

2. Does the United States have the right to intervene in Cuban affairs? Make an argument for and against.

3. On the Internet using a search engine, see whether you can reach *Granma*, the official Cuban government newspaper. What does it say about the United States' violation of its sovereignty?

4. On the Internet using a search engine, type "Andrew Reding, 'Playing into Castro's Hands,'" *Washington Post*, 23 May 2001. (You can also go to http://www.washingtonpost.com, accessed 26 July 2003, and search the newspaper.) The article states, "Sens. Jesse Helms (R-N.C.) and Joseph Lieberman (D-Conn.) introduce legislation to allocate $100 million in aid to Cuban opposi-

tion groups, with the objective of fostering democracy in Cuba." Why does the author believe this is playing into Castro's hands? Discuss.

5. Go to an Internet search engine and type "Juan O. Tamayo, 'Crisis Shook Exile Lobby Embargo Foes Scored Points,' *Miami Herald*, 25 April 2000." (Or go to http://www.miami.com/herald, accessed 26 July 2003.) Why were there predictions of a major improvement of 41 years of animosity between the United States and Cuba? What does the author think? What changes, if any, have occurred? Why did the Cuban exiles consider it Clinton's betrayal?

6. Go to an Internet search engine and type "Philip P. Pan and Michael A. Fletcher, 'Other Latinos More Divided over Fate of Cuban Boy,' *Washington Post*, 10 April 2000." (Or go to http://www.washingtonpost.com, accessed 26 July 2003.) The question of whether the United States should continue its aggressive policy toward Cuba has become embroiled in domestic politics, which has split the U.S. Latino population. For example, the recognition of Cuba by Mexico and the case of Elián González badly split the community. Many Latinos thought the boy should be returned to his father in Cuba while Cuban Americans generally supported his staying in the United States. Do you think they should have returned him to his father? Why or why not?

7. Compare the issues of the embargo, Elián González, and Guantánamo. How are they alike and how are they interrelated?

8. Dissect the *For* and *Against* arguments of this chapter. Do you believe that U.S. citizens should support the embargo? Do you believe they think the United States should get out of Guantánamo?

9. Read Max J. Castro, "Grumpy Old Men: The Aging Exile Leaders Who Are Trying to Keep Elián González in the United States Have a Lot in Common with Their Anti-Democratic Nemesis, Fidel Castro," *salon.com*, 6 April 2000, http://www.salon.com/news/feature/2000/04/06/cubans, accessed 26 July 2003. Does a person's opinion about this issue depend on his or her age?

10. Do you believe that other U.S. Latinos should have supported the Miami Cubans? If so, why? If not, why?

11. Some scholars say that the embargo actually helps keep Castro in power. Go to an Internet search engine and type, "Cato Policy Analysis" or http://www.cato.org, accessed 26 July 2003. What is the Cato Institute's position?

12. *El Súper* (1979, directed by L. Ichaso and Orlando Jimenez-Leal) is a humorous and touching story of Cuban exiles living in a basement apartment in New York. *The Pérez Family* (1995, directed by Mira Nair) is about Cubans arriving in Miami and the problems of reunions with family members whom they have not seen in 20 years. Critically review these films.

13. Make a chart showing reasons for and against the Cuban embargo. Would you end it? Why or why not?

14. Make a chart listing reasons for and against getting out of Guantánamo Bay. Should the United States leave? Why or why not?

## NOTES

1. WFDY Fifteenth Assembly Resolution on International Solidarity, http://www.wfdy.org/english/assembly-15/15-international-solidarity.html, accessed 25 July

2003; Commission on Human Rights, Fifty-fifth session. "Summary Record of the Fourth Meeting. Held at the Palais des Nations, Geneva, on Wednesday, 24 March 1999, at 10 A.M.," http://www.igc.org/deepdish/lastgrad, accessed 25 July 2003.

2. Jay Moore, "End of the Century: Is Colonialism Over?," *Editor's Bullhorn,* 28 December 1999; "National Bipartisan Commission on Cuba, U.S.–Cuba History," 1998, http://www.uscubacommission.org/history2.html, accessed 3 August 2003; U.S. Department of State, Bureau of Population, Refugees, and Migration, http://www.cal.org/corc/, accessed 3 August 2003; Barbara Robson, "The Cubans: Their History and Culture," Refugee Fact Sheet Series, no. 12, *Center for Applied Linguistics Refugee Service Center,* 1996, http://www.culturalorientation.net/cubans/, accessed 3 August 2003; "The Economic History of Cuba," *World History Archives,* http://www.hartford-hwp.com/archives/43b/index-c.html, accessed 3 August 2003.

3. "National Bipartisan Commission on Cuba, U.S.–Cuba History," 1998, http://www.uscubacommission.org/history2.html, accessed 3 August 2003; U.S. Department of State, Bureau of Population, Refugees, and Migration, http://www.cal.org/corc/, accessed 3 August 2003; Barbara Robson, "Cubans Their History and Culture," Refugee Fact Sheet Series, no. 12, *Center for Applied Linguistics Refugee Service Center,* 1996, http://www.culturalorientation.net/cubans/, accessed 3 August 2003; "The Economic History of Cuba," *World History Archives,* http://www.hartford-hwp.com/archives/43b/index-c.html, accessed 3 August 2003.

4. Ibid.

5. Ibid.

6. Ibid.

7. The U.S. Government/CANF Propaganda Machine, http://members.attcanada.ca/~dchris/CubaFAQ105.html, accessed 25 July 2003.

8. Rodolfo F. Acuña, "Los cubanoamericanos de Miami," *La Opinion,* 23 April 2000.

9. Max J. Castro, "Grumpy Old Men : The Aging Exile Leaders Who Are Trying to Keep Elián González in the United States Have a Lot in Common with Their Anti-Democratic Nemesis, Fidel Castro," *salon.com,* 6 April 2000, http://archive.salon.com/directory/topics/immigration/, accessed 25 July 2003.

10. "Cubans in Miami," Sociology 338: Latinos in the U.S., http://www.princeton.edu/~sociolog/syllabi/centeno_lecture_notes_cubans.html, accessed 25 July 2003.

11. "Cuban Discord and Helms-Burton," 19 July 1996, http://www.earlham.edu/~pols/ps 17971/weissdo/HelmsB.html, accessed 25 July 2003; "Cuba Solidarity against the Blockade," http://cubaproject.freeservers.com/lazy_helms_burton.html, accessed 25 July 2003.

12. "Cuban Discord and Helms-Burton," 19 July 1996, http://www.earlham.edu/~pols/ps 17971/weissdo/HelmsB.html, accessed 25 July 2003; Cuban American National Foundation, http://www.canfnet.org/, accessed 25 July 2003.

13. "WCVI Celebrates Latino Issues Conference with New Direction on Public Policy Strategy," http://www.wcvi.org/press_room/press_releases/tx/pr_conf_101201.html, accessed 25 July 2003.

14. Philip P. Pan and Michael A. Fletcher, "Other Latinos More Divided over Fate of Cuban Boy," *Washington Post,* 10 April 2000.

15. Ibid.

16. Ibid.

17. "Ending the Cuban Embargo: One Step Forward, Two Steps Back," *Global*

*Exchange Newsletter* (winter 2001), http://www.globalexchange.org/campaigns/cuba/US-Cuba/cubaWin2000NL.html.

18. Miguel A. Gayoso, soc.culture.cuba, 13 September 1997, http://xld.com/public/cuba/embargo.htm, accessed 25 July 2003.

19. Ibid.

20. Miguel A. Gayoso, soc.culture.cuba, 13 September 1997, http://xld.com/public/cuba/embargo.htm, accessed 25 July 2003; Christopher Marquis, "Cuban American Lobby on the Defensive," *New York Times,* 30 June 2000, http://www.ciponline.org/cuba/newsarchives/june2000/nyt063000.htm, accessed 25 July 2003.

21. Jeff Jacoby, "The Cuban Embargo's Moral Justification," *Boston Globe,* 2 April 1998, http://www.nocastro.com/embargo/jeffjby.htm, accessed 25 July 2003.

22. James M. Lindsay, "Why Are Cuban Americans Singled Out as an Ethnic Lobby? Getting Uncle Sam's Ear/Will Ethnic Lobbies Cramp America's Foreign Policy Style." *Brookings Foreign Policy Studies* 20, no. 1 (2002): 37–40, http://www.brook.edu/dybdocroot/press/REVIEW/winter2002/lindsay.htm, accessed 25 July 2003.

23. Ibid.

24. Ibid.

25. Elián Archives, http://www.nocastro.com/archives/Eliánindex.html, accessed 25 July 2003.

26. "Is It Fashionable to Hate Cubans-Americans?" 27 April 2000, http://www.lasculturas.com/aa/aa042700a.php, accessed 25 July 2003.

27. Ibid.

28. Philip Pullella, "Pope Urges U.S. to 'Change' Cuban Embargo," 21 January 1998, http://64.21.33.164/CNews/y98/jan98/22e4.htm, accessed 25 July 2003.

29. Terra Lawson-Remer, "Yes! Lift the Cuban Embargo," *La Verdad,* in Cato Center for Trade Policy Studies, http://www.freetrade.org/issues/cuba.html, accessed 25 July 2003.

30. Ibid.

31. Philip Peters, "A Policy toward Cuba That Serves U.S. Interests," *Cato Policy Analysis,* no. 384 (November 2000), http://www.cato.org/cgi-bin/scripts/printtech.cgi, accessed 25 July 2003.

32. Ibid.

33. Ibid.

34. Jeff Jacoby, "The Cuban Embargo's Moral Justification," *Boston Globe,* 2 April 1998, http://www.nocastro.com/embargo/jeffjby.htm, accessed 25 July 2003.

35. "Cuban Exile Says Cuban Bombings Financed by U.S. Lobby Group," 12 July 1998, http://64.21.33.164/CNews/y98/jul98/13e3.htm.

36. Max J. Castro, "Grumpy Old Men : The Aging Exile Leaders Who Are Trying to Keep Elián González in the United States Have a Lot in Common with Their Anti-Democratic Nemesis, Fidel Castro," *salon.com,* 6 April 2000, http://archive.salon.com/news/feature/2000/04/06/cubans/print.html, accessed 25 July 2003. This article talks about his experiences in Miami during the Elián impasse. "Why are they so obsessed with Fidel Castro that hatred of him and his system seems to outweigh all other values, even parental rights and, if you believe those who promise violence if Elián is removed from his uncle's Miami home, the rule of law? And why do they use language and tactics, including stifling dissent, that strike Americans as undemocratic and invite comparison with Castro and his regime?" He attributes it to "gerontocracy. The oldest, most traumatized, most bitter generation is still the largest and most powerful group

of Cubans."; "American Schizophrenia over Cuba and Elián," 31 March 2000. Also at *Boston Review: A Political and Literary Forum,* http://www.lasculturas.com/aa/aa033100a.php. "The United States can't seem to decide how bad life is in Cuba. I was always indoctrinated that communism was evil, especially the Soviet Union and Cuba. China was a whole other world of malfeasance. I was also taught that the American Indigenous people were better off after Manifest Destiny."

37. Interview with Cuban Ambassador Olga Chamero Trias, "Cuba against the Odds," *India's National Magazine* 16, no. 8 (1999), http://www.flonnet.com/fl1608/16081110.htm, accessed 25 July 2003.

38. Aaron P. Lukas, "It's Time, Finally, to End the Cuban Embargo," *Cato Institute's Center for Trade Policy Studies,* http://www.freetrade.org/pubs/articles/al-12-14-01.htm, accessed 25 July 2003.

39. Eugene J. Carroll, Jr., Rear Admiral, U.S. Navy (ret.), Deputy Director, "Faulty US Policy toward Cuba," Center for Defense Information, http://www.cdi.org/issues/cuba/faulty.html, accessed 25 July 2003; Bergen Organization, http://www.bergen.org/AAST/Projects/Cuba/other.html, accessed 25 July 2003. "The embargo is not at all widely supported, even by America's allies. For years, the United Nations has made resolutions opposed to the embargo. The only countries who side with the United States are Israel and Uzbekistan. The anti-American sentiment is also growing as it becomes evident that the embargo is not achieving its goal. Thirty-two members of the Organization of American States (all but the U.S.) voted against Helms-Burton as a violation of international law."

40. Cuban Committee for Democracy, http://www.us.net/cuban/cuban%20affairs/president.html, accessed 25 July 2003.

41. George J. Church, "Cubans, Go Home: Clinton Is Determined to Turn the Rafters Back Rather than Open Talks with Fidel Castro," *Time Magazine,* 1994, http://www.time.com/time/archive/preview/from_redirect/0,10987,1101940905-165006,00.html, accessed 25 July 2003.

42. Rodolfo F. Acuña, "Los Cubanoamericanos de Miami," *La Opinion,* 23 April 2000.

## SELECTED WORKS

Boswell, Thomas, and James Curtis. *The Cuban-American Experience. Culture, Images and Perspectives.* Totaowa, N.J.: Rowman and Allanheld, 1984.

Cuban American National Foundation, http://www.canfnet.org/ accessed 25 July 2003.

Eckstein, Susan, and Lorena Barberia. Grounding Immigrant Generations in History: Cuban Americans and Their Transnational Ties." *International Migration Review* 36, no. 3 (Fall 2002): 799ff.

"Ending the Cuban Embargo: One Step Forward, Two Steps Back." *Global Exchange Newsletter* (winter 2001), http://www.globalexchange.org/campaigns/cuba/US-Cuba/cubaWin2000NL.htm, accessed 26 July 2003.

Granma Internacional, http://www.granma.cu/, accessed 26 July 2003.

Grenier, Guillermo J., Lisandro Pérez, and Nancy Foner. *Legacy of Exile, The Cubans in the United States.* Allyn & Bacon New Immigrants Series. New York: Allyn & Bacon, 2003.

Jacoby, Jeff. "The Cuban Embargo's Moral Justification." *Boston Globe,* 2 April 1998.

Lindsay, James M. "Why Are Cuban Americans Singled Out as an Ethnic Lobby? Getting Uncle Sam's Ear / Will Ethnic Lobbies Cramp America's Foreign Policy Style." *Brookings Foreign Policy Studies* 20, no. 1 (2002): 37–40.

Lukas, Aaron P. "It's Time, Finally, to End the Cuban Embargo." *Cato Institute's Center for Trade Policy Studies,* http://www.freetrade.org/pubs/articles/al-12–14–01.htm, accessed 25 July 2003.

Marquis, Christopher. "Cuban American Lobby on the Defensive." *New York Times,* 30 June 2000.

Pan, Philip P., and Michael A. Fletcher. "Other Latinos More Divided over Fate of Cuban Boy." *Washington Post,* 10 April 2000.

Pérez, Louis A. *On Becoming Cuban: Identity, Nationality, and Culture.* New York: HarperTrade, 2001.

Peters, Philip. "A Policy toward Cuba That Serves U.S. Interests." *Cato Policy Analysis,* no. 384 (2000), http://www.cato.org/pubs/pas/pa-384es.html, accessed 25 July 2003.

Refugee Service Center, http://www.cal.org/RSC; http://www.cal.org/rsc/cubans/HISTO2.htm, accessed 25 July 2003.

"The U.S. Government/CANF Propaganda Machine," http://members.attcanada.ca/~dchris/CubaFAQ105.html, accessed 25 July 2003.

U.S. Naval Station, Guantánamo Bay, Cuba, http://www.nsgtmo.navy.mil, accessed 25 July 2003.

# 10

# U.S. MILITARY BASES IN PUERTO RICO

## BACKGROUND

The case of the sovereignty of Puerto Rico differs from that of Cuba because Puerto Rico is part of the United States. Nevertheless, the people of Puerto Rico want the U.S. Navy to stop using the island of Vieques for target practice. The Navy says that Vieques is irreplaceable, and the Navy needs Vieques for purposes of national security. The United States also has military installations, which are unpopular with the Puerto Rican people, on the island of Puerto Rico, but again, U.S. military authorities say that they need the installations for national security.[1] As with the other Latino issues, this chapter discusses the issue of who is right and wrong. Here, the discussion is whether or not the United States should respect the sovereignty of Puerto Ricans and get its military installations out of Vieques and Puerto Rico.

Puerto Rico, an island 100 miles long and 35 miles wide, has 931 people per square mile, which makes it one of the most densely populated places on earth. Puerto Rico is 60 percent more densely populated than El Salvador, which is the most densely populated country on the Latin American mainland. In addition, because Puerto Rico's terrain is quite mountainous, only half the land is suitable for farming. Puerto Ricans have only one-fourth acre of farmland per person, which is not much when compared with the United States, which has about four and one-half acres of farmland per person. In dispute is the island of Vieques, which is six miles off Puerto Rico's east coast and is strategically in the center of the Antilles chain. Vieques has 33,000 acres of land, which is significant in a country as densely populated as Puerto Rico.

## History

Puerto Rico did not have as strong an independence movement as Cuba in 1898. Sentiment was divided on the island ranging from those favoring staying within the Spanish Empire where they were recognized as Spaniards to those who wanted independence and those wanting annexation to the United States. The latter view was supported by the island's plantation owners, who welcomed the opportunity to annex to the United States because of the passage of the Dingley Tariff, which put an import tax on sugar.

At the end of the Spanish American War, the Puerto Rican people had no say in question of annexation to the United States. The Treaty of Paris signed by Spain and the United States made Puerto Rico a U.S. possession. It was a time when the United States was expanding its markets and naval bases and was well on the road to becoming a world power.

Under Spanish rule, Puerto Ricans had been unconditionally Spaniards. Puerto Ricans had full representation in the Spanish legislature, all males could vote, and the island could pass its own tariffs. In contrast, under the Foraker Act of 1900 changed this, and Puerto Ricans were not entitled to the protection of the U.S. Bill of Rights nor American citizenship, despite the fact that U.S. laws applied in Puerto Rico. The Foraker Act also opened Puerto Rico to American investors and encouraged Anglo American monopolization of the island's resources.[2] North American investors bought cane lands in Puerto Rico and formed corporations to process sugar. Eventually five of them cornered 40 percent of the sugar cane lands of the island. Meanwhile, the production of coffee fell after 1898.

The sugar boom killed the manufacturing of cigars in homes and small shops. Added regulation resulted in cigars being made almost exclusively in big workshops owned by the tobacco companies. The small family cigar makers either went out of business or became wage laborers for large companies. The modernization of farming converted Puerto Rico into one large plantation, which was overdependent on a single crop, making it vulnerable to natural disasters such as storms and to U.S. quotas of sugar. Ownership of land became more concentrated under U.S. rule: the rich got richer while the poor got poorer as the internal market gave way to imports.

The demise of small farms and jobs in urban centers triggered an uprooting of Puerto Rican workers and their families who migrated to the United States where large growers and industrialists recruited Puerto Ricans to fill the shortage of labor created by the 1917 Literacy Act and the 1921 and 1924

Immigration Acts that cut European immigration to a trickle. This movement was facilitated in 1917 when Congress made Puerto Ricans United States citizens.

Widespread discontent gripped the island, which contributed to the growth of Puerto Rican nationalism and communism. A number of academics and professionals formulated an economic strategy known as the Chardón Plan in 1934, named for the university chancellor who presided over the meetings. The plan called for the expropriation of corporate plantations of more than 500 acres, a limit established by the Foraker Act that the United States never enforced. The intention was to distribute land among workers to diversify crop production and enhance traditional agriculture through methods and techniques recommended by agronomists.

The Depression of the 1930s led to the rise of Luis Muñoz Marín and the Popular Democratic Party. In the 1940 elections, the Popular Democrats gained control of the Puerto Rican Senate and later the House of Representatives. Muñoz Marín was the first elected governor of Puerto Rico in 1948. Previous governors had been appointed by the President of the United States. Muñoz Marín launched Operation Bootstrap, designed to industrialize the island by granting tax-exempt status to new factories. Operation Bootstrap created thousands of new jobs, however, not enough since more than 100,000 Puerto Ricans moved to the U.S. mainland during the 1950s. In 1952, Puerto Rico became a self-governing commonwealth of the United States, and that same year Puerto Rico organized programs to preserve and promote traditional Puerto Rican cultural traditions. In the years that followed, the Institute of Puerto Rican Culture consolidated these cultural projects. Puerto Rico enjoyed relatively good prosperity until the 1970s when fuel crises economically depressed the island. There were some bright spots as the pharmaceutical industry developed beyond the original expectations, but other industries, such as electronics, did not keep the pace, and the island's economy was not able to absorb the booming population.

Relations with the United States often were problematic. Many Puerto Ricans became disgruntled when the media reported stories of sterilization programs. In the years after World War I, the United States government, the medical community, and the local government of Puerto Rico initiated a sterilization program as a form of birth control. They designed the program to end overpopulation, which Americans blamed for unemployment and poverty in Puerto Rico. In 1937, despite opposition from Puerto Ricans and the Catholic church, a private organization allegedly supported by the U.S. government opened 23 birth control clinics. Sterilization, which the United States had banned for other than strictly medical purposes, became an alternative method of birth control, along with contraceptives. Critics say that although the sterilization programs seemed voluntary, women were often unaware of the irreversibility of sterilization, and doctors and hospitals put subtle pressure on women to undergo the procedure. The targeted women came overwhelmingly from the lower classes. Moreover, there were no restrictions on the age, health, or the number of children the woman already had. Critics say that by 1965, the programs had sterilized one-third of the female population of the island. Authorities also experimented with techniques developed in Puerto Rico in other Latin American countries such as Colombia and Bolivia with the support of U.S. government agencies and private organizations.[3]

Despite U.S. development programs, other difficulties gripped Puerto Rico as agriculture became even more commercialized, leaving only subsistence and truck farming. Unemployment reduced many Puerto Ricans to using food stamps and accelerated migration to the mainland.[4] Increasingly Puerto Rican entrepreneurship was limited to industries such as food processing, furniture manufacture, printing, publishing, construction materials, and producing farm products for local consumption.

Meanwhile, the deindustrialization of the United States affected Puerto Ricans as U.S. manufacturers sent their products to Asia and then to Mexico to be assembled by cheap labor. As a consequence, Puerto Rico lost employment in the textile, apparel, footwear, and tobacco industries while gaining limited jobs in the pharmaceutical, computer, and electronics industries. The outcome was that during the 1970s the number of Puerto Ricans living in the United States grew by some 600,000 people, or by 41 percent, to 2,014,000.[5] Puerto Ricans, both on the island and on the mainland, increasingly became disillusioned with the United States, which helped Europe with the Marshall Plan and the Middle East with large foreign aid packages, while Puerto Rico remained a stepchild to the United States.

### The Vieques Question

The name Vieques comes from the Indian word *bieque,* meaning small island. The Taino Indians inhabited Vieques before 1493. The Spaniards finally abandoned Vieques in 1843. In the second half of the 1800s, Vieques experienced a great sugar boom with landowners importing black slaves from the neighboring British islands. Like the rest of Puerto Rico, Vieques became part of the United States in 1898.

Workers there, along with those on the island of Puerto Rico, struggled against the sugar oligarchy, and in 1915 agricultural workers affiliated with the American Federation of Labor conducted a strike that engulfed Vieques and Puerto Rico. On Vieques police killed several workers and opened fire on hundreds of strikers. The strike lasted four years. Meanwhile, the population of Vieques reached about 12,000 people.

When the U.S. Navy arrived in 1941, 10,362 people lived on the island and the island produced 8,000 tons of sugar annually. The Navy expropriated more than three-fourths of Vieques—26,000 of Vieques' 33,000 acres—including most of the land used for farming. The construction of the base killed the sugar industry and thousands of small farmers were uprooted, most of whose families had occupied the island for generations. The U.S. government paid large landowners a fixed price of $20 or $30 for their houses, forcing more than 800 worker-families to leave. The pretext for the low payments was that the workers could not prove legal title to their land. In many cases, the Navy gave the displaced families 24 to 48 hours to abandon the island. Some workers stayed and took part in the construction of the Navy base. However, after the initial building boom, the jobs went away. After World War II Puerto Rico tried to revive farming but failed, and Vieques was a dying island.[6]

Led by Puerto Rican intellectual Pedro Albizu Campos, Puerto Ricans vigorously protested the U.S. Navy's occupation of Vieques. In a series of articles, Albizu Campos accused the Navy of carrying out a policy of genocide against the Puerto Rican people on Vieques. The presence of thousands of Marines further heightened antagonism in the 1950s and 1960s. In 1953, Marines beat Pepé Christian, a 70-year-old storekeeper, to death and left his 73-year-old friend Julio Bermúdez seriously injured. The old men had refused to sell the Marines more rum. Naval authorities acquitted the Marines. Two years later, 13-year-old Chuito Legrand stepped on a mortar shell while he and three friends were playing near a dairy farm. Cries of "*Yanqi* (Yankee) go home!" filled the island. According to critics, the Navy reacted arrogantly. In 1961 the Department of the Navy unilaterally proposed to abolish the municipality of Vieques. The Governor of Puerto Rico, Muñoz Marín, responded, "We know of no truly comparable action in American history." Three years later, the Navy threatened to expropriate the southern coast of Vieques.[7] In 1975, the Navy dropped a cruise missile next to a school, and in October 1993 the Navy dropped five 500-pound bombs that missed their targets and landed one mile from the Isabel Segunda village.

Tensions climaxed on April 19, 1999, when the Navy accidentally dropped two 500-pound bombs over the Observation Tower, killing a civilian guard and injuring four others. Puerto Ricans protested against the U.S. Navy. On May 26 of that year, the Navy admitted having accidentally fired 263 rounds of shells loaded with depleted uranium. They recovered only 57 of the shells. In protest the Catholic church of Vieques set up a campsite and chapel at Playa Yayi. On July 4, Puerto Ricans held a march on Vieques attended by

Puerto Rican protesters from the Cayo la Yayi Colec-
tivity start a new occupation of a strip of land in 2002
where the U.S. Navy returned on May 4, 2000. After
a group of protesters staged an act of civil disobedi-
ence for almost a year, a Federal Court decided that
the land did not belong to the U.S. Navy, and that it
was part of Vieques, and that the arrests made on that
date were illegal. Residents of Vieques mounted a
new camp aimed to disrupt military operations. (AP/
Wide World Photos)

50,000 people. Various political, religious, and civic groups showed their
support. The pressure mounted as human rights groups joined the protest.

On August 29, 2001, the people held a local non-binding referendum.
Sixty-eight percent voted to ask the Navy to stop the bombing immediately
and leave the island (30 percent voted for the Navy to stay and continue the
bombing.) Under an arrangement with President Bill Clinton, the Navy
would cease all training on the Vieques naval training range by May 2003.
Still, the Navy announced that not only would it continue the bombing until
May 2003, but it also announced that the next maneuver would be full scale.
This did not end the controversy, and subsequent congressional bills would

Protesters are led off by federal agents, at Camp Yayi on the U.S. Naval bombing range on the island of Vieques, Puerto Rico, 2000. (AP/Wide World Photos)

allow the Navy to continue training under terms proposed by the Secretary of the Navy, who may close the Vieques training range if the Secretary could find alternative equivalent or superior training facilities.[8] Live bombs could be used at the discretion of the Navy. The 1999 executive order signed under former President Clinton allowed training on Vieques only with inert bombs, after a bomb killed a Puerto Rican civilian. The Navy resumed training with dummy bombs, which triggered an international uproar. The Navy and the supporters of the training argued that Puerto Rico belonged to the United States and that the Navy needed Vieques for the training. This fragile agreement, however, ended after the terrorist attack on the Twin Towers in New York City on September 11, 2001.

Opponents say the bombings have already caused a death, and the Navy is doing irreparable ecological damage to the small island. The rate of cancer among the residents of Vieques is 27 percent higher than on the island of Puerto Rico.[9] Lastly, scholars complain that Vieques remains the site of important archaeological work in the Caribbean region. Archaeologists found amulets featuring the Andean condor, thought to have been crafted in Vieques around 2,000 years ago. The Navy's control impeded this excavation.[10]

### Are Puerto Ricans American?

Puerto Ricans fought in every major U.S. war of the twentieth century, and Puerto Ricans fought with distinction. Today, Puerto Rico is a commonwealth of the United States and elects its own governor. Puerto Ricans are citizens of the United States but cannot vote for president and do not have representation in the U.S. Congress—ironically rights that they would have if still under Spain. Technically, Puerto Ricans can pass their own laws, but its laws are subordinate to those of the United States. That is, Puerto Ricans cannot pass a law that conflicts with the U.S. Constitution or enter a treaty with a foreign country.

Because of inequality and racism, Puerto Ricans have not fully assimilated into the United States. This segregation consequently has contributed to a strong national identity. As one writer puts it, "Puerto Rico's heart is not American. It is Puerto Rican. The national sentiment of Puerto Ricans is entirely devoted to our patria, as we call our homeland in Spanish, our language. We are Puerto Ricans in the same way that Mexicans are Mexicans and Japanese are Japanese. For us, 'we the people' means we Puerto Ricans."[11]

Pedro Albizu Campos, founder of Puerto Rico's modern independence movement, said in the 1930s that the United States was "interested in the cage, not the birds."[12] Albizu Campos, a Harvard-educated scholar influenced by the Irish independence struggle, challenged American rule. Albizu Campos led the Nationalist Party and pressured the Liberal Party to declare independence as one of its priorities. In 1936 under the wartime Sedition Act of 1918, the United States indicted Albizu Campos and other Nationalist leaders, sentencing him to a federal penitentiary in Atlanta for almost a decade. In 1937, Gen. Blanton Winship, the U.S.-appointed governor, ordered police to fire on a group of unarmed Nationalist Party members in the city of Ponce in Puerto Rico, killing 22 and wounding 97. This repression contributed to the end of the Nationalist Party and the purging of *independistas* (independents) from the ranks of other parties. The United States established the Commonwealth of Puerto Rico in 1948–52.

In 1950, after his release from prison, Albizu Campos organized armed attacks on Blair House in Washington, where President Harry Truman was living, and on the U.S. Congress in 1954. The Puerto Rican government labeled the Nationalist Party members and more than a thousand leaders and members of the Puerto Rican Independence Party (PIP) as subversives. Most independists did not favor armed struggle, yet the United States imprisoned them on illegal arrest warrants. The police collaborated with U.S. intelligence agencies and compiled a huge blacklist of independence supporters.[13] These actions seemed to have suppressed the *independista* movement until the question of Vieques revived it.

In 1952, 81 percent of Puerto Rican voters backed the commonwealth in a yes-or-no referendum. In 1993, 49 percent of Puerto Ricans voted for a commonwealth and 46 percent for statehood. While only 4 percent voted for independence, many Puerto Ricans say that this vote was significant in history.[14] Although most Puerto Ricans do not favor independence, there has been an independence movement throughout the American period.

## SHOULD THE UNITED STATES GET ITS MILITARY BASES OUT OF PUERTO RICO?

### For

The question of Vieques has moved more people toward the issue of Puerto Rican Independence than any other event in recent history. Puerto Ricans are drawing the correlation between Europe's colonization of third-world countries and their status as a colony of the United States and concluding that Puerto Rico is not a full partner in the American Republic. The 1999 death of Vieques resident David Sanes was attributed to stray bombs. However, this is not the first time the Navy killed a Puerto Rican accidentally.[15]

The most difficult thing to accept in this dispute is the indifference and arrogance of Americans. Many in Congress are not defending the rights of the Puerto Rican people and have no intention of sticking their necks out. Since September 11, 2001, things have gotten worse, and dissidents are afraid to be labeled as terrorists. The United Nations Special Committee on Decolonization, for the first time in 28 years, passed a resolution on the issue of Puerto Rican sovereignty on Vieques.[16] Yet U.S. authorities insist they have the right to endanger life on the island, although the world community, including the United Nations, has condemned the U.S. actions on Vieques.

In addition, the Naval bombing has had environmental consequences. The cancer rate in Vieques is much higher than elsewhere in Puerto Rico, and many rare diseases have appeared among the people. The bombing has contaminated and destroyed the coral reefs, mangroves, and lagoons and has seriously damaged the Vieques fishing industry, the livelihood of many islanders. The Navy has reduced the ability of the people of Vieques to farm, fish, or attract tourists, and in return it only provides a mere 92 local jobs (custodial work, maintenance, and security). Because of this unemployment has worsened.[17] Even if the military leaves, 14,000 acres of Vieques would go to the Department of the Interior, leaving almost nothing to the people. What would be left is unexploded bombs, trash, and contaminated beaches.

Even so, the United States has not agreed to clean up Vieques after six decades of intensive bombing. Nothing seems to deter the Navy. The Navy is planning to build giant fuel-storage tanks, floating piers, and troop barracks on the beaches and coastal areas of Vieques. Amidst all this, the Navy has admitted to causing the death of a whale and to releasing tiny strands of silica glass, used to confuse radar, into the atmosphere.[18] It is doubtful whether the United States would treat one of its 50 states in a similar manner.

Despite universal disapproval and a de-escalation of the tension during the Clinton administration, the Navy has gotten the green light from George W. Bush to expand its activities. Congress has not checked this activity and passed legislation stipulating that the navy will not vacate Vieques until a better site is found. In case of a national emergency, the Navy could keep its facilities.[19] In April 2002, the Navy resumed its bombing exercises. Both the destroyer USS *Mahan* and the guided-missile frigate USS *Barry* conducted ship-to-shore training.

Within a week, protests of these training exercises resumed, and federal authorities arrested 14 people for trespassing. The total arrested grew to the hundreds. Military authorities used gas on the protesters; the pretext was that the protestors allegedly threw rocks, which eyewitnesses dispute. Police Col. César García contradicted the Navy account: "I witnessed the incident, and there was no rock-throwing. Right now, my superiors are on the phone to complain to the Navy about the situation."[20] Meanwhile, a news blackout about the Vieques crisis occurred in the United States. In the entire first week of April 2002, *Lexis-Nexis,* a news media reporting service, reported only 14 newspaper items, mostly short blurbs, on the resumption of the war exercises. The *Los Angeles Times* carried a 71-word item on April 2 and a 62-word item on April 7. The *New York Times* did no better.

In the year 2001, U.S. District Judge José Fuste sentenced Bronx Democratic Party chief Roberto Ramírez, City Councilman Adolfo Carrion, and state Assemblyman José Rivera to 40 days each after convicting them in a quick trial of misdemeanor trespassing charges. Rubén Berrios, the leader of the Puerto Rican Independence Party, received a four-month sentence. Sen. Norma Burgos, a former secretary of state and then vice president of the island's pro-statehood party, and José Aponte, mayor of the town of Carolina and president of the Puerto Rican mayors association, were both arrested. Puerto Rican entertainers and sports figures such as singers Ricky Martin, Marc Anthony, José Feliciano, Benicio del Toro, Detroit Tigers outfielder Juan González, middleweight boxing champion Felix Trinidad, and golfer Chi Chi Rodríguez all called for the Navy's withdrawal in full-page advertisements in the *New York Times* and *Washington Post.*[21] Gov. Sila María Calderón and most of the Puerto Rican legislature have called on the Navy to get out and passed a noise abatement law that made the bombing exercises illegal.

After September 11, the situation worsened. Attorney General John Ashcroft and the Bush administration initiated a get-tough policy; those arrested for the first time got a minimum of 40 days in jail. Gov. Calderón, who was elected largely because of a promise to force the Navy to leave immediately, backed down and said she supported a deal endorsed by President Bush for the Navy to leave by May 2003. Even the promise of the Navy to cut exercises to 90 days a year and limit ammunition to inert bombs has been set aside because of September 11.[22]

The Puerto Rican people have spoken with one voice, telling the American Congress to get out of both Vieques and Roosevelt Roads, the military base on the big island.[23] Puerto Rico's 3.8 million U.S. citizens want equality, dignity, and full self-government as first-class citizens. Puerto Rico has endured territorial status longer than any other American territory without becoming either independent, as with the Philippines, or a state, as in the case of Alaska and Hawaii.[24] The American people must realize that the Cold War has ended in Europe; the Soviet threat is over. U.S. nuclear weapons and troops are no longer needed internationally for the defense of the United States.[25]

### Against

The navy accidentally killed a Puerto Rican civilian in Vieques during a bombing exercise in April 1999. That was unfortunate, but it is the sovereign right of the United States to permit the Navy to continue to use the island as a bombing range and for combat training until 2093. The Navy says Vieques is the crown jewel of its dozen-or-so training ranges. It is unique and the only such site where the Navy can rehearse land, air, and amphibious assaults all at once because it is free from commercial air and sea traffic.

People on the mainland also have to suffer inconveniences; the price of freedom is high. How many Americans have died so Puerto Ricans and other American citizens can live free?[26] What does Puerto Rico mean overall to the United States? Why is it important to this defense? Strategically, this is the largest and most populated of a cluster of five Caribbean islands. Between the Dominican Republic and the Virgin Islands, it controls the Mona Passage, a key shipping lane to the Panama Canal. It has the finest natural harbor in the area. Vice Admiral William J. Fallon, commander of the U.S. Second Fleet, said, during congressional hearings in September 1999, that the Vieques site was irreplaceable.

Most Puerto Ricans acknowledge that jobs and the economy are what is most important to them. In the 1990s, more than 90 percent voted for statehood or continued commonwealth status.[27] There were probably nuclear weapons at the military base at Roosevelt Roads;[28] however, they were part of a war effort to combat communism and terrorism. Moreover, troops in Puerto Rico are vital because of the Cuban revolution of 1959. Puerto Rican bases are ideal for naval training and counterinsurgency training. They have served as a springboard for U.S. invasions in the Dominican Republic, Panama, and Grenada. The best military minds say that Vieques is irreplaceable. In more than 50 years of combat training exercises, there has never been a civilian casualty outside the Vieques range, and, until quite recently, there had never been a casualty on the range. The entire range complex at Vieques gives senior commanders the opportunity to train, evaluate, and improve combat readiness. It will save lives.

Again, the Navy has tried to live up to agreements, and the loss of life has been minimal. In more than 55 years, only one death has occurred on the island. This has been blown out of proportion by militants who have manufactured the crisis. The Puerto Rican press is filled with exaggerated stories about the environmental disasters at Vieques and Roosevelt Roads.

U.S. corporations such as General Electric, Johnson & Johnson, Abbott Laboratories, and many textile firms have made substantial investments there. Their contribution has brought one of the highest standards of living in the Caribbean, and indeed, in all of Latin America. Puerto Ricans have benefited from being U.S. citizens and have moved to the mainland at will, a freedom coveted by many other people.[29]

American taxpayers subsidize Puerto Rico's commonwealth at the rate $13 billion a year. Puerto Ricans cannot blame the United States for all of Puerto Rico's problems. Perhaps Puerto Ricans should have fewer infants. High population cuts down economic opportunities and because of this almost 3 million Puerto Ricans have moved to the mainland—primarily to New York, California, Florida, Texas, and Connecticut. Puerto Ricans can do this because Puerto Ricans are American citizens. There is a price for these political and civic advantages not available to foreign immigrants. It is not the fault of Americans that Puerto Ricans have been slower to assimilate into "American society than any other Spanish-speaking immigrant group, and their ambivalence toward full 'Americanization' sets Puerto Rico apart as a unique domestic and foreign policy problem."[30]

The problem is one of a handful of radicals. President Bill Clinton catered to Puerto Rican radicals. In 1999, Clinton offered clemency to 16 Puerto Rican militants of the outlawed Armed Forces for National Liberation (Fuerzas Armadas Liberacion National Puertoriqueña—FALN) imprisoned for more than a hundred bombings in the 1970s and early 1980s. Clinton did this because he wanted the Puerto Rican vote. This type of leniency encourages disrespect for the law.

The closing of bases worldwide has hurt the defense capability of the United States.[31] Puerto Ricans must learn that there is a price for being an American and that they must carry their share of the defense burden.

George W. Bush gave the Navy flexibility with use of the Vieques range. Technically the Navy could cease all training on the Vieques naval training range by May 2003, but that is only if the Secretary of the Navy can find a suitable alternative. Americans are going to have to rethink Vieques after the events of September 11 and consider what is in the best interests of America.[32]

## POSTSCRIPT

As this book goes to press, the U.S. Navy, after nearly 60 years of using Vieques as a bombing and artillery range, announced that it was formally turning over the 15,000 acres along with 3,100 acres on the western side of the island, which will become the Caribbean's largest wildlife refuge. It ended four years of intense protests about the environmental and safety hazards that the range presented. The fallout from this affair still divides many Americans with many interpreting the withdrawal as compromising the security of the United States; they condemn the protestors for not supporting America in its time of need. On the other hand, many Puerto Ricans and environmentalists are bitter that the withdrawal took so long. Hundreds of people in the past three years alone, according to the critics of U.S. policy, had to go to jail, and thousands more suffer the environmental fallout.

## QUESTIONS

1. How does the case of Puerto Rico differ from that of Cuba? How does it differ from California?

2. How did Puerto Rico become part of the United States? How did Puerto Ricans become U.S. citizens? What is colonialism? Was and is Puerto Rico a colony of the United States? Is the United States violating the sovereignty of Puerto Rico? (If more information is necessary to answer these questions, go to the Internet.)

3. Find Vieques on a map. Why is Puerto Rico concerned about Vieques?

4. Go to an Internet search engine and type, "Roosevelt Roads, Puerto Rico." Select two articles in favor of the United States' retaining troops there and two against. What do the articles say about it?

5. Who was Dr. Pedro Albizu Campos? (Go to the Internet to find out more.) Why would he be revered by many Puerto Ricans? Why would the Federal Bureau of Investigation have a file on him? Would you agree with his statement that the United States was "interested in the cage, not the birds"? What did he mean?

6. Why would the controversy over Vieques help the independence movement? Why would non-Americans view the controversy with different eyes?

7. What are arguments for pulling U.S. troops out of Roosevelt Roads and Vieques? Do you agree with them? Why or why not?

8. What are arguments against pulling our troops out of Roosevelt Roads and Vieques? Do you agree with them? Why or why not?

9. The film *Popi* (1969, directed by Arthur Hiller) tells the story of a Puerto Rican widower with two kids in New York City who decides to take them to Miami, put them on a raft, and pass them off as Cuban refugees. View the film and explain why the father would want to make his boys Cuban.

10. View the PBS special *The Double Life of Ernesto Gómez* (1999, directed by Gary Weimberg and Catherine Ryan) in which 15-year-old Ernesto Gómez, raised by a Mexican family, describes his feelings when he finds out he is not Mexican and that his birth mother, Dylcia Pagán, a Puerto Rican nationalist, was imprisoned in 1980.

11. Try to get the newest documentary on Vieques called, *When the Little Becomes Big* (2002, directed by Marien Pérez Rivera). What insight does the documentary offer?

12. Why would Puerto Ricans be angry about the sterilization programs? Compare with other forced sterilization programs in the United States historically.

13. Have they resolved the issue of the sovereignty of the Puerto Rican people? Why or why not?

14. Does the case of Puerto Rico differ from that of other member states of the United States of America? How is it the same and how is it different?

15. On 1 May 2003 the press reported the U.S. Navy is considering alternative sites for use as a bombing range: Pinecastle naval bombing range in Florida's Ocala National Forest near Jacksonville Naval Air Station (382,000 acres), Avon Park Air Force range in south-central Florida (106,000 acres), and several others. What do you think will be the reaction of the people living near those sites?

16. What is the duty of the U.S. Navy to Vieques now? Do they have a moral duty to clean up Vieques? If so, do you believe this will happen?

17. Do you believe that the U.S. Navy would have left Vieques without the protests? What will happen with the bases on the island of Puerto Rico?

18. There is a Spanish saying, "Palo dado ni Díos lo quita" (not even God can take away the hurt caused by a blow). How does this saying apply to the issue of Vieques and other issues covered in this book?

## NOTES

1. Jay Moore, "End of the Century: Is Colonialism Over?" *Editor's Bullhorn*, 28 December 1999, http://www.neravt.com/left/moore4.htm, accessed 25 July 2003.

2. Foraker Act (Organic Act of 1900). U.S. President McKinley signed a civil law that established a civilian government in Puerto Rico. The new government had a

governor and an executive council appointed by the President, a House of Representatives with 35 elected members, a judicial system with a Supreme Court, and a nonvoting Resident Commissioner in Congress. Puerto Rico became the United States' first unincorporated territory.

3. Sara Hoerlein, "Female Sterilization in Puerto Rico," http://www.puertorico.com/forums/showthread.php3?threadid=5486, accessed 25 July 2003; Philip R. Reilly, *The Surgical Solution: A History of Involuntary Sterilization in the United States* (Baltimore and London: The John Hopkins University Press, 1991); Ana María García, "La Operacion," L.A. Film Project, 1985.

4. Fernando Pico, "Let Puerto Rico Decide. (Chronology of Puerto Rico's History Since Before 1898 and the Need to Let the Country Decide on its Future Economic and Social Policies) (Editorial)," *America* 178, no. 19 (1998): 3ff.

5. Gary Martin, "Puerto Rico's Economy: History and Prospects," *Business America* 8, 25 November 1985, 7(3).

6. Wanda Bermúdez, "Brief History Vieques 1998," http://www.vieques-island.com/history.shtml, accessed 25 July 2003.

7. Robert Rabin, "Vieques: Five Centuries of Struggle and Resistance," http://www.vieques-island.com/board/navy/rabin.html, accessed 25 July 2003.

8. "Gov. [Pedro] Rossello's Letter to the President Accepting Agreement," *Puerto Rico Daily News*, 31 January 2000, http://www.englishfirst.org/vieques/viequesrossello13100.htm, accessed 25 July 2003; "Text of Clinton's Vieques Statement," *The Associated Press*, 3 December 1999, http://www.vieques-island.com/navy/clinton.html, accessed 25 July 2003.

9. "Cancer In Vieques," *Fire*, 4 August 1999, http://www.fire.or.cr/cancer.htm, accessed 25 July 2003; Matthew Chapman, "Cancer Surge on Bomb Range Island: US Forces Have Trained in Vieques for 60 years," *BBC News*, 4 February 2001, http://news.bbc.co.uk/hi/english/world/americas/newsid_1152000/1152449.stm, accessed 25 July 2003.

10. Robert Rabin, "Vieques: Five Centuries of Struggle and Resistance," *Travel Guide to Vieques*, http://www.vieques-island.com/board/navy/rabin.html, accessed 25 July 2003.

11. Rubén Berrios Martínez, "Puerto Rico's Decolonization: The Time Is Now," *Foreign Affairs* 76, no. 6 (1997): 100ff.

12. Ibid.

13. Ibid.

14. Ibid.

15. African Perspective Staff, "Puerto Rico: Bombing Exercises Resume," *African Perspective*, http://www.africanperspective.com/html44/CtW.html#n3, accessed 25 July 2003.

16. Cat Lazaroff, "UN Committee Supports End to U.S. Navy Bombing on Vieques," *Navy News & Undersea Technology* 17, no. 29 (2000): 3ff, http://www.viequeslibre.addr.com/articles/un2000.html, accessed 4 August 2003.

17. Links to sites about Vieques: http://soconnell.web.wesleyan.edu/courses/ees335/field%20trip/vieques_links.html, accessed 4 August 2003; Wanda Bermúdez, "Brief History of Vieques," *Travel Guide to Vieques, 1998*, http://www.vieques-island.com/history.shtml, accessed 4 August 2003; The U.S. Navy and Vieques: Fact vs. Fiction, http://www.geocities.com/viequeswar/viequespuertorico.html, accessed 4 August 2003.

18. "Will the Navy Leave Vieques? (Truthful or Expedient?)," *The Other Side* 37, no. 6 (2001): 8ff; "Don't Mess with Texas (Navy Abandons Consideration of Padre Island National Seashore as Replacement for Bombing Range on Puerto Rican Island of Vieques) (Brief Article)," *Sierra* 86, no. 6 (2001): 71ff.

19. "Will the Navy Leave Vieques? (Truthful or Expedient?)," *The Other Side* 37, no. 6 (2001): 8ff.

20. Dr. Victor M. Rodríguez, "Coronel de la Policia Desmiente al Navy. U.S. Navy Uses Gas on Puerto Rico Protesters," e-mail, 6 April 2002; "In Brief / Puerto Rico; Nun, Priest Arrested in Latest Vieques Protest," *Los Angeles Times*, 7 April 2002.

21. Juan González, "No Mercy for Vieques Protesters," *In These Times*, 25 June 2001, 11.

22. "Protests Greet Resumption of Navy Bombing on Vieques," *New York Times*, 2 April 2002.

23. Rubén Berrios Martínez, "Puerto Rico's Decolonization: The Time Is Now," *Foreign Affairs* 76, no. 6 (1997): 100ff.

24. Self-Determination Legislation, H.R. 856 The United States-Puerto Rico Political Status Act. H.R. 856 Bill seeks to resolve the status issue by addressing the Puerto Rico legislature's request for a self-determination process guaranteeing the island's decolonization by means of a federally sponsored plebiscite in 1998. http://www.puertorico-herald.org/legislat.shtml, accessed 25 July 2003.

25. Daniel B. Schirmer, *Republic or Empire: American Resistance to the Phillippine War* [electronic book], (Cambridge, Mass: Schenkman Publishing, 1972), available at Revised Boondocks Net Edition, 2003, http://www.boondocksnet.com/centennial/solidar.html, accessed 25 July 2003.

26. Alvin Z. Rubinstein, "The Case against Puerto Rican Statehood," *ORBIS* 45, no. 3 (2001): 415ff.

27. J. Michael Waller, "Fidel Fuels Fires of Vieques Quarrel. (Castro, Activist Groups Want U.S. Military out of Puerto Rico)," *Insight on the News* 17, no. 27, (2001): 20ff.

28. Naval Station Roosevelt Roads, Puerto Rico, http://www.navstarr.navy.mil/, http://www.atlanticfleet.navy.mil/cb-viequesfence.htm, accessed 25 July 2003.

29. Alvin Z. Rubinstein, "The Case against Puerto Rican Statehood." *ORBIS* 45, no. 3 (2001): 415ff.

30. Ibid.

31. Ibid.

32. Lisa Troshinsky, "DoD Nixes Vieques Referendum; V-22 Suffers Setback. (Department of Defense)(Statistical Data Included)," *Navy News & Undersea Technology* 18, no. 50 (2001): 1ff.

## SELECTED READINGS

Barreto, Amilcar Antonio. *Vieques, the Navy and Puerto Rican Politics*. Gainesville, Fla.: Florida University Press, 2002.

Bermúdez, Wanda. "Brief History Vieques 1998," http://www.vieques-island.com/history.shtml. Accessed 25 July 2003.

Berrios Martínez, Rubén. "Puerto Rico's Decolonization: The Time Is Now." *Foreign Affairs* 76, no. 6 (1997): 100ff.

Fernández, Ronald. *Prisoners of Colonialism: The Struggle for Justice in Puerto Rico.* New York: Common Courage Press, 1994.

González, Juan. *Harvest of Empire: A History of Latinos in America.* New York: Penguin, 2001.

———. "No Mercy for Vieques Protesters." *In These Times,* 25 June 2001.

Laó-Montes, Agustín, and Arlene Dávila, eds. *Mambo Montage: The Latinization of New York City* New York: Columbia University Press, 2001.

Lazaroff, Cat. "UN Committee Supports End to U.S. Navy Bombing on Vieques." *Navy News & Undersea Technology* 17, no. 29 (2000): 3.

Matos Rodriguez, Félix V., and Linda C. Delgado. *Puerto Rican Women's History: New Perspectives.* Armonk, N.Y.: M. E. Sharpe, 1998.

Moore, Jay. "End of the Century: Is Colonialism Over?" *Editor's Bullhorn,* 28 December 1999, http://www.neravt.com/left/moore4.htm. Accessed 25 July 2003.

Murillo, Mario. *Islands of Resistance: Vieques, Puerto Rico, and U.S. Policy.* New York: Seven Stories Press, 2001.

Naval Station Roosevelt Roads, Puerto Rico, http://www.navstarr.navy.mil. Accessed 25 July 2003.

Rabin, Robert. "Vieques: Five Centuries of Struggle and Resistance," http://www.vieques-island.com/board/navy/rabin.html. Accessed 25 July 2003.

Rodríguez, Clara E. *Puerto Ricans. Born in the U.S.A.* Boulder, Colo.: Westview Press, 1991.

Roy-Fequiere, Magali. "Contested Territory: Puerto Rican Women, Creole Identity, and Intellectual Life in the Early Twentieth Century (Special Issue: Puerto Rican Women Writers)." *Callaloo* 17, no. 3 (summer 1994): 916ff.

Rubinstein, Alvin Z. "The Case against Puerto Rican Statehood." *ORBIS* 45, no. 3 (2001): 415ff.

Spencer, Jack. "The Importance of Vieques Island for Military Readiness." Washington, D.C.: The Heritage Foundation, 16 February 2001. Http://www.heritage.org/Research/NationalSecurity/BG1411.cfm. Accessed 25 July 2003.

Suro, Roberto. *Strangers among Us: Latinos' Lives in a Changing America.* New York: Vintage Books, 1999.

Troshinsky, Lisa. "DoD Nixes Vieques Referendum; V-22 Suffers Setback. (Department of Defense) (Statistical Data Included)." *Navy News & Undersea Technology* 18, no. 50 (2001): 1ff.

"U.S. Navy Leaves Vieques after 60 Years of Bombing." *Hispanicsurf.com.* 1 May 2003. Http://www.hispanicsurf.com/newsroom/navy_leaves_vieques_after_60years-050103.htm. Accessed 4 August 2003.

"Will the Navy Leave Vieques? (Truthful or Expedient?)." *The Other Side* 37, no. 6 (2001): 8ff.

# RESOURCE GUIDE

## SELECTED BOOKS AND ARTICLES

"1990. Eugenic and Racist Premise of Reproductive Rights and Population Control." http://www.hsph.harvard.edu/Organizations/healthnet/SAsia/depop/Chap7.html. Accessed 4 August 2003.

Acuña, Rodolfo F. *Anything but Mexican: Chicanos in Contemporary Los Angeles.* London: Verso, 1996. Deals with contemporary Los Angeles and U.S. Mexicans.

———. *Occupied America: A History of Chicanos.* 5th ed. New York: Longman, 2003. A general history of U.S. Mexicans. Latter chapters deal with Central Americans.

———. *Sometimes There Is No Other Side: Chicanos and the Myth of Equality.* Notre Dame, Ind.: Notre Dame University Press, 1998. Question of affirmative action and the culture wars in the United States.

Allen, Theodore W. "'Race' and 'Ethnicity': History and the 2000 Census." http://eserver.org/clogic/3-1&2/allen.html. Accessed 4 August 2003.

Arcilla, Jose S. S. J., "Roots: The Philippines in the 1600s." *BusinessWorld* (Philippines), 21 February 2000.

Arias, Elizabeth. "Change in Nuptiality Patterns among Cuban Americans: Evidence of Cultural and Structural Assimilation?" *International Migration Review* 35, no. 2 (2001): 525. Deals with Cuban Americans and question of Americanization.

Asimov, Nanette. "One in 7 California Teachers Unqualified; Programs Designed to Lure Credentialed Instructors." *San Francisco Chronicle,* 7 December 2000.

———. "One in 7 of State's Teachers Uncredentialed; Poorest Children Stuck with the Least Qualified." *The San Francisco Chronicle,* 12 December 2001. Article deals with the disparate treatment and education of Latino students.

Baker, Stephen. "The Coming Battle for Immigrants." *Business Week*, 26 August 2002, 138–40.

Balderama, Francisco E., and Raymond Rodríguez. *Decade of Betrayal: Mexican Repatriation in the 1930s*. Albuquerque, N.Mex.: University of New Mexico Press, 1995. Discusses the repatriation and deportation of a million Mexicans during the 1930s.

Barreto, Amilcar Antonio. *Vieques, the Navy and Puerto Rican Politics*. Gainesville, Fla.: Florida University Press, 2002. Good analysis of the political implication and context of the Vieques struggle for self-determination.

Beltrán, Gonzalo Aguirre. *La Población Negra de México: Estudio Ethnohistórico*. Xalapa: Universidad Veracruzana, 1992.

Bermúdez, Wanda. "Brief History Vieques 1998." http://www.vieques-island.com/his indx.html. Accessed 4 August 2003.

Berrios Martínez, Rubén. "Puerto Rico's Decolonization: The Time I Now." *Foreign Affairs* 76, no. 6 (1997): 100ff. Deals with independence for Puerto Rico.

Booth, William. "America's Racial and Ethnic Divides One Nation, Indivisible: Is It History?" First in a series of occasional articles. *Washington Post*, 22 February 1998. Part of a national series exploring racial and ethnic tensions in the United States.

Boswell, Thomas, and James Curtis. *The Cuban-American Experience. Culture, Images, and Perspectives*. Totaowa, N.J.: Rowman and Allanheld, 1984. A dated but important look at the Cuban American experience.

Brazil, Eric. "Sending Dollars to Latin America: Wiring Money Home—Cheaply Credit Unions Cut Costs for Immigrants." *San Francisco Chronicle*, 24 June 2001.

Brimelow, Peter. *Alien Nation: Common Sense about America's Immigration Disaster*. New York: Random House, 1995. An immigrant from England, Brimelow is a leading voice for the exclusion of third-world immigration to the United States. Brimelow is cited by most nativist organizations.

Buchanan, Patrick J. *The Death of the West: How Dying Populations and Immigrant Invasions Imperil Our Country and Civilization*. New York: Thomas Dunne Books, 2002. A far-right-of-center voice who is for closing the southern border with Mexico using military troops there.

Bunzel, John H. "The Nation; Post-Proposition 209; The Question Remains: What Role for Race?" *Los Angeles Times*, 8 December 1996. A leader in the debate on affirmative action.

Carrera, Mahali M. "Locating Race in Late Colonial Mexico. (Social Structure)." *Art Journal* (fall 1998).

Casimir, Leslie. "Census: 36 Percent of City Foreign-Born." *New York Daily News*, 21 November 2001.

Castro, Max J. "Grumpy Old Men: The Aging Exile Leaders Who Are Trying to Keep Elián González in the United States Have a Lot in Common with Their Anti-Democratic Nemesis, Fidel Castro." *salon.com*, 6 April 2000, http://archive.salon.com/directory/topics/immigration/. Accessed 25 July 2003.

Castro, Max J., and Thomas D. Boswell. "The Dominican Diaspora Revisited: Dominicans and Dominican-Americans in a New Century." *Political and Social Issues PymesDominican.com*, 4 August 2003. Http://www.pymesdominicanas.com/english/articles/paper53_nsc.htm. Accessed 4 August 2003.

Chávez, Leo R. "The Power of the Imagined Community: The Settlement of Undocumented Mexicans and Central Americans in the United States." *American Anthropologist* 96, no. 1: 52–73.

———. *Shadowed Lives: Undocumented Immigration in American Society.* San Diego: Harcourt Brace Jovanovich College Publishers, 1992.

Cockcroft, James D. *Latinos in the Making of the United States.* Franklin Watts, 1999. Written for high school students, it is a basic history of Latinos in the United States.

Cohen, Carl. *Naked Racial Preference: The Case against Affirmative Action.* Boston: Madison Books, 1995. Presents the argument against affirmative action.

Cordero-Guzmán, Hector R., Robert C. Smith, and Ramon Grosfoguel, eds. *Migration, Transnationalization, and Race in a Changing New York.* Philadelphia: Temple University Press, 2001. Interviews and quantitative analyses to explore the lives of Haitians, Dominicans, Salvadorans, Chinese, Puerto Ricans, Indian Americans, Jamaicans, Peruvians, Mexicans, Ecuadorians, and other immigrants in New York City.

Cornelius, Wayne, with Yasuo Kuwahara. *The Role of Immigrant Labor in the U.S. and Japanese Economies: A Comparative Study of San Diego and Hamamatsu, Japan.* San Diego, Calif.: Center for U.S.-Mexican Studies, University of California, San Diego, 1998. A balanced view of immigration and its problems.

Cruz, Jose E. *Identity and Power: Puerto Rican Politics and the Challenge of Ethnicity.* Philadelphia, Pa.: Temple University Press, 1998. Explores Puerto Rican identity politics and argues that instead of fragmentation and instability, identity politics helped mobilize the group and increases accountability from political leaders in Hartford, Connecticut.

Curtis, Bob. "The 'Race' Question on the U.S. Census Is Racist. Why This Is So and What to Answer Instead." http://sodabob.com/Constitution/Census.asp. Accessed 4 August 2003.

Dávila, Arlene. *Latinos Inc.: The Marketing and Making of a People.* Berkeley, Calif.: University of California Press, 2001. The role of corporate America in forging the Latino identity and cultivating the "Hispanic market."

de la Garza, Rodolfo, Louis DeSipio, F. Chris Garcia, John Garcia, and Angelo Falcon. *Latino Voices: Mexican, Puerto Rican, and Cuban Perspectives on American Politics.* Boulder, Colo.: Westview, 1992. Discusses the political status of Latinos during the early 1990s.

Delgado, Hector L. *New Immigrants, Old Unions: Organizing Undocumented Workers in Los Angeles.* Philadelphia, Pa.: Temple University Press, 1993. Deals with labor unions and immigrants.

Delgado, Richard. *The Rodrigo Chronicles: Conversations about America and Race.* New York: New York University Press, 1995. A fictional conversation between a law student and his professor, discussing the question of affirmative action and civil rights. Although fictional, it is factual and heavily footnoted. Easy reading, and concepts are qualified by the story line.

Duignan, Peter. "Bilingual Education: A Critique." Hoover Institution, http://www.hoover.stanford.edu/publications/he/22/22a.html. Accessed 26 July 2003. A case against bilingual education from a scholar from the Hoover Institution, which has been at the forefront of the campaigns against immigrant rights, affirmative action, and bilingual education.

"Eighteen Calif. School Districts Sued; Shoddy Classrooms, Textbook Shortages, Teacher Quality Cited." *The Washington Post,* 13 December 2000.

Fears, Darryl, and Claudia Deane. "Biracial Couples Report Greater Tolerance: U.S. Survey Finds Acceptance Weakest among Whites." *The Washington Post,* 8 July 2001, http://www.post-gazette.com/headlines/20010708biracialnat2p2.asp. Accessed 4 August 2003.

Federation for American Immigration Reform. "Fairness to Americans and Legal Immigrants Requires Opposing Another Amnesty for Illegal Aliens." July 2000, http://www.fairus.org/html/07431007.htm. Accessed 4 August 2003.

———. "Immigrants and Public Health: Why Immigration is a Health Care Concern." http://www.fairus.org/html/04149711.htm. Accessed 4 August 2003.

———. "Why Amnesty for Illegal Aliens Was—and Remains—a Bad Idea." May 1997, http://www.fairus.org/html/04134705.htm. Accessed 4 August 2003.

Fernández, Ronald, Serafin Méndez Méndez, and Gail Cueton. *Puerto Rico Past and Present: An Encyclopedia.* Westport, Conn.: Greenwood Press, 1998. Puerto Rico, A to Z.

Fletcher, Michael A. "Interracial Marriages Eroding Barriers." *Washington Post,* 28 December 1998. Http://www.washingtonpost.com/wp-srv/national/daily/dec98/melt29.htm. Accessed 26 July 2003. Deals with interracial marriages and changing attitudes.

Gándara, Patricia. "Choosing Higher Education: Educationally Ambitious Chicanos and the Path to Social Mobility." *Education Policy Analysis Archives* 2, no. 8 (May 1994), http://epaa.asu.edu/epaa/v2n8.html.

Gándara, Patricia, and Elias Lopez. "Latino Students and College Entrance Exams: How Much Do They Really Matter?" *Educational Administration Abstracts* 34, no. 4 (1999): ff. The authors deal with the college entrance examination in relation to Latino students.

Gándara, Patricia, and Leiani Osugi. "Educationally Ambitious Chicanas." *Thought & Action: The NEA Higher Education Journal* 10, no. 2 (1994): 7ff. Article by a premier Mexican American educator on the factors affecting Mexican American women in graduate education.

García, Alma M. *The Mexican Americans.* Westport, Conn.: Greenwood Press, 2002. Profiles the immigration and settling patterns of new Mexican immigrants.

García, Jorge J. E., and Pablo De Greiff, eds. *Hispanics/Latinos in the United States: Ethnicity, Race, and Rights.* New York: Routledge, 2000. An anthology of articles on Latinos written by scholars from the disparate groups.

Garcia, Sonia R. "Motivational and Attitudinal Factors amongst Latinas in U.S. Electoral Politics." *NWSA Journal* 13, no. 2 (2001): ff. Draws differences in the voting patterns of Latino males and females.

Garza, Hedda, and James Cockcroft. *Latinas: Hispanic Women in the United States.* University of New Mexico Press, 2001. A revised edition on Latinas geared at middle and high school students.

Gilbertson, Greta A., Joseph P. Fitzpatrick, and Lijun Yang, "Hispanic Intermarriage in New York City: New Evidence from 1991." *International Migration Review* 30, no. 2 (summer 1996): 445ff.

Gonzales, Patrisia, and Roberto Rodríguez. "Census Facilitates 'Demographic Genocide.'" Column of The Americas, Universal Press Syndicate, week of 17 March 2000. This husband and wife team is one of the best sources for contemporary views on Latinos in the United States; in this article they write on the designation of Latinos as *white* on the census.

González, Juan. *Harvest of Empire: A History of Latinos in America.* New York: Penguin Books, 2000. One of the best general treatments of U.S. Latinos put into contemporary context.

————. "No Mercy for Vieques Protesters." *In These Times,* 25 June 2001. One of the few comprehensive articles on the controversy over Vieques.

González-Pandon, Miguel. *The Cuban Americans.* Westport, Conn.: Greenwood Press, 1998. Overviews the immigration and adjustment of Cubans in the United States post 1965.

Gordon, Milton. *Assimilation in American Life: The Role of Race, Religion and National Origins.* New York: Oxford University Press, 1964. The classic but dated work on assimilation in the United States.

Gorkin, Michael, Marta Pineda, and Gloria Leal. *From Grandmother to Granddaughter: Salvadoran Women's Stories.* Berkeley, Calif.: University of California Press, 2000. Narrative of nine women of El Salvador who share life experiences, exploring tensions and joys.

Grenier, Guillermo J., Lisandro Pérez, and Nancy Foner. *Legacy of Exile: The Cubans in the United States.* Allyn & Bacon New Immigrants Series. New York: Allyn & Bacon, 2003. Brief overview of Cuban Americans.

Grieco, Elizabeth M., and Rachel C. Cassidy. *Overview of Race and Hispanic Origin.* U.S. Census Brief, March 2001. Http://www.census.gov/prod/2001pubs/c2kbr01-1.pdf. Accessed 24 July 2003. It is recommended that the reader download this article. Also see, http://www.census.gov/population/www/cen2000/phc-tb.html. Accessed 4 August 2003. Both sites summarize the findings of the 2000 census and give excellent summaries.

Gurza, Agustin. "Vowing to Love, Honor and Preserve Cultures." *Los Angeles Times,* 31 October 2000.

Guthrie, Julian. "Bilingual-Education Showdown; California Board Is Considering Modifications of Prop. 227 Law." 22 March 2002.

Gutiérrez, David G. *Walls and Mirrors: Mexican Americans, Mexican Immigrants, and the Politics of Ethnicity.* Berkeley, Calif.: University of California Press, 1995. Deals with first compared to second generation tensions.

Guzmán, Betsy. *The Hispanic Population. Census 2000 Brief.* U.S. Census Bureau, May 2001. Http://www.census.gov/prod/2001pubs/c2kbr3sp.pdf. Accessed 24 July 2003. Essential eight-page report that is the best short treatment of Latinos in the United States; it is recommended that the reader download this article.

"Habla Ingles, Por Favor: Ron Unz Has Battled Bilingual Ed out West. Now He Takes on the Nation's Largest School District—New York." *Newsweek,* 12 March 2001, 64.

Hamilton, Nora, and Norma Stoltz Chinchilla. *Seeking Community in a Global City: Guatemalans and Salvadorans in Los Angeles.* Philadelphia, Pa.: Temple University Press, 2001. Draws from extensive interviews of Salvadoran and Guatemalan community members and leaders in Los Angeles. Deals with contemporary migration. Provides invaluable statistics.

Haney López, Ian F. "Race, Ethnicity, Erasure: The Salience of Race to LatCrit Theory." LatCrit: Latinas/os and the Law: A joint symposium by *California Law Review* and *La Raza Law Journal. California Law Review* 85, no. 5 (1997):

1143–211. Haney Lopez is a law professor and a member of the LatCrit school, which critically looks at race and its impact on the law.

———. *Racism on Trial: the Chicano Fight for Justice.* Cambridge, Mass.: Belknap Press, 2003. This book tells the story of the Chicano movement in Los Angeles by following two criminal trials, including one arising from the student walk-outs.

Hegstrom, Edward. "Poll Discerns Anti-Amnesty Sentiment: Just 29% of Texans Favor It for Illegal Immigrants." *Houston Chronicle,* 10 September 2001. Http:// www.americanpatrol.com/POLLS/Polls002.html. Accessed 26 July 2003. Reports on findings of poll on undocumented immigration.

Hernández, David Manuel. "Divided We Stand, United We Fall: Latinos and Immigration Policy." *Perspectives in Mexican American Studies Annual* 6 (1997): 80ff. A scholarly look at immigration policy.

Hoerlein, Sara. "Female Sterilization in Puerto Rico." Http://www.puertorico.com/ forums/showthread.php3?threadid=5486. Accessed 4 August 2003.

Hwang, Sean-Shong, Kevin M. Fitzpatrick, and David Helms. "Class Differences in Racial Attitudes: A Divided Black America?" *Sociological Perspectives* 41, no. 2 (1998): 367ff. Very useful study on how class affects racial attitudes. Mostly deals with African Americans.

Jacoby, Jeff. "The Cuban Embargo's Moral Justification." *Boston Globe,* 2 April 1998, http://www.nocastro.com/embargo/jeffjby.htm. Accessed 4 August 2003.

Johnson, Kevin R. "'Melting Pot' or 'Ring of Fire'? Assimilation and the Mexican American Experience." LatCrit: Latinas/os and the Law: A joint symposium by *California Law Review* and *La Raza Law Journal. California Law Review* 85, no. 5 (1997): 1259–313. Johnson, a law professor, discusses his experiences as a product of an Anglo father and Mexican mother.

Kasindorf, Martin, and Haya El Nasser. "Impact of Census' Race Data Debated." *USA Today,* 13 March 2001. Http://www.usatoday.com/news/nation/census/ 2001-03-13-census-impact.htm. Accessed 26 July 2003. One of the many journal articles on the findings of the 2000 census.

Kiely, Kathy. "Importance of Foreign Aid Is Hitting Home." *USA Today,* 4 December 2001. Http://www.usatoday.com/news/sept11/2001/12/04/foreignaid-usat.htm. Accessed 26 July 2003. Discusses foreign aid and how it affects public policy.

Klein, Dianne. "Curbs on Illegal Immigration Are 'Social Sin,' Mahony Says." *Los Angeles Times,* 11 December 1993. Deals with views of Cardinal Roger Mahony and the anti-immigrant campaign.

Krashen, Stephen. "Bilingual Education: Arguments For and (Bogus) Arguments Against." Georgetown University Roundtable on Languages and Linguistics, May 6, 1999. Http://ourworld.compuserve.com/homepages/jwcrawford/ Krashen3.htm. Accessed 26 July 2003. Excellent article defending bilingual education. The most comprehensive arguments for the programs.

Kull, Andrew. *The Color Blind Constitution.* Cambridge: Harvard University Press, 1992. The leading constitutional scholar on race and the constitution. According to Kull, a color-blind society is attainable or even desirable. Traces legal argument for color-blindness and concludes "the Constitution is not color-blind and never was."

Laó-Montes, Agustín, and Arlene Dávila, eds. *Mambo Montage: The Latinization of New York City.* New York: Columbia University Press, 2001. A fascinating anthology on the disparate Latino groups in New York City. The Puerto Ricans eclipse the other groups, which is natural because of their numbers.

"Latinos in the United States." *The National Association of Hispanic Journalists,* http://www.nahj.org/resourceguide/chapter_3c.html. Accessed 26 July 2003. An excellent overview of disparate groups by Latino reporters. A practical guide for placing the disparate groups.

Lazaroff, Cat. "UN Committee Supports End to U.S. Navy Bombing on Vieques." *Navy News & Undersea Technology* 17, no. 29 (2000): 3ff. Http://www. viequeslibre.addr.com/articles/un2000.html. Accessed 4 August 2003.

Liebman, Alex. "How'd That Guy Get in, Anyway?" *Argos* 1, no. 2 (summer 1998). Http://www.gofast.org/argos-summer-1998/article3.htm. Accessed 4 August 2003.

Lindsay, James M. "Why Are Cuban Americans Singled Out as an Ethnic Lobby? Getting Uncle Sam's Ear/Will Ethnic Lobbies Cramp America's Foreign Policy Style." *Brookings Foreign Policy Studies* 20, no. 1 (2002): 37–40. Deals with the propriety of Cuban Americans lobbying for an anti-Castro foreign policy. Makes analogies with other ethnic groups.

Logan, John R. "Choosing Segregation: Racial Imbalance in American Public Schools, 1990–2000." 11–14. Http://mumford1.dyndns.org/cen2000/SchoolPop/ SPReport/page1.html. Accessed 4 August 2003.

———. *The New Latinos: Who They Are, Where They Are.* Lewis Mumford Center, 10 September 2001. Http://mumford1.dyndns.org/cen2000/HispanicPop/ HspReport/HspReportPage1.html. Accessed 26 July 2003. Revises the under-counts in the 2000 census; it is recommended that the reader download this article. The new immigrants are those other than the Mexican Americans, Puerto Ricans, and Cuban Americans.

———. "How Race Counts for Hispanic Americans." Lewis Mumford Center for Comparative Urban and Regional Research. University at Albany, 14 July 2003. Http://mumford1.dyndns.org/cen2000/BlackLatinoReport/Black-Latino01.htm. Accessed 24 July 2003. This article analyzes how class and where Latino students live determines what they call themselves or whether they consider themselves white or nonwhite.

López-Garza, Marta, and David R. Díaz, eds. *Asian and Latino Immigrants in a Restructuring Economy: The Metamorphosis of Southern California.* Stanford, Calif.: Stanford University Press, 2001. Eighteen chapters with 21 authors, the anthology gives an overview of settlements of Asians and Latinos in Southern California.

Luis, William. *Culture and Customs of Cuba.* Westport, Conn.: Greenwood Press, 2000. An in-depth, scholarly look at Cuban society.

Mahler, Sarah J., and Nancy Foner, eds. *Salvadorans in Suburbia: Symbiosis and Conflict.* New York: Allyn & Bacon, 1996. A 100-page overview of Salvadorans in the United States. Reviews the civil war and the diaspora of Salvadorans and their status in the United States. Showcases Salvadorans on Long Island.

Mann, Eric, and Kikanza Ramsey, "The Left Choice Is the Best Choice." *Community/ Labor Strategy Center* [author is one of the founders of this group]. Http:// www.thestrategycenter.org/AhoraNow/body_mannramsey_an1_part1.html.

Matos Rodríguez, Felix V., and Linda C. Delgado, *Puerto Rican Women's History: New Perspectives.* Armonk, N.Y.: M. E. Sharpe, 1998. One of the few histories of Puerto Rican women and one of the best on Latinas.

Mayer, Jr., Vincent Villanueva. "The Black Slave on New Spain's Northern Frontier: San Jose De Parral 1632–1676." Ph.D. diss., University of Utah, 1975.

McDaniel, Antonio. "The Dynamic Racial Composition of the United States. An American Dilemma Revisited." *Daedalus* 124, no. 1 (1995): 179ff. This is a scholarly article on the question of race and the tensions it produces.

McDonnell, Patrick J. "Mexicans Change Face of U.S. Demographics Census: Study Shows Latinos on Rise, Settling in Many Parts of Country." *Los Angeles Times,* 10 May 2001.

———. "State's Diversity Doesn't Reach Voting Booth." *Los Angeles Times,* 11 November 1994.

———. "Study Seeks to Debunk Stereotypes of Latinos." *Los Angeles Times,* 21 October 1994. Talks about how Latinos, especially immigrants, lack health insurance. A study by David E. Hayes-Bautista of UCLA shows that despite not having insurance, immigrants do not use public health facilities as often as other groups.

Menchaca, Martha. *Recovering History Constructing Race: The Indian, Black, and White Roots of Mexican Americans.* Austin: University of Texas Press, 2001.

Menjivar, Cecilia. *Fragmented Ties: Salvadoran Immigrant Networks in America.* Berkeley, Calif.: University of California Press, 2000. An ethnographic study of the complex immigrant social networks among Salvadorans in the United States.

———. "Living in Two Worlds? Guatemalan-Origin Children in the United States and Emerging Transnationalism." *Journal of Ethnic and Migration Studies* 28, no. 3 (July 2002): 531ff.

Mentzer, Marc S. "Minority Representation in Higher Education: The Impact of Population Heterogeneity." *Journal of Higher Education* 64, no. 4 (1993): 417ff. Deals with the numbers of Latinos in higher education.

"Metropolitan Racial and Ethnic Change Initiative Census 2000." Lewis Mumford Center for Comparative and Urban Regional Research. Http://mumford. cas.albany.edu/MumfordContact/censusbrochure.pdf. Accessed 24 July 2003.

Mills, Jon K., Jennifer Daly, Amy Longmore, and Gina Kilbride, "A Note on Family Acceptance Involving Interracial Friendships and Romantic Relationships." *The Journal of Psychology* 129, no. 3 (May 1995): 346ff.

Morales, Rebecca, and Frank Bonilla, eds. *Latinos in a Changing U.S. Economy: Comparative Perspectives on Growing Inequality.* Newbury Park: Sage Publications, 1993. A collection of articles on how the changes in the economy are affecting the various Latino groups.

"More than Half of Teens Who Date Have Dated Interracially: Study." *Jet,* 24 November 1997, 32ff.

Murillo, Mario. *Islands of Resistance: Vieques, Puerto Rico, and U.S. Policy.* New York: Seven Stories Press, 2001. A short history on the controversy on Vieques.

Newton, Lina Y. "Why Some Latinos Supported Proposition 187: Testing Economic Threat and Cultural Identity Hypotheses." Hispanics in America at 2000; statistical data included. *Social Science Quarterly* 81, no. 1 (2000): 180–93. Although Latinos overwhelmingly voted against Proposition 187, a sizable minority supported it. Why?

Nobles, Melissa. *Shades of Citizenship Race and the Census in Modern Politics.* Stanford: Stanford University Press, 2000. Deals with the question of race and the census.

Norwood, Charlie. "The Hidden Catalyst Behind America's Rising Number of Un-insured." January 2001. Article available through Congressional Staff. Http://www.house.gov/norwood/. Accessed 4 August 2003.

Oboler, Suzanne. *Ethnic Labels, Latino Lives: Identity and the Politics of (Re)presentation in the United States.* Minneapolis, Minn.: University of Min-neapolis Press, 1995. Analyzes the meaning, role, and implications of ethnic labels on people's lives and in their struggle for citizenship rights and social justice in contemporary U.S. society.

Offner, Paul. "What's Love Got to Do with It? Why Oprah's Still Single. (Society and Opportunities for African American People)." *Washington Monthly* 34, no. 3 (2002): 15–19. Deals with the question of why successful Latinas are marrying out.

Owens, Eric. "Mexicans Want America's Southwest." National Freedom Association, http://www.nationalfreedomassociation.org/news/0001.html. Accessed 4 Au-gust 2003.

Pabst, Georgia. "Census Data Show Impact for Latinos but Future Work Force Continues to Struggle, Group's Report Says." *Milwaukee Journal Sentinel,* 16 July 2001. Http://www.jsonline.com/news/census2000/jul01/census 16071501.asp. Accessed 4 August 2003.

Paley, Grace. *A Dream Compels Us: Voices of Salvadoran Women.* South End Press, 1990. Testimonies of Salvadoran women.

Pan, Philip P., and Michael A. Fletcher. "Other Latinos More Divided over Fate of Cuban Boy." *Washington Post,* 10 April 2000. Deals with the divisions in the various Latino communities over Elián González.

Pardo, Mary. *Mexican American Women Activists: Identity and Resistance in Two Los Angeles Communities.* Philadelphia, Pa.: Temple University Press, 1998. Socio-logical analysis of two Mexican American communities and women leaders in them. Strong on the variable class differences.

Patterson, Orlando. "Race by the Numbers." *New York Times,* 8 May 2001. Http://www.racematters.org/racebythenumbers.htm. Accessed 26 July 2003. African American scholar Oscar Patterson has been one of the leading voices against bilingual education and including Latinos as members of minority groups. Pat-terson seems to be saying that Latinos are pushing to be number one using the fiction of being nonwhite while they designate themselves as white.

———. *Rituals of Blood: Consequences of Slavery in Two American Centuries.* New York: Basic Books, 1998.

Pérez, Louis A. *On Becoming Cuban: Identity, Nationality, and Culture.* New York: HarperTrade, 2001. Explores the interaction between the United States and Cuba from the 1850s to the 1950s and how North American products, ideas, and pursuits from movies to baseball had an impact on Cuba. Argues that the American way of life was crucial in forming the Cuban national identity.

Pérez y González, María. *Puerto Ricans in the United States.* Westport, Conn.: Green-wood Press, 2000. Good overview of Puerto Ricans coming to the United States post 1965.

Porter, Rosalie Pedalino. "The Case against Bilingual Education: Why Even Latino Parents Are Rejecting a Program Designed for Their Children's Benefit." *The Atlantic Monthly* 281, no. 5 (1998): 28–39. Atlantic Online, May 1998, http://www.theatlantic.com/issues/98may/biling.htm, accesssed 25 July 2003.

Prewitt, Kenneth. "Demography, Diversity, and Democracy. The 2000 Census Story." *Brookings Review* 20, no. 1 (winter 2002): 6–9.

"Protests Greet Resumption of Navy Bombing on Vieques." *New York Times,* 2 April 2002.

Puente, Maria, and Gale Holland, "Deep Vein of Anger in California / Prop. 187 Reinforcing Divisions." *USA Today,* 11 November 1994.

Pullella, Philip. "Pope Urges U.S. to 'Change' Cuban Embargo." 21 January 1998. Http://64.21.33.164/CNews/y98/jan98/22e4.htm, accesscd 25 July 2003.

Pycior, Julie Leininger. *LBJ and Mexican Americans: The Paradox of Power.* Austin: University of Texas Press, 1997.

Pyle, Amy, Patrick J. McDonnell, and Hector Tobar. "Latino Voter Participation Doubled Since '94 Primary." *Los Angeles Times,* 4 June 1998.

Qian, Zhenchao. "Who Intermarries? Education, Nativity, Region, and Interracial Marriage, 1980 and 1990." Statistical data included. *Journal of Comparative Family Studies* 30, no. 4 (1999): 579ff. A scholarly article on interracial marriage in the 1980s and 1990s.

Rabin, Robert. "Vieques: Five Centuries of Struggle and Resistance." Http://www. vieques-island.com/board/navy/rabin.html, accessed 25 July 2003.

Reilly, Philip R. *The Surgical Solution: A History of Involuntary Sterilization in the United States.* Baltimore and London: The Johns Hopkins University Press, 1991.

Reuters News Service. "Majority of Babies Born in California Are Hispanic." *Deseret News,* 20 December 2001.

Rodríguez, Cindy. "Latinos Give U.S. New View of Race." *Boston Globe,* 2 January 2000. Http://www.boston.com/dailyglobe2/002/metro/Latinos.give.US.view. of.race + .shtm. Accessed 26 July 2003.

Rodríguez, Clara E. *Changing Race: Latinos, the Census, and the History of Ethnicity in the United States.* New York: New York University Press, 2000. An excellent look at Latinos and the census.

———. *Puerto Ricans: Born in the U.S.A.* Boulder, Colo.: Westview Press, 1991. A balanced history of Puerto Ricans by a prolific Boriqua writer.

Rodríguez, Gregory. "150 Years Later, Latinos Finally Hit the Mainstream." *New York Times,* 15 April 2001. Also available at http://www.newamerica.net/index. cfm?pg = article&pubID = 178. Accessed 26 July 2003. Applauds the entrance of Latinos into the American middle class.

———. "English Lesson in California: In the Face of a Ballot Challenge, Support for Bilingual Education Is Wavering." *The Nation* 266, no. 14 (April 1998): 15–18.

Rodríguez, Roberto. "California Has Another Proposition.(Ron Unz Initiative to Ban Bilingual Instruction)." *Black Issues in Higher Education* 14, no. 23 (January 1998): 11.

Rohrlich, Ted. "Mahoney Says Prop. 187 Poses Threat to Moral Principles." *Los Angeles Times,* 9 October 1994.

Rojas, Aurelio. "Growers Hire Illegals with Impunity; Workers Pay the Price for Lax INS Scrutiny of Farm Industry." *The San Francisco Chronicle,* 19 March 1996. Http://www.sfgate.com/chronicle/special/immigration/. Accessed 26 July 2003. Talks about the abuses of agribusiness vis-á-vis farm workers.

Roy-Feguiere, Magali. "Contested Territory: Puerto Rican Women, Creole Identity, and Intellectual Life in the Early Twentieth Century (Special Issue: Puerto Rican Women Writers)." *Callaloo* 17, no. 3 (summer 1994): 916ff.

Rubinstein, Alvin Z. "The Case against Puerto Rican Statehood." *ORBIS* 45, no. 3 (2001): 415ff. Makes arguments as to why Puerto Rico should not get statehood.

Russo, Francine. "When Love Is Mixing It Up: More Couples Are Finding Each Other across Racial Lines—and Finding Acceptance." *Time,* 19 November 2001. Http://www.time.com/time/archive/preview/from_redirect/0,10987,1101011 119-184008,00.html. Accessed 26 July 2003. A romantic view of interracial dating.

Saad, Lydia. "Americans Clearly Oppose Amnesty for Illegal Mexican Immigrants; Poll Analyses: Few Favor Increasing Immigration More Generally." *Gallup News Service,* 6 September 2001, http://www.gallup.com/poll/releases/ pr010906.asp, accessed 26 July 2003.

Sachs, Susan. "The World: What's in a Name? Redefining Minority." *New York Times,* 11 March 2001. Political scientists and immigration experts debate whether Latinos are a minority group in meaning typically applied to blacks, that is, an oppressed group with common historic grievances against white society.

Samora, Julián, and Richard A. Lamanna. "Mexican Americans In A Midwest Metropolis: A Study of East Chicago." In *Forging a Community: The Latino Experience in Northwest, Indiana, 1919–1975,* James B. Lane and Edward J. Escobar, eds. Chicago: Cattails Press, 1987.

Santa Ana, Otto. *Brown Tide Rising: Metaphors of Latinos in Contemporary American Public Discourse.* Austin, Tex.: University of Texas Press, 2002. Applies cognitive metaphor theory to an extensive natural language data taken from *Los Angeles Times* and other media. Shows how metaphorical language portrays Latinos as invaders, outsiders, burdens, parasites, diseases, animals, and weeds. Relates to Proposition 187 and 209.

Schlesinger, Jr., Arthur M. *The Disuniting of America: Reflections on a Multicultural Society.* New York: W. W. Norton, 1992. Schlesinger contends that identity politics and history are disuniting America. Talks about the superiority of Western culture.

Shorris, Earl. *Latinos Biography of a People.* New York: Norton, 1992. A very readable biographical study of Latinos.

Shuit, Douglas. "Study Finds Latinos to Be Group Most Lacking in Health Coverage." *Los Angeles Times,* 19 July 1994.

Skerry, Peter. "The Black Alienation: African Americans vs. Immigrants." *The New Republic,* 30 January 1995. Http://www.brook.edu/dybdocroot/Views/Op-Ed/ Skerry/19950130.htm. Accessed 4 August 2003.

———. *Counting on the Census? Race, Group Identity, and the Evasion of Politics.* Washington, D.C.: Brookings Institute Press, 2000. A conservative perspective on the 2000 census and its meaning.

———. *Mexican Americans: The Ambivalent Minority.* New York: Free Press, 1991.

Smith, Becky. "Illegal Aliens: To Teach or Not to Teach." EDUC 420, Professional Teacher and American School Mary Washington College, http://www. altenforst.de/faecher/englisch/immi/illegal.htm, accessed 26 July 2003.

Smith, Denise, and Renee E. Spraggins. *Gender: 2000.* U.S. Census, September 2001. Http://www.census.gov/prod/2001pubs/c2kbr01-9.pdf. Accessed 4 August

2003. Deals with differences among women in the various racial groups; it is recommended that the reader download this article.

Specht, Jim. "Recent Laws Bring Wave of Newcomers; Policy of Reuniting Families Shapes Decade-Long Influx." *Chicago Sun-Times,* 8 December 1996.

Stannard, David E. "Genocide in the Americas: Columbus's Legacy." *The Nation* 255, no. 12 (1992): 430ff.

Stefanic, Jean, and Richard Delgado. *No Mercy. How Conservative Think Tanks and Foundations Changed America's Agenda.* Philadelphia, Pa.: Temple University Press, 1996. Excellent book on the funding of anti-immigrant and race organizations and foundations. Traces the origin of funds for groups such as English only.

Sundaram, Anjalo, and George Gelber, eds. *A Decade of War: El Salvador Confronts the Future.* New York: Monthly Review Press, 1991.

Suro, Roberto. "Mixed Doubles. (Interethnic Marriages and Marketing Strategy.) (Statistical Data Included)." *American Demographics,* November 1999. Puerto Rican specialist in interracial marriages.

———. *Strangers among Us: Latinos' Lives in a Changing of America.* New York: Vintage Books, 1999. *Washington Post* reporter Roberto Suro deals with Latino immigration to America and issues such as poverty, bilingual education, and the relationship of Latinos to blacks.

"Taxpayers Should Not Have to Subsidize College for Illegal Aliens." Federation of American Immigration Reform, http://www.fairus.org/html/04182108.htm. Accessed 4 August 2003.

Torres-Saillant, and Ramona Hernández. *The Dominican Americans.* Westport, Conn.: Greenwood Press, 1998. Overviews the immigration patterns, adaptation, and contributions of Dominicans post 1965.

Tyson, Ann Scott. "Young Love Bridges Race Divide." *Christian Science Monitor,* 3 December 1997. Http://www.csmonitor.com/durable/1997/12/03/us/us.4. html. Accessed 4 August 2003.

Unz, Ron. "California and the End of White America." *Commentary* 108, no. 4 (1999): 17ff. The force behind the campaign against affirmative action. The article is revealing because it betrays hints of racial motives to his campaign.

Vincent, Theodore G. *The Legacy of Vicente Guerrero, Mexico's First Black Indian President.* Gainesville: University Press of Florida, 2001.

Walton-Raji, Angela. "African–Native American Genealogy Forum." http://www. african-nativeamerican.com/. Accessed 4 August 2003.

West, Cornell. *Race Matters.* New York: Vintage, 1994. A collection of essays on race.

Wolf, Eric. *Sons of the Shaking Earth: The People of Mexico and Guatemala—Their Land, History, and Culture.* Chicago: Phoenix Books, 1959.

Woodward, Jr., Ralph Lee. *Central America: A Nation Divided.* 2d ed. New York: Oxford University Press, 1985.

Yzaguirre, Raul. "Census Shows Disparity in Education of Latino Children." *Hispanic Online HispanicMagazine.com,* April 2001, www.hispanicmagazine.com/2001/ apr/Forum. Accessed 4 August 2003.

## WEB SITES

### How to Conduct Internet Searches for Latino Material

Research via the Internet on Latinos is relatively simple. Any of the search engines, for example, AOL, Yahoo, Google, will do. The researcher merely has to type in "Latino," "Hispanic," or in some cases "Chicano," and the related Web sites will pop up. The researcher may also use alternatives such as "Mexican American," "Puerto Rican American," "Salvadoran American," and so on, or just drop the word "American." To narrow the search to a specific question, use "Latino women," "Latino lawyers," and so forth. The search may also include "Latinos and the 2000 census," "Latinos and bilingual education," "Latinos and interracial dating," and so on. Considerable material exists, for example, on Viéques and on Puerto Rico. The female and male points of view can be found by adding "male" or "female" as variables.

Bilingual Education Web Sites, http://www.ecsu.ctstateu.edu/depts/edu/textbooks/bilingual.html. Accessed 26 July 2003. Developed by the ERIC Clearinghouse on Urban Education at Columbia Teachers College and the National Clearinghouse for Bilingual Education.

Boricua.com, http://www.boricua.com/. Accessed 26 July 2003. A newsletter in Internet form that serves as a gateway to other Puerto Rican sites.

Centro de Estudios Puerto Riqueños, http://www.centropr.org/. Accessed 26 July 2003. The Web site for CUNY Hunter College. Has access to research materials, the journal, and the Puerto Rican Studies Programs.

Chávez, Linda, http://www.lasculturas.com/aa/bio/bioLindaChavez.php. Accessed 26 July 2003. Las Culturas is a conservative Web site spinning Latino issues with conservative perspective. Linda Chávez is a Latina Republican.

CUNY Dominican Studies Institute, http://www.ccny.cuny.edu/dsi. Accessed 26 July 2003. This is the Web site for the Dominican Studies Institute.

English for Children, http://www.onenation.org/. Accessed 26 July 2003. This is an English-only Web site, which is against bilingual education.

Hoover Institution, http://www.hoover.stanford.edu/publications/he/22/22a.html. Accessed 26 July 2003. The Stanford University–based think tank states that its mission is to promote "The principles of individual, economic, and political freedom; private enterprise; and representative government were fundamental to the vision of the Institution's founder." It has been the leader in producing research against affirmative action, bilingual education, and immigrant rights.

José Angel Gutiérrez Papers, 1959–90. University of Texas, San Antonio Archives, http://www.lib.utsa.edu/Archives/Manuscripts/ms24.html. Accessed 4 August 2003.

José Angel Gutiérrez, "Texas Political History Collection." Special Collections and Archives, University of Texas, Arlington, http://libraries.uta.edu/SpecColl/polhist.html. Accessed 4 August 2003.

Lewis Mumford Center for Comparative Urban and Regional Research, http://www.albany.edu/mumford. Accessed 28 July 2003.

Mexica Nation, http://www.mexica.net. Accessed 27 July 2003. Web site of a Chicano nationalist group.

National Committee for Pay Equity, http://www.feminist.com/fairpay/monori/html. Accessed 26 July 2003.

National Council of La Raza, http://www.nclr.org/. Accessed 26 July 2003.
Pew Hispanic Center, http://www.pewhispanic.org/index.jsp. Accessed 27 July 2003.
  Mission is to improve understanding of the diverse Latinos in the United States
  and to chronicle Latinos' growing impact on the nation.
Puerto Rican Legal Defense and Education Fund, http://www.prldef.org/. Accessed
  26 July 2003.
Raza Unida Homepage, http://larazaunida.tripod.com. Accessed 27 July 2003. The
  oldest Chicano political party in the United States. Questions can be directed
  to Genaro Ayala at pnlrunm@yahoo.com.
Salsa Puerto Riqueña, http://www.geocities.com/sd_au/articles/sdhsalsapr.htm. Accessed 26 July 2003. Series of articles on salsa.
Steve Sailer Archive, "Importing Mexico's Worsening Racial Inequality," http://
  www.vdare.com/sailer/sailer_mexico_part2.htm. Accessed 26 July 2003. A
  leading anti-immigrant Web site. Articles on the far side of exaggeration.
Tomás Rivera Policy Institute, http://www.trpi.org. Accessed 26 July 2003.
Unz, Ron, Web Page, http://www.onenation.org/. Accessed 26 July 2003. Unz is the
  main force against bilingual education in the United States.
Vega García, Susan A. "Recommended U.S. Latino Websites Diversity & Ethnic Studies," http://www.public.iastate.edu/~savega/us_latin.htm. Accessed 26 July
  2003. Excellent source for additional Web sites.
Voice of Citizens Together, http://www.americanpatrol.com/. Accessed 26 July 2003.
  This group claims that Latinos in the United States are plotting to return the
  country to Mexico.

## FILMS/VIDEOS

Many of the films listed here can be obtained through your public library or the local
video store.

*Alambrista!* 1979. Directed by Robert M. Young. Tragedies suffered by unauthorized
  immigrants crossing the border.
*American Me* 1992. Directed by Edward James Olmos. Story of the Mexican Mafia
  at Folsom prison in California.
*And the Earth Did Not Swallow Him* 1994. Directed by Severo Perez. In 1952 a
  Mexican American family is struggling to survive, working as migrant laborers
  in fields from Texas to Minnesota.
*Ballad of an Unsung Hero* 1983. Directed by Isaac Artenstein. Life story of Pedro J.
  Gonzalez is made into a film. Concentrates on California in 1930s.
*The Ballad of Gregorio Cortez* 1982. Directed by Robert M. Young. Gregorio Cortez
  shoots and kills a sheriff in self-defense and is chased for the next 11 days by a
  posse of 600 Texas rangers.
*Born in East L.A.* 1987. Writer/director Cheech Marin, who was born in the United
  States, is accidentally deported to Mexico without identification or knowledge
  of Spanish.
*Break of Dawn* 1988. Written and directed by Isaac Artenstein. Life story of Pedro J.
  Gonzalez, who championed the cause of Mexican Americans in California dur-
  ing the Depression years.
*Calle 54* 2000. Directed by Fernando Trueba. Documentary on salsa.
*Chicana* 1979. Directed by Sylvia Morales. Mexican murals, rare photographs, and doc-

umentary footage trace the traditional and the emerging roles of Mexican/ Chicanas from pre-Columbian times to the late 1970s.

*Chicano! History of the Mexican American Civil Rights Movement* 1996. Four parts. PBS series examining the Mexican American civil rights movement. See National Latino Communication Center, www.nlcc.com.

*Chicano Park* 1988. Directed by Marilyn Mumford and Mario Berrera. Documentary on San Diego's Logan Heights barrio to preserve a park.

*Chulas Fronteras* 1978. Directed by Les Blank and Chris Strachwitz. Documentary on the music and culture of Mexican Americans in southern Texas.

*Colors* 1988. Directed by Dennis Hopper. Two cops try to bring peace to gang war on the streets of Los Angeles.

*Crossover Dreams* 1985. Directed by Leon Ichaso. Comedy about a salsa singer who tries to cross over into the pop music mainstream and takes advantage of everyone he meets on his way to the top.

*The Double Life of Ernesto Gomez* 1999. Directed by Gary Weimberg and Catherine Ryan. Fifteen-year-old Ernesto Gomez, raised as a Mexican, finds out his birth mother was Dylcia Pagan, a Puerto Rican patriot imprisoned in 1980.

*El Norte* 1983. Directed by Gregory Nava. Guatemalan brother and sister flee Guatemala, encountering numerous obstacles, and finally arrive in Los Angeles without documents.

*El Súper* 1979. Directed by L. Ichaso and Orlando Jimenez-Leal. A humorous and touching story of Cuban exiles living in a basement apartment in New York.

*Fear and Learning at Hoover Elementary* 1997. Directed by Laura Angélica Simón. A documentary on the impact of anti-immigrant legislation on Latino elementary school children.

*I Am Joaquin* (Yo Soy Joaquin) 1969. Directed by Luis Váldez and produced by El Teatro Campesino. Dramatization of the Chicano poem of the same title by Rodolpho "Corky" Gonzales about the Chicano experience from Cortés to farm workers' struggle.

*La Bamba* 1987. Written and directed by Luis Valdez. Seventeen-year-old Ritchie Valens's rise to rock 'n' roll stardom and his early death.

*La Ciudad* (The City) 1998. Directed by David Riker. Four stories about recently arrived undocumented immigrants from Mexico and Latin America to New York City.

*The Lemon Grove Incident* 1985. Directed by Paul Espinoza. Documentary of efforts in the Mexican American community to gain educational rights and end segregation.

*Lone Star* 1996. Directed by John Sayles. Murder-mystery explores interpersonal and interracial tensions in Rio County, Texas.

*Los Siete de la Raza* 1969. Director unknown. Struggle of mostly Central American youth in the Mission district of San Francisco who were recruiting street kids into a Brown College studies program. Victims of a press and police campaign to clean up the Mission, they were accused of killing an undercover police officer. The campaign to free them leads to the creation of Los Siete de la Raza, a self-help political organization to fight for the rights of "Brown people."

*Miami-Havana* 1992. Directed by Estela Bravo. Documentary on tensions on Cuban American and Cuban families separated by the political conflict.

*Mi Familia* (My Family) 1995. Directed by Gregory Nava. A romantic view of a Mexican American family vis-à-vis several generations.

*Milagro Beanfield Wars* 1988. Directed by Robert Redford. About the encroachment on the communal lands of New Mexicans by land developers and the struggle for the survival of the culture.

*Mi Vida Loca* (My Crazy Life) 1994. Directed by Allison Anders. Rival Latino gangs in Los Angeles feud.

*Nueba Yol* 1995. Directed by Angel Muniz. A Dominican immigrant to New York and his daily struggles in a strange land, devoid of the comforts of his native customs, language, and culture.

*The Pérez Family* 1995. Directed by Mira Nair. Cubans arriving in Miami and the problems of reunions with family members whom they have not seen in 20 years.

*Popi* 1969. Directed by Arthur Hiller. Puerto Rican widower from New York decides to take his two kids to Miami, put them on a raft, and pass them off as Cuban refugees.

*The Ring* 1952. Directed by Kurt Neumann. Chronicles the fate of Tomas, a Mexican American living in a Los Angeles barrio, and his attempts to break out of poverty.

*Salt of the Earth* 1954. Directed by Herbert Biberman. A semi-documentary of Mexican American zinc miners in New Mexico and how women save the strike.

*Scarface* 1983. Directed by Brian DePalma. Tells the story of the violent career of a small-time Cuban refugee hoodlum and his building of Miami's cocaine empire.

*Short Eyes* 1987. Directed by Robert M. Young. Based on work of Miguel Pinero. Life in a New York county jail and the tensions between different racial groups.

*Selena* 1997. Directed by Gregory Nava. Story of the late Tejana singer Selena.

*Stand and Deliver* 1987. Directed by Ramon Menendez. Jaime Escalante, a math teacher at Garfield High in East Los Angeles, motivates students to achieve in mathematics.

*Strangers in the City* 1962. Directed by Rick Carrier. The story of Puerto Rican immigrants to New York City. How two siblings had to struggle against insurmountable odds.

*This Rebel Breed* 1960. Directed by Richard L. Bare. Two undercover cops infiltrate gangs to stop narcotics trafficking.

*Vieques: An Island Forging Futures* 2000. Director Johanna Bermudez Ruiz. Documentary on Vieques.

*West Side Story* 1961. Directed by Robert Wise and Jerome Robbins. Musical based on the Romeo and Juliet story, set in New York's West Side slums during the late 1950s; involves tensions between a Puerto Rican gang and a white gang.

*When the Little, Becomes Big* 2002. Directed by Marien Perez Rivera. On the Vieques controversy.

*Yo Soy Chicano* 1972. Directed by Jesús Salvador Treviño. The Chicano movement.

*Zoot Suit* 1981. Directed by Luis Valdez. Based on the infamous Sleepy Lagoon case of 1942 and the injustices of the trial.

## ORGANIZATIONS

There are literally thousands of local Latino organizations with views ranging from the far left to the far right. This guide lists major centers from which the reader can compile a list of local organizations. For example, most campuses with students of Mexican extraction have chapters of the Movimiento Estudiantil Chicanos de Aztlan (MEChA). The departments or centers have links to this or other campus organizations. They also carry links to local community organizations.

AfroCubaWeb, http://www.afrocubaweb.com/. Accessed 26 July 2003. Access by subscription at http://groups.yahoo.com/group/afrocubaweb/. Accessed 26 July 2003.

CARECEN (the Central American Resource Center), http://www.carecen-la.org/, accessed 26 July 2003 (Los Angeles), http://www.icomm.ca/carecen/, accessed 26 July 2003 (New York), http://www.carecensf.org/about.html, accessed 26 July 2003 (San Francisco), http://www.carecendc.org/, accessed 26 July 2003 (Washington, D.C.).

Central American Research and Policy Institute (CARPI), California State University Northridge, http://www.csun.edu/~bc60904/carpi.html, accessed 26 July 2003.

Central American Web site, California State University Northridge, http://www.csun.edu/~bc60904/CAS.html, accessed 26 July 2003. Program http://www.csun.edu/~bc60904/menu.html, accessed 26 July 2003.

Centro de estudios Puertorriqueños, Hunter College/CUNY, http://www.centropr.org/, accessed 26 July 2003.

The César E. Chávez Center for Interdisciplinary Instruction in Chicana & Chicano Studies, http://www.sscnet.ucla.edu/chavez/, accessed 26 July 2003.

The Chicana and Chicano Studies Department, California State University, Northridge, http://www.csun.edu/~hfchs006/, accessed 26 July 2003.

CLNET, University of California Riverside, http://clnet.ucr.edu/, accessed 26 July 2003.

Cuban American National Foundation, http://www.canfnet.org/, accessed 26 July 2003.

Cuban Research Institute, Florida International University, http://lacc.fiu.edu/cri/, accessed 26 July 2003.

CUNY Dominican Studies Institute, http://www.ccny.cuny.edu/dsi/, accessed 26 July 2003.

Esperanza Center, http://www.esperanzacenter.org/, accessed 27 July 2003. A progressive, grassroots cultural organization, advocating/affirming the lives and struggles of young people of color, women, lesbians, gays, the working class, and the poor.

Inter-University Program for Latino Research, http://www.nd.edu/~iuplr/, accessed 26 July 2003.

Julian Samora Research Institute, Michigan State University, http://www.jsri.msu.edu/, accessed 26 July 2003.

Latin American and Caribbean Center, Florida International University, http://lacc.fiu.edu/, accessed 26 July 2003.

Lewis Mumford Center for Comparative Urban and Regional Research, http://www.albany.edu/mumford, accessed 28 July 2003.

MALDEF (Mexican American Defense and Education Fund), http://www.maldef.org/, accessed 26 July 2003.

Mexica Nation, http://www.mexica.net/, accessed 27 July 2003. Web site of Chicano nationalist group.

NALEO (National Association of Latino Elected and Appointed Officials), http://www.naleo.org/, accessed 26 July 2003.

National Council of La Raza, http://www.nclr.org/, accessed 26 July 2003.

National Network for Immigrant and Refugee Rights, http://www.nnirr.org/, accessed 27 July 2003.

Pew Hispanic Center, http://www.pewhispanic.org/index.jsp, accessed 27 July 2003. Mission is to improve understanding of the diverse Latinos in the United States and to chronicle Latinos' growing impact on the nation.

Puerto Rican Legal Defense and Education Fund, http://www.prldef.org/, accessed 26 July 2003.

Radio Bilingue, Latino Community Radio Network, http://www.radiobilingue.org/, accessed 26 July 2003.

Raza Unida Homepage, http://larazaunida.tripod.com, accessed 27 July 2003. The oldest Chicano political party in the United States. Questions can be directed to Genaro Ayala at pnlrunm@yahoo.com.

SALEF (The Salvadoran-American Leadership and Education Fund), http://www.salef.org/, accessed 26 July 2003.

Southwest Voter Registration and Education Project, http://www.svrep.org/, accessed 26 July 2003.

Tomás Rivera Policy Institute, http://www.trpi.org/, accessed 26 July 2003.

Willie C. Velasquez Institute, http://www.wcvi.org/, accessed 26 July 2003.

## LATINO NEWS MEDIA SOURCES

Most newspapers have Web sites. The following are a sampling of Latino newspapers or those with heavier Latino coverage. Internet searches can be made on any of these Web sites that have archives.

"Chicano/Raza Sites," http://www.geocities.com/CapitolHill/1884/chr-links.htm, accessed 4 August 2003.

"Directory of Central America News Sources," *planeta.com,* 1 July 2003, http://www.planeta.com/ecotravel/period/pubcent.html, accessed 4 August 2003.

*Hispanic Link: News Service,* http://www.hispaniclink.org/, accessed 4 August 2003.

*Granma* (Cuba), http://www.granma.cu/, 4 August 2003.

*La Opinión* (Los Angeles), http://www.laopinion.com, accessed 4 August 2003.

"Puerto Rican Newspapers," *allyoucanread.com,* http://www.allyoucanread.com/news.asp?id = c66, accessed 8 August 2003.

# INDEX

# ABOUT THE AUTHOR

RODOLFO F. ACUÑA is Professor of Chicana/o Studies at California State University, Northridge.

CPSIA information can be obtained
at www.ICGtesting.com
Printed in the USA
FSHW021104260821
84026FS

9 780313 361432